Transformational Leadership for Rapid School Improvement

Kevin Perks
EDITOR

Foreword by Terry Hofer
Afterword by Charles S. Dedrick

TEACHERS COLLEGE PRESS
TEACHERS COLLEGE | COLUMBIA UNIVERSITY
NEW YORK AND LONDON

THE COUNCIL*of*
SCHOOL SUPERINTENDENTS
LEADERS · EDUCATORS · ADVOCATES

LEAF
Leadership for Educational
Achievement Foundation, Inc.
LEAD · EDUCATE · ACHIEVE

WestEd.org

Published simultaneously by Teachers College Press,® 1234 Amsterdam Avenue, New York, NY 10027; WestEd, 730 Harrison Street, San Francisco, CA 94107; New York State Council of School Superintendents, 7 Elk Street, 3rd Floor, Albany, NY 12207; and Leadership for Educational Achievement Foundation (LEAF), 7 Elk Street, 3rd Floor, Albany, NY 12207.

WestEd is a nonpartisan, nonprofit agency that conducts and applies research, develops evidence-based solutions, and provides services and resources in the realms of education, human development, and related fields, with the end goal of improving outcomes and ensuring equity for individuals from infancy through adulthood. For more information, visit WestEd.org.

Library of Congress Cataloging-in-Publication Data

Names: Perks, Kevin, editor.
Title: Transformational leadership for rapid school improvement / Kevin
  Perks ; foreword by Terry Hofer.
Description: New York : Teachers College Press, [2024] | Includes
  bibliographical references and index.
Identifiers: LCCN 2023043510 (print) | LCCN 2023043511 (ebook) | ISBN
  9780807769546 (paper : acid-free paper) | ISBN 9780807769553 (hardcover :
  acid-free paper) | ISBN 9780807782316 (ebook)
Subjects: LCSH: School improvement programs—United States. | Educational
  leadership—United States. | Educational change—United States.
Classification: LCC LB2822.82 .T695 2024 (print) | LCC LB2822.82 (ebook) |
  DDC 371.2/070973—dc23/eng/20231129
LC record available at https://lccn.loc.gov/2023043510
LC ebook record available at https://lccn.loc.gov/2023043511

ISBN 978-0-8077-6954-6 (paper)
ISBN 978-0-8077-6955-3 (hardcover)
ISBN 978-0-8077-8231-6 (ebook)

Printed on acid-free paper
Manufactured in the United States of America

This book is dedicated to all students, at every stage of their learning journey, striving to achieve their limitless potential, particularly those who have been historically underserved and marginalized.

This book is also dedicated to our educational leaders who also strive daily to support everyone in their educational communities and to build systems that are able to provide what our students need. This is no small feat. The problems the future brings are myriad and unknown, and it will be up to our current students to solve them.

This book is also dedicated to all of us who care about our future. The burden to prepare our youth rests on all of our shoulders. Our students are the light; it is all of our burden to keep this flame blazing.

Contents

Foreword

"You work to turn around schools. How do you do it?"

Recently, I received a voicemail from a new teacher asking how he could help his school turn around. I had a long drive ahead and plenty of time to talk, so I took the call and engaged in the conversation.

As director of WestEd's Center for School Turnaround and Improvement, I receive many calls of this kind. Most of the inquiries on the topic come from folks who have worked in education for decades, at state, district, and school levels. So I was particularly curious about the perspective of this young teacher. He was eager for the answer—*The* answer.

Vincent Mays, principal at Jeehdeez'a School in northern Arizona, put it this way, "If you can always reframe the problem, you can always find a path forward."

That sounds about right.

I have been privileged to work with clients on school turnaround efforts throughout the United States and with the Bureau of Indian Education. Most schools seek external support once to accelerate progress. Each school has a unique context and a unique array of strengths and needs. No two schools are identical, and neither is the approach. Continuously identifying and re-framing the problems helps to motivate and inspire a viable path forward.

But, too often, the path forward falls short of expectations. When this happens over and over, through multiple leadership changes, it is under-standable how some staff members could become less optimistic over time. School turnaround does not proceed in an upward linear direction.

Kevin Perks and I have engaged side-by-side in this work for a decade. Together, we have worked to create opportunities for educators to draw on their prior knowledge and experiences to rethink and reframe challenges, of-ten using protocols to help focus the process. These opportunities are always enriched through a knowledgeable other from the district, the school, or an external partner. Or, the conversations can be enriched through recent train-ing, coaching, or professional reading.

The release of the Four Domains for Rapid School Improvement by the Center for School Turnaround in late 2017 created a new opportunity for enriching those conversations. We started to reframe conversations with inquiry questions in the areas of turnaround leadership, talent development, instructional transformation, and culture shift. This proved to be powerful for generating fresh ideas from educators and has since become a staple of the work.

Generating ideas can be fun, but implementing multiple ideas while running a school is challenging. I worked with Edgar Lin, a successful turnaround principal in the South Bronx, to scan the research for guidance on this topic. Ultimately, we came up with a definition of our own for distributed leadership, "Enlisting others to advance a vision through the purposeful alignment of practices that are grounded in shared mission, beliefs, values and goals."

The purposeful alignment of practices.

Building capacity for educators to align practices is not easy. To begin, leaders must provide a clear vision if they are going to successfully enlist followers. They must sell the vision to well-educated and experienced staff members as a viable solution. A vision that prioritizes one of the four domains, or one or more of the 12 practice areas within the domains creates a "big tent" for school faculty members to come together—in other words, to find a purposeful alignment of practices.

The common vocabulary of the Four Domains for Rapid School Improvement can be a springboard for more granular and contextualized ideas that span roles and responsibilities throughout a school.

Each chapter in this book represents a potential path forward. Finding a path that works in your context may have lifelong implications for one student, scores of students, or an entire student body.

At first glance, the concept of generating conditions that result in lifelong implications may not square with the use of the word "rapid" in the title. Many of the ideas in the book require the development of new systems and a multiphase plan to introduce, refine, and sustain the system. Other ideas in this book can generate new opportunities for students before the sun goes down tomorrow night. I hope you find both: impactful ideas that can be rapidly implemented and inspiring approaches that meet the moment.

Though there may be no easy answer to the question of "how do you do it," the pathways are limitless. Climb under this big tent, and let's brainstorm where to begin.

—Terry Hofer, EdD
Director of School Improvement, WestEd

Acknowledgments

Putting together an edited book like this is no small feat and truly takes a village. Although the many people to acknowledge and mention is longer that the space here provides, I will do my best. My apologies to anyone not directly mentioned.

First a huge thank you to every author who helped contribute to the chapters in this volume. I am constantly humbled by your brilliance. I have learned so much from you through the contributions you have shared in this book and beyond. I am excited that your hard work and valuable guidance will receive a larger audience. It has been a privilege working with every one of you.

Next, a huge thank you to Vrenali Banks and everyone at the Leadership for Educational Achievement Foundation (LEAF), Inc. and the New York State Council of School Superintendents (NYSCOSS) who supported this project and partnered with us at WestEd to provide valuable resources and insights to educational leaders across New York for the past decade. This book would not exist without your partnership.

This book would also not exist without the support of WestEd and all the leaders and staff who supported its creation. There are too many to name; however, I would like to make special note of Stephen Hamilton who got this entire project started a decade ago with his foresight. Steve, you saw the promise long before I did. Also, a special acknowledgment goes out to Noel White and his team, who helped review and edit the drafts of the articles that became the chapters in this book. This effort would have taken twice as long without their masterful eyes. I have experienced firsthand how they can take my roughest prose and help craft it into something coherent, and even elegant. Also, my thanks to Danny Torres, who has provided valuable guidance all along the way.

Of equal importance in helping make this book a reality are all of my colleagues in the Quality Schools and District team at WestEd, as well as my colleagues on other teams across the agency. In particular, I would like to acknowledge Sofia Aburto, Robin Ahigian, Johanna Barmore, Terry Hofer, Susan Levenson, Cerelle Morrow, Marias Paredes, Bob Rosenfeld, Melissa

Strand, and Susan Villani. I am daily grateful to work with some of the best and most deeply committed people in the education field.

Another acknowledgment goes out to my Teachers College Press editor, Allison Scott. Navigating the ins and outs of producing a book like this is not easy. I have greatly appreciated how your leadership and guidance allowed me to stay focused on the content.

Finally, I would like to acknowledge and thank my family, whose support has never waned, even when projects like this consume more time that one might like. Similarly, a thank you to the families of all who helped with this endeavor. Contributing to a work such as this takes dedication and commitment. I have no doubt that this book would not have been able to come to fruition as well without this support.

Introduction

"There is always light. If only we're brave enough to see it. If only we're brave enough to be it."[1]

THE CHALLENGE

Being a school or district leader has arguably never been more difficult. As most educational leaders quickly learn, one of their primary responsibilities is to provide leadership that works to continuously improve outcomes for all of their students, particularly those who have been historically marginalized and underserved. This requires constantly striving to enhance educational systems and working to support the continuous growth of all staff in improving their professional practices. Since the COVID-19 pandemic, this task has become even more challenging as leaders deal with such obstacles as increasing gaps in achievement, rising absentee rates, the impact of trauma resulting from the pandemic, ongoing staffing shortages, and limited or hostile family and community engagement. These are just a few of the myriad hurdles educational leaders are trying to overcome on a daily basis.

The political landscape has not made the work of school and district leaders easier either. For example, recent policy shifts in many states have made it more difficult for school and district leaders to support LGBTQ+ and gender nonconforming students. Confusion about critical race theory has pitted families against the schools that serve their children when it is more important than ever for schools and families to be working in partnership. The long-lasting impact has exacerbated the need to focus on the safety and social-emotional well-being of not only students but educational staff as well. Given the many challenges like this that educators face, school and district leaders need all the support they can get.

---

1 Gorman, A. (2021). The Hill We Climb: The Amanda Gorman poem that stole the inauguration show. *The Guardian*. https://www.theguardian.com/us-news/2021/jan/20/amanda-gorman -poem-biden-inauguration-transcript

The burden to lead educational efforts in local communities should not fall solely on the shoulders of district and school leaders. Nor should they have to reinvent the wheel at every turn. This book is intended to be a resource to educational leaders who are charged with rapidly improving their schools and districts. In these pages, leaders will find guidance, support, and resources across a range of topics and issues that they are likely to be dealing with. Although this book does not seek to address everything a district or school leader needs to know, we have striven to include topics that many leaders are likely to be contending with and to provide practical and actionable guidance.

AUDIENCE

So, who is the book written for, and what is included in it? It is written for any and all educators interested in improving schools and who are in a position to do so. Within this broader group, it is specifically geared to district and school leaders who are, or will be, in charge of leading improvement efforts in their local contexts. However, other educational leaders – such as leaders within state education agencies, foundations that support schools and districts, as well as local stakeholders interested in improving schools – will probably find many, if not all, the topics in this book relevant and useful.

BACKGROUND

Most of the chapters in this book began as articles written in partnership between the Leadership for Educational Achievement Foundation, Inc. (LEAF, Inc.) and WestEd. LEAF is an arm of the New York State Council of School Superintendents (NYSCOSS) and is an organization that provides professional learning to superintendents and their leadership teams across the state of New York. LEAF's programs are research-based, aligned to the needs of the field, and responsive to changing expectations for school leaders.

WestEd is a nonpartisan research, development, and service agency that works with education and other communities across the country to promote excellence, achieve equity, and improve learning for all children, youth, and adults, particularly those who have been historically underserved. WestEd's staff provide a broad range of services focused on generating knowledge and applying evidence and expertise to help educators and leaders at all levels improve policies, systems, and practices on behalf of all learners.

For the past decade, WestEd and LEAF have partnered together to provide bimonthly articles that provide practical guidance for district and school leaders focused on building their knowledge and capacity to support improvement on a wide range of topics and issues. This book compiles a collection of these articles refreshed for this book. All of these articles-turned-chapters support some facet of school or district improvement and are written by educational experts, including current and former school and district leaders, as well as expert researchers and practitioners at WestEd who work daily with educators and educational leaders across the country to support their school improvement efforts.

HOW THIS BOOK IS ORGANIZED

It is no secret that there are many challenges that have plagued educational leaders for years. To state a few more examples, culturally and linguistically diverse students have historically faced unique barriers within our nation's education system that continue to persist (Noltemeyer & Mcloughlin, 2012). The children most at risk for academic failure have been and continue to be children of color, specifically African American and Latinx youth, as well as children impacted by poverty (e.g., Jackson & Addison, 2018). Also, improving math and reading achievement for students has always been a chronic challenge, and this has only been exacerbated by the pandemic (Mervosh, 2022).

Against this backdrop of myriad challenges, the chapters in this book are intended to build the capacity of superintendents, principals, and other educational leaders to be transformational leaders who are increasingly able to rapidly improve schools and address persistent challenges like those described previously. When we use the term *transformational leader*, we are describing leaders who are able to substantively enhance and improve educational systems and educator practices in order to achieve better and longer-lasting outcomes for all of their students. When we use the term *rapid*, we are referring to changes and improvements that can happen and get started relatively quickly within educational systems at the school or district level. The term *rapid* is not meant to imply that substantive and enduring improvements are quick and easy, but rather that the pathway to impactful improvement for students can have multiple starting points and is within the reach of all educational leaders. With this in mind, the chapters in this book have been chosen because they provide knowledge, insights, and approaches that school and district leaders can use and that research and scholarship have shown to accelerate a positive impact on school- and district-level systems, and practices that will benefit students.

Although many challenges persist, a broad and deep body of research indicates that there are practices that play significant roles in helping to drive rapid improvements in schools. In 2017, the federally funded Center on School Turnaround (CST) established a systems framework that synthesizes what a broad body of research indicates are some of the most effective practices for driving rapid school improvement (Ryan Jackson et al.,

2018). This framework, comprised of multiple practices, is organized into the Four Domains of Rapid School Improvement. This framework is used as the overarching organizing structure for this book. This framework is described briefly in the following section.

THE FOUR DOMAINS OF RAPID SCHOOL IMPROVEMENT

The Four Domains of Rapid School Improvement (see Figure I.1) is a research-based framework that school and district leaders can use to guide and support effective and sustainable change in schools. These domains were developed based on research and best practices in educational leadership and have been shown to be effective in driving positive outcomes for students (Center for School Turnaround & Improvement, 2017). Each domain identifies a specific area of focus for educational leaders and includes three specific

Figure I.1. The Four Domains of Rapid School Improvement

Four Domains for Rapid School Improvement
A SYSTEMS FRAMEWORK

Turnaround Leadership
Prioritize improvement and communicate urgency
Monitor short- & long-term goals
Customize and target support to meet needs

Culture Shift
Build a culture focused on student learning and effort
Solicit and act upon stakeholder input
Engage students and families

Student-centered, Equity-driven

Talent Development
Recruit, develop, retain, and sustain talent
Target professional learning opportunities
Set clear performance expectations

Instructional Transformation
Diagnose and respond to student learning needs
Provide rigorous evidence-based instruction
Remove barriers and provide opportunities

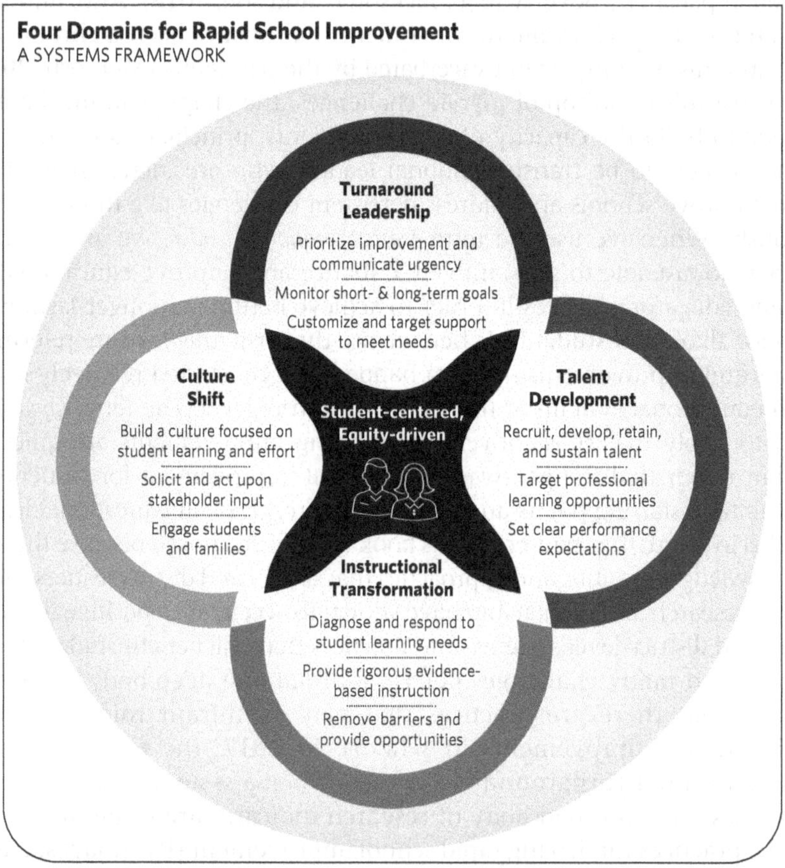

practices to help leaders drive improvements in schools. A brief summary of each domain and its practices follows.

Turnaround Leadership

The first domain of the framework, turnaround leadership, emphasizes the important roles leaders play in driving improvement efforts. This domain emphasizes the importance of leaders being committed to prioritizing and elevating achievement. Effective transformational leaders who successfully lead substantive improvement efforts are those who routinely communicate the urgent need for improvement so that all students receive the high-quality education they deserve. They are also highly focused on achieving equity for all students, particularly those historically underserved. Turnaround leaders are also successful at supporting and empowering other leaders and staff to develop, implement, and monitor the progress of plans that are grounded in data and have been strategically designed to address students' needs.

Talent Development

Whereas the domain of turnaround leadership emphasizes the importance of leadership that understands and has the capacity to drive rapid improvement, the second domain recognizes that leaders will not be successful if they are unable to build and support teams that can effectively implement improvement efforts. Therefore, the second domain emphasizes the importance of attracting, hiring, and retaining high-quality staff. This includes recruiting a talented and diverse workforce of teaching staff and other educational personnel comprised of individuals who deeply understand the lived experiences and needs of the students they are serving. Strong leaders also set clear expectations for all staff and actively work to understand their needs. With this understanding, the most successful leaders are able to simultaneously set high expectations for staff and support their social and emotional well-being. This includes developing a culture of continuous learning that provides staff with routine opportunities to engage professional learning designed to improve professional practices, particularly those aligned with student goals and needs.

Instructional Transformation

The third domain recognizes the essential role that high-quality, evidence-based instruction plays in supporting student success. Everything else does not matter if not all students are routinely being taught well. Thus, transformational leaders are able to ensure that all students have access to and the opportunity to receive engaging and rigorous teaching through evidence-based instructional practices. Additionally, they are able to ensure that all education systems are able to identify and respond to student needs, particularly needs that are not met by a strong core instructional program. When barriers arise, effective leaders are also able to leverage existing assets to overcome these obstacles.

Culture Shift

Just as the common adage "It takes a village" implies, the fourth domain of rapid school improvement emphasizes the importance of having a supportive, engaged, and collaborative educational community committed to excellence and achievement for all students. This domain recognizes the importance of having a positive culture and climate where all educational stakeholders from educators to students to families to community members are all intensely focused on the learning and well-being of students. Transformational leaders assiduously work to build a strong community of partners, and they actively solicit and respond to input from all stakeholders. Most importantly, they are highly effective at engaging families as school partners to support their children's success, particularly parents of students who have traditionally been marginalized, disadvantaged, and/or have suffered trauma.

In sum, the Four Domains of Rapid School Improvement provide a comprehensive framework the school and district leaders can use to support planning and implementing school improvement initiatives. It is important to also point out that all four domains and the key practices within them intersect and work to support each other. For example, when transformation leaders work to ensure staff needs are met and when they provide high-quality professional learning (Domain 2), this helps to create a positive culture intent on improvement (Domain 4). Similarly, effectively communicating the urgency of improvement (Domain 1) is essential to engaging stakeholders in the work of improving outcomes for students (Domain 4). Thus, by addressing specific aspects of each domain, leaders can begin to create a cohesive and integrated approach that drives rapid improvement. In addition, by focusing on improvement and turnaround leadership, talent development, instructional transformation, and shifting culture to promote excellence and equity, educational leaders can create the conditions necessary for student success and improved educational outcomes.

HOW TO READ THIS BOOK

This book is divided into four main sections aligned to the Four Domains of Rapid School Improvement. Each section begins with an introduction to the chapters within it and provides a brief overview of the topics addressed therein and how they align with the given domain. The introduction to each section also concludes with some guiding questions for readers to consider and reflect on before and as they read. Readers also do not need to read the chapters in a linear fashion. However, two recommended approaches include scanning the chapter titles and reading the topics that resonate the most or identifying one of the four domains to focus on and exploring the chapters in that section. In both cases, it will be beneficial to read the section introductions first.

Each chapter is also written to encourage reflection and discussion by providing questions and prompts throughout for readers to consider. Each chapter begins with Before Reading prompts that prepare readers to cognitively engage in the topic it will address. In addition, all of the chapters also include Pause and Reflect prompts to encourage reflection as readers engage with the content in each chapter. Finally, every chapter ends with a Further Reflect and Take Action section that provides prompts that encourage readers to reflect further and/or take actionable next steps related to the topic.

The interactive questions and prompts throughout all of the chapters are designed to encourage a thoughtful, reflective, and interactive reading experience. While the questions should work well for those reading this book independently, we highly encourage readers to read this book in collaboration with others as a book group or professional learning community. In collaborative contexts, the questions and prompts can be used to foster conversations, before, during, and after everyone has read a chapter.

REFERENCES

Center for School Turnaround & Improvement. (2017). *Four domains for rapid school improvement: A systems framework*. WestEd.

Jackson, C., & Addison, K. L. (2018). Understanding the relationships between poverty, school factors and student achievement. *Montgomery County Public Schools*. https://files.eric.ed.gov/fulltext/ED598342.pdf

Mervosh, S. (2022). The pandemic erased two decades of progress in math and reading. *The New York Times*. https://www.pro-memoria.info/wp/wp-content/uploads/The-Pandemic-Erased-Two-Decades-of-Progress-in-Math-and-Reading-Sarah-Mervosh-The-New-York-Times.pdf

Noltemeyer, A. L., & Mcloughlin, C. S. (2012). *Disproportionality in education and special education: A guide to creating more equitable learning environments*. Charles C. Thomas Publisher.

Ryan Jackson, K., Fixsen, D., & Ward, C. (2018). *Four domains for rapid school improvement: An implementation framework*. Center on School Turnaround at WestEd.

Part I

INTRODUCTION— TURNAROUND LEADERSHIP

The first domain of the Four Domains of Rapid School Improvement focuses on turnaround leadership. It prioritizes three research-based practices that school and district leaders should emphasize when leading substantive improvement efforts. These include prioritizing improvement and communicating its urgency, monitoring short- and long-term goals, and customizing and targeting support to meet needs. All three of these practices work together to support intentional and deliberate improvement planning. For example, they emphasize the importance of determining which areas of improvement need to be prioritized for supporting growth and increases in positive outcomes for all students. The practices also point out that it is not enough to have priorities; they need to be communicated frequently and often with urgency. To do this, leaders also need to develop actionable improvement plans to support implementation of improvement efforts so progress toward short- and long-term goals can be monitored. When this is done well, it builds the capacity of school and district leaders to leverage resources and adjust efforts to continuously ensure that improvement work is targeting student needs more nimbly.

As briefly discussed in the introduction to this book, it is important to clarify that the term "turnaround" in the title of Domain 1 is not meant to imply that the research-based practices just mentioned only apply to schools that are struggling the most and that are engaged in comprehensive turnaround efforts. The term is meant to emphasize that the research-based practices in this domain have been found to work in all contexts, even those that may be the most challenging.

The four chapters in this section have been selected to help build the capacity of school leaders to drive impactful improvement efforts. The first chapter in this section, Chapter 1 "Leading with Empathy: Leveraging an Essential Leadership Trait," emphasizes the importance of leaders leading with empathy. In this chapter, Dr. Michael Nagler argues that we cannot expect to substantively improve and sustain progress if we do not routinely strive to understand the experiences of others, particularly as they relate to changes leaders make in the spirit of improvement. For example, communicating the urgency of improvement efforts is likely to fall on deaf ears if we are unable to empathize with the experiences of students and staff alike. Similarly, how can we effectively target the needs of individuals if we do not strive to understand what they are going through?

Building on the first chapter, Chapter 2, "Culturally Responsive Schools Start with Culturally Responsive Leaders" describes the importance role school and district leaders play in leading and modeling cultural responsiveness. In this chapter, Dr. Saroja Warner defines what it means to be a culturally responsive leader and explains how "creating schools that are culturally responsive is more critical than ever for achieving educational equity" for all students. In addition, culturally responsive leaders must also be able to communicate the importance of developing the cultural responsiveness of all teachers and the value of culturally responsive teaching. As readers engage with this chapter, they are encouraged to consider how being culturally responsive can help leaders set meaningful and achievable improvement goals, communicate the urgency of working to meet those goals, and develop plans that will effectively target support to meet staff and student needs.

Chapter 3, "Is an Equity Audit in Your Future?" provides readers with an introduction to equity audits, including what they are and why education leaders should consider them. In short, equity audits provide a means to identify areas of inequity. Targeting these areas helps leaders know where to prioritize improvement and what to communicate urgency about. Additionally, a significant body of research indicates that when leaders identify areas of inequity and target improvement in these areas, all students benefit.

The final chapter in Section 1, Chapter 4, "Planning and Implementing a Special Education Program Review," describes a process for conducting a review of a district's special education program. In particular, conducting a review allows districts to understand their strengths and challenges to better customize and target supports to meet students' needs. The results of reviews can have a wide range of benefits including improved instruction, a culture more focused on student learning, and deeper engagement from parents and community.

Prior to reading, readers are encouraged to consider and discuss the following questions about the chapters in this section.

- How would you define empathy, and why do you think it is important for educational leaders to have? How might empathy help to drive and sustain improvement efforts?
- What does it mean to you to be a culturally responsive leader? How does being a culturally responsive leader help to drive and sustain improvement efforts? To what extent and how do leaders in your school or district model cultural responsiveness?
- How would you define equity, and why is it essential in education? What do you think is entailed in an equity audit, and to what extent has your district engaged in this process before?
- To what extent has your school or district recently engaged in a review of your special education systems and practices? What do you think are your school's or district's strengths in this area? What do you think are the greatest opportunities for improvement?

CHAPTER 1

Leading With Empathy
Leveraging an Essential Leadership Trait

Michael P. Nagler

Before Reading

- Why is it important for leaders to practice empathy?
- What does the phrase *leading with empathy* mean to you?
- Describe the relationship between the concepts of empathy, innovation, and equity in education.

INTRODUCTION

The Greek philosopher Heraclitus is credited with saying, "The only constant in life is change." I wonder if he could have ever imagined a world with artificial intelligence, cellular phones, Zoom meetings, and the fourth industrial revolution? Technology has created a pace of change that is, and will continue to be, exponential. When you add the ambiguity of a global pandemic, the result has left us with a polarized society, fueled by social media "echo chambers" and extreme politics at every level to which even school boards are not immune.

Given all of this, it is not surprising that education leaders during the past few years have had some extremely challenging moments, especially school superintendents and other district leaders. In my experience as a superintendent, I have found that change within education, particularly change focused on improvement, is particularly difficult to manage because public schools tend to be institutions that resist change. In truth, they may be one of the most nostalgic and traditional institutions in society. Still, the pandemic forced educational leaders to grapple with implementing a range of new technologies and solutions, but now we find ourselves within a political

13

backdrop that is forcefully urging a "return to normal." Thus, how do leaders successfully navigate a landscape that is simultaneously urging them to both improve and find innovative solutions to do so that meet the growing needs of students, while at the same time pushing them to maintain a status quo? I've found that one of the most successful tools in dealing with this tension is empathy.

"Seek first to understand, then be understood" (Covey, 2004). Whether you're listening to staff, students, families, or other interested parties—putting yourself in "their shoes" is imperative in leadership. The capacity to understand others and move away from "your own autobiography" (Covey, 2004) is a lynchpin to successfully navigating the tense and ambiguous times we live in. Moreover, it is a skill we need to teach our students. As Dr. Michele Borba encourages us to ask, "Which competencies and practices will 'future proof' students—or at least prepare them to the best extent possible?" (2022). At the top of her list and mine is empathy because as she states, "Empathy is essential to future proofing because it boosts human traits like trust, creativity, communication, prosocial behaviors, and resilience—traits that will be key in the fourth industrial revolution."

WHAT IS EMPATHY? WHAT THE RESEARCH SAYS

Empathy in leadership isn't a new concept. For example, you could make a case that servant leadership and transformational leadership require empathy—but the word is not used in the definition of those types of leaders. Brower states that empathy "may not be a brand new skill, but it has a new level of importance and the fresh research makes it especially clear how empathy is the leadership competency to develop and demonstrate now and the future of work" (Brower, 2021, p. 6). She also states that, "Great leadership requires a fine mix of all kinds of skills to create the conditions for engagement, happiness and performance, and empathy tops the list of what leaders must get right" (Brower, 2021 p. 2).

What has changed that makes empathy so critical? The very nature of workers and the workplace. For example, research conducted by Businessolver found that 70 percent of employees feel empathy in leadership decreases turnover rates. In addition, 76 percent think empathy drives productivity. When you are an empathetic executive, you develop strong relationships with your employees, grow your organization, and create a legacy you can be proud of in the process. Yet, the same study found that only 63 percent of team members feel like their CEO is empathetic (Miller, 2022).

Empathy as a leadership trait is also often overlooked. For example, Holt and Marques (2011) found that empathy tends to be undervalued by leaders and suggest that this paradigm needs to shift. Even more recently, this lack of appreciation for empathy is a fault that the Center for Creative Leadership (2023) believes should be rectified. They write that "Empathic leadership means having the ability to understand the needs of others, and being aware of their feelings and thoughts. Unfortunately, it has long been a soft skill that's overlooked as a performance indicator. Our research, however, has shown that today's successful leaders must be more 'person focused' and able to work well with people from varying teams, departments, countries, cultures, and backgrounds."

Given all of this, how do leaders use and cultivate empathy in their leadership style? Stephen Covey argues that it starts with listening.

> Empathic listening involves much more than registering, reflecting, or even understanding the words being said . . . In empathic listening, you listen with your ears, but you also, more importantly, listen with your eyes and your heart. You listen for feeling, meaning. You listen for behavior. You use your right brain as well as your left. You sense, you intuit, you feel. Empathic listening is so powerful because it gives you accurate data to work with. Instead of projecting your own autobiography and assuming thoughts, feelings, motives, and interpretation, you're dealing with the reality inside another person's head and heart. You're listening to understand. You're focused on receiving the deep communication of another human soul. (Covey, 2004, pp. 252–253)

As the foregoing research indicates, it is pretty clear that empathy is an effective skill that is necessary in leadership, but why is it particularly important for educational leaders today, and how can they build their capacity to lead with empathy?

WHY EMPATHY FROM EDUCATION LEADERS IS IMPORTANT

Empathy is typically considered to be the capacity to be aware of and understand how others are feeling. The term is often used to describe a person's innate capacity for understanding others and how they are feeling. For example, a person might be described as having empathy for others. Or, someone might be described as being empathic—which means they intuitively understand others and how others are feeling, and they are able to communicate this understanding through their words and actions. This way of thinking of empathy suggests that empathy is more than a trait or characteristic that people have; it suggests that empathy is also a way of acting, a way of behaving, a way of leading.

From this perspective, leading with empathy is an active approach to leadership that requires working proactively to deeply understand the experiences of stakeholders in the educational community. It is essential for improvement because it encourages leaders to embrace a growth mindset that drives them to better understand the problems and challenges people are facing. As leaders increasingly understand the experiences of others, they may be better prepared to engage in an innovative process of design thinking that includes analyzing the problems and challenges, developing new ideas and prototypes, testing these for success and failure, and repeating the process as needed. This process entails, in part, leaders creating systems for collecting feedback about how well changes and solutions are working. As most leaders know, innovation is not typically something that is done right the first time. Innovating requires trial and error until the desired change is achieved. Leading with empathy also can mean having a tolerance, an acceptance, and even an appreciation for failed attempts to innovate that occur along the way to learning.

For example, during the pandemic, many schools shifted to online and distance learning. As a result, some families with multiple children were quickly overwhelmed as each child needed support from adults at home. In some schools, students were given way too much work; in others, they received hardly any. Leaders who developed systems of feedback early on were able to learn about these challenges that stakeholders were experiencing, and the leaders were able to quickly adapt and adjust to ease the transition to remote learning. Leaders who did not work actively to understand were not able to adjust as quickly, making the shift to remote learning more challenging and stressful for students, families, teachers, and staff.

Although empathy allows education leaders to understand how changes are impacting individuals throughout the educational community, empathic understanding also can be the springboard for identifying innovations that can provide effective solutions to challenges. If leaders do not actively work to understand how disruptions are impacting families and how families are feeling and experiencing change, they will be less effective in identifying solutions to address known and unknown challenges. Similarly, they will not be able to see opportunities when they arise. For example, I found a silver lining during the pandemic. After communicating regularly with staff and families, I noticed that distance learning provided an excellent and very real opportunity to help students enhance their independence, self-regulation, and executive functioning by emphasizing the teaching of skills like goal-setting, establishing routines, and regularly reflecting on the learning progress. These are skills which transcend any content students are required to learn and, as such, became priorities of focus for instruction. Thus, listening to the challenges that students and families were facing presented an opportunity to reprioritize the instructional focuses to better meet the realities students were dealing with.

In short, when empathy helps drive change, it may foster innovation and also help strengthen equity. When empathy is not a driving force within change, equity and innovation can be seen as transactional demands that are done for the leaders rather than for the learners or those supporting learners.

Pause and Reflect

- Why do you think empathy is often undervalued in leadership?
- Why is empathy essential to improvement?
- What forces work to prohibit an empathic approach to leadership?
- What strategies or approaches could leaders take to integrate empathy into their routine practice?

BUILDING CAPACITY TO LEAD WITH EMPATHY

Leading with empathy is like any other skill or muscle, and it requires deliberate practice to strengthen the ability to act with empathy in professional practice. In alignment with current literature about growth mindset (Dweck, 2016), we believe that empathy is not a fixed quality leaders have but a skill they can hone. Similarly, as much as the skill of leading with empathy can be strengthened, it can also atrophy all too easily. The following paragraphs suggest three steps leaders can take to build their capacity to lead with empathy, particularly in times of disruption and ambiguity. These suggestions come from my own experiences and from conversations with other educational leaders.

Deliberately Engage With Diverse Perspectives

A key practice that district and school leaders can take to lead with empathy is to deliberately seek and routinely engage with diverse perspectives. Since empathy is about understanding others, the most direct way to learn how others are feeling is to break out of one's own daily bubbles and engage with other people who are in different circumstances.

I constantly ask myself—where am I getting my information? How am I distilling it? District and school leaders are bombarded with information daily, and social media is playing an increasingly influential role (Suciu, 2019). Given this rise in electronic information, it is ever important that educational leaders connect with individuals from the educational community who have different experiences and points of view. This diversity of perspective is essential.

In his article "Echo chambers and epistemic bubbles," C. Thi Nguyen (2020) points out that many people live in epistemic bubbles and echo chambers in which information is filtered to comport with one's own views and biases. People tend to read books, watch shows, and follow news channels that align with their ways of thinking, and the algorithms of online platforms are designed to filter information so people see mainly what they want to see. An epistemic bubble exists when relevant but divergent views and information are filtered out and excluded. When leaders live in epistemic bubbles, they lack the range of information needed to problem-solve. Another danger is that epistemic bubbles encourage overconfidence because the only information one receives will tend to reinforce preexisting ideas and beliefs. Nguyen distinguishes epistemic bubbles from echo chambers, which are even more dangerous in that they not only filter out differing views but also encourage a distrust of divergent beliefs and opinions. Educational leaders should work to prevent being trapped in such "bubbles" or "chambers," and this work begins with actively engaging with others who have different perspectives and experiences.

So how can you have a presence on social media and not contribute to the echo chamber? Social media posts allow parents and stakeholders to visually see what is occurring behind the walls of our schools. In the absence of facts people make things up—so provide the facts. Media posts should be structured around your school mission, vision, and beliefs. It also provides an opportunity for leaders to interact with students and teachers, further strengthening empathy. Do you welcome feedback? You can't seek to understand if you don't provide opportunities for people to speak. Another strategy some leaders are using is surveying students and families about their feelings and beliefs about the school and district. We administer a climate survey every year and hold annual presentations to the public on the results. Principals and school administrators are then required to create action steps and plans to address concerns raised in the survey.

Practice Active Listening

As mentioned previously, leading with empathy entails actively listening and striving to understand others' experiences while engaging *with* them. Active listening means truly working to understand how others may be perceiving their world and feeling differently about it than the listener (e.g., see Engel, 2018). This level of understanding does not occur quickly; it requires building trust that can develop only by taking the time to thoughtfully engage in conversations focused on generating deeper understanding about how changes are affecting others. In short, it cannot be rushed. For example, one of my greatest challenges as a superintendent in a diverse community in New York was to find solutions to address the challenge of an increasing number of Spanish-speaking families entering the school system with students who did not speak any English and/or had little or no formal education. As the number of families entering the school system grew, it became clear that the existing systems and practices were not able to meet the needs of this growing population. A variety of solutions were attempted that did not fully address key challenges related to this issue. It was only by continually engaging key stakeholders through surveys, thought exchanges, and ongoing conversations that the district developed a dual language program and began hiring teachers with similar life experiences to those of the students. It was in large part through active listening that district and school leaders were able to deeply understand the needs of these students and their families in order to build a system that worked better for them. It took time for the team to grow their brains around all the issues.

Sometimes, simple questions can serve to begin building trust and start engaging in deep conversations that have the potential to build the understanding and empathy that lead to greater innovation and equity. Examples include the following:

- How is it going?
- How are you feeling about . . . ?
- What is working best?
- What is not working?
- What would work better?
- What can be done differently?

Sometimes one or two of these questions are all that is needed to communicate a powerful message of empathy and to begin developing a deeper understanding of others.

Work Collaboratively to Design Solutions

A third practice that can help educational leaders lead with empathy logically flows from engaging with diverse perspectives and active listening. In addition to engaging in these two practices, empathic leaders also work collaboratively with and empower others to generate solutions. I strongly believe that active listening often requires engaging in multiple conversations and sustaining them over time. Our current iteration of post pandemic practices is the launch of Synergy@Mineola High School. Synergy is a new structure of high school that eliminates periods and allows students to control their own time, space, and pace of work. We launched this project based on focus groups with students and teachers using the concept of a minimal viable product (MVP). An MVP is a common method used by start-ups when launching a product. They don't wait for a product to be perfect; instead they knowingly launch an "unfinished" product to purposefully determine what to fix first. They know a product will be "buggy" after the launch but also know the feedback they receive will be targeted—allowing for purposeful changes directly implemented based on customer feedback. Better solutions come from soliciting feedback from the users. Our Synergy team meets weekly to iterate new methodology and change and modify the systems we created. We also involve students in the concept of co-creation to better deliver a solution that works for everyone.

Forces That Restrain Leading With Empathy

The three practices suggested in this chapter may strike some readers as common sense. Many readers may have encountered similar recommendations in other contexts and discussions. All the more reason to embrace these recommendations. However, a key point which is perhaps less intuitive is that empathy plays a considerable role in supporting equity and innovation. And given the importance of empathy, it is helpful to consider some of the forces that discourage leaders from leading with empathy. The following points describe a few such forces, along with suggestions for how leaders can mitigate these as barriers to empathy.

Time. One of the biggest forces that can dissuade leaders from leaning into empathy more intentionally is time. When COVID-19 hit and schools were forced to close, leaders did not have a lot of time to engage with others, to actively listen, and to problem-solve as collaboratively as they may have desired. Nonetheless, the need to react quickly is not a novel dilemma for leaders. To mitigate against a lack of time, some leaders have developed sustainable habits and feedback systems that allow them to routinely engage with diverse groups of stakeholders in ongoing problem-solving. This approach includes creating a schedule of routine engagements with diverse stakeholders, like weekly coffee talks with parents, or blocking off weekly times to reach out and talk with students, families, or staff members.

The Bubble Effect. As described in this chapter, district and school leaders can easily become isolated in an epistemic bubble or, worse, an echo chamber. Particularly when implementing new changes or initiatives, leaders may perceive a change more optimistically than stakeholders. For example, when leaders develop plans and begin implementation, much of the energy can be focused on the process of implementation itself. Empathic leaders can mitigate against this tendency by actively working to find out both how well the changes are working and how the changes are being received by others.

Discomfort With What One Might Find. Anyone seeking to expand their own perspective and better understand the experiences of those in their educational community is likely to become aware of new challenges and then feel responsible for taking on those challenges. Leading with empathy implies leaning forward into challenges. And the most difficult kind of problem to solve is one that is not fully understood. (Just ask teachers how we are going to prepare students for the world of work when we don't know what jobs will exist in the future.) However, the more one leads with empathy, the better one can understand, and the greater the likelihood of being effective in dealing with disruption while fostering innovation and ensuring equity is sustained.

CONCLUSION

For many district and school leaders, the need to improve and innovate rapidly and to be insistent about ensuring equity may never have been greater. As this chapter argues, and I have found over 14 years as a superintendent, empathy can be essential to making both possible, and leaders can actively enhance their empathic skill by applying it to shepherd their communities and foster the trust that is needed to navigate the turbulent waters of the current period. Such a perspective does not come easily, and mitigating against forces that discourage leading with empathy takes deliberate effort. Leaders do not always get empathy right, and unfortunately it can also be argued that there is currently a dearth of empathy on a broader scale. Empathy may not be a defining characteristic of the current zeitgeist. However, district and school leaders have a powerful opportunity and essential role to lead with empathy to address the many challenges that currently face their communities. The current conditions also constitute an opportunity to model for students how to effectively embrace uncertainty and change in a way that gives hope for a future that is better than the past.

Reflect Further and Take Action

- How did the chapter's information, ideas, and activities affirm, expand, or challenge your prior understanding about empathy?
- What is your current level of practice as it relates to empathy? What about other leaders in your context?
- Based on your reading, what actions or steps can you take moving forward?

REFERENCES

Borba, M. (2022). Future-proofing students. *ASCD, 79*(8), 18–23.

Brower, T. (2021). Empathy is the most important leadership skill according to research. *Forbes.* Accessed November 9, 2022. https://www.forbes.com/sites /tracybrower/2021/09/19/empathy-is-the-most-important-leadership-skill -according-to-research/

Center for Creative Leadership. (2023). The importance of empathy in the workplace. Accessed February 20, 2023. https://www.ccl.org/articles/leading-effectively -articles/empathy-in-the-workplace-a-tool-for-effective-leadership/

Covey, S. R. (2004). Habit 5: Seek first to understand, then to be understood. In *The 7 habits of highly effective people: Powerful lessons in personal change* (pp. 235–260). Free Press.

Dweck, C. (2016). What having a "growth mindset" actually means. *Harvard Business Review, 13*, 213–226.

Engel, J. (2018). How empathic and active listening can improve workplace communication. *Forbes*. https://www.forbes.com/sites/forbescoachescouncil/2018 /12/19/how-empathic-and-active-listening-can-improve-workplace-communi cation/#61686f651f3c

Holt, S., & Marques, J. Empathy in leadership: Appropriate or misplaced? An empirical study on a topic that is asking for attention. *Journal of Business Ethics, 105*(1), 95–105. https://doi.org/10.1007/s10551-011-0951-5

Miller, H. L. Why empathetic leadership is the most effective leadership style. *Leaders.com*, July 6, 2022. https://leaders.com/articles/leadership/empathetic -leadership/

Nguyen, C. T. (2020). Echo chambers and epistemic bubbles. *Episteme, 17*(2), 141– 161. https://philpapers.org/archive/NGUECA.pdf

Suciu, P. (2019). More Americans are getting their news from social media. *Forbes*. https://www.forbes.com/sites/petersuciu/2019/10/11/more-americans-are -getting-their-news-from-social-media/#6e1eda33e179

CHAPTER 2

Culturally Responsive Schools Start With Culturally Responsive Leaders

Saroja R. Warner

Pause and Reflect Before Reading

- Where do you see diversity in your educational community?
- How would you define cultural competence?
- And, what do you think it means to be culturally responsive as an educator?

INTRODUCTION

In 2020, two pandemics scourged our nation, creating unrest and turmoil in all aspects of life, including education. The COVID-19 global pandemic illuminated, and exacerbated, inequities in educational opportunities for students. As schooling quickly transitioned universally to virtual environments, the inefficiencies of our education system became apparent: students (and teachers) without access to broadband internet service or access to WiFi and computers, and teachers ill-equipped to implement effective virtual curriculum, pedagogies, and practices. Many students who were already disengaged in education offered in physical school buildings disappeared altogether in the virtual learning environments that replaced them during the pandemic. And concerns are that loss of learning for students has impacted particular students disproportionately: students of color, students from low socioeconomic backgrounds, students with different abilities, and English language learners.

The second pandemic, systemic racism, has existed for centuries and entered the forefront of our collective consciousness as a result of the national spotlight and media coverage of the police killings of Black citizens including Ahmaud Aubrey, Breonna Taylor, and George Floyd. Amid the battle against an invisible enemy, COVID-19, Black people across the nation faced and continue to face a very real and present danger to their lives from the (in)justice system resulting in the ignition of the global Black Lives Matter movement, which played a significant role in shifting the public discourse around race, antiracism, and education.

In today's context, creating schools that are culturally responsive is more critical than ever for achieving educational equity and improving our schools. Across the nation, education leaders are leveraging culturally responsive teaching as the umbrella under which schools are focusing their improvement efforts. To accomplish this, they are implementing a number of educational equity strategies that include developing students' social and emotional skills, supporting students with diverse abilities, and implementing bullying prevention, trauma-informed teaching, and restorative justice practices. Culturally responsive teaching is an approach to teaching that emphasizes "using the cultural knowledge, prior experiences, frames of reference, and performance styles of ethnically diverse students to make learning encounters more relevant and effective for them" (Gay, 2010, p. 31). School and district leaders who promote culturally responsive practices play a central role in developing teachers' own culturally responsive practices and creating culturally responsive school environments that are inclusive, affirm students' identities, and support positive academic and social outcomes.

Pause and Reflect

- What do you know about culturally responsive teaching?
- What do you know about culturally responsive school environments?
- Based on what you know, what are the benefits of both for supporting student learning and outcomes?

CHARACTERISTICS AND BEHAVIORS OF CULTURALLY RESPONSIVE LEADERS

Emerging research on culturally responsive leaders (CRLs) provides insights into what school and district leaders should know and do to create, maintain, and sustain culturally responsive school environments that support educational equity (Gilbert et al., 2022; Khalifa et al., 2016; Rice-Boothe, 2022; Skrla et al., 2004). This chapter describes five key characteristics and behaviors of CRLs:

1. Routinely engage in critical self-awareness of cultural identity and implicit bias

2. Intentionally recruit, hire, and retain culturally responsive teachers
3. Promote a culturally responsive and inclusive school culture
4. Mentor and model culturally responsive teaching
5. Engage with students, families, and communities in culturally responsive ways

Routinely Engage in Critical Self-Awareness of Cultural Identity and Implicit Bias

For school and district leaders who are invested in becoming more culturally responsive, the first step is to engage routinely in practices aimed at developing self-awareness and interrogating their own implicit biases. Each person's biases affect their judgments and behaviors, and this phenomenon holds true for everyone, regardless of race, gender, or any other aspect of identity. In other words, educators of color are not immune from implicit biases that have the potential to adversely influence their practice.

School leaders who are culturally responsive consistently engage in critical reflection about who they are as humans and the assumptions they have about the people and contexts in which they lead (Gooden & Dantley, 2012; Johnson, 2006). For example, when leaders adopt and enact a culturally responsive orientation to data inquiry, they are better equipped to address implicit biases that influence their interpretations of student data and their perceptions of information more broadly about students and their families (Skrla et al., 2004). This means recognizing that there are multiple information domains for gathering data beyond conventional measures of academic performance that include data about students' schooling experiences and personal stories and experiences (Warner, 2021). Understanding the whole child—students' experiences with schools and in proximity to schools—from an asset-based perspective better equips culturally responsive leaders to identify systems, structures, and practices that inhibit equity in their schools and to identify culturally responsive approaches for countering and ultimately dismantling barriers to equity.

Additional strategies for promoting critical self-awareness and identity development include writing cultural and racial autobiographies, participating in educational plunges, and journaling on critical topics of culture (Brown, 2004; Gooden & O'Doherty, 2015; Jean-Marie et al., 2009). *The Culturally Responsive Leadership Framework* (2022), by the Leadership Academy, in the "Additional Resources" section at the end of this chapter identifies research-based leadership actions that have been shown to support creating more culturally responsive learning environments for every student. The first action recommended in this resource focuses on equity and access and includes reflection on personal beliefs, biases, assumptions, and behaviors as a routine practice.

Pause and Reflect

1. To what extent do you and/or leaders you work with routinely engage in critical self-reflection of implicit bias?
2. What specific examples from your own or your colleagues' practices can you identify that are aligned to this characteristic?
3. What new behaviors or practices might you try in your own leadership context to be a culturally responsive leader?

Intentionally Recruit, Hire, and Retain Culturally Responsive Teachers

CRLs promote and sustain environments that are stable enough to attract culturally responsive teachers and to support the further development of those teachers. Research suggests that good teachers will eventually leave schools that have ineffective school leaders (Grissom et al., 2021; Grissom & Keiser, 2011; Leithwood et al., 2004).

Since being an effective leader includes having cultural competence, CRLs must be committed to recruiting and retaining culturally responsive teachers. CRLs can do so through the application and hiring process by using interview protocols and performance tasks to determine if teachers demonstrate cultural competence. Additionally, retaining culturally responsive teachers is best accomplished when CRLs create safe learning environments for both teachers and students, environments in which cultural diversity is valued, continuous improvement is the norm, and high expectations abound.

You might start simply by looking around and listening in your school building. For example, when you stand in the hallway or cafeteria, what do you see? Is student work prominently visible throughout the building? Are a variety of cultures, experiences, and languages represented on walls, in classrooms, and in office spaces? What do you hear? Are students, teachers, and staff smiling and laughing?

CRLs can go further by making sure their instructional resources are of high quality, which includes being culturally responsive as well. The Culturally Responsive Curriculum Scorecard in the "Additional Resources" section at the end of this chapter includes a comprehensive set of rubrics for reviewing and evaluating the quality of cultural responsiveness within a district's existing curriculum resources and materials.

Pause and Reflect

- To what extent do you and/or leaders you work with deliberately recruit, hire, and retain culturally responsive teachers?

- What is the current level of practice in your district(s) and schools related to this characteristic of a culturally responsive leader?
- What specific examples from your own or your colleagues' practices can you identify that are aligned to this characteristic?

Promote a Culturally Responsive and Inclusive School Culture

Consistent with Standard 5 of the Professional Standards for Educational Leaders (National Policy Board for Educational Administration, 2015), CRLs build and maintain safe, caring, and healthy school environments that meet the academic, social, emotional, and physical needs of each student (Khalifa et al., 2016). They create and sustain school cultures in which each student is known and sees their culture reflected in the curriculum and throughout the school; students and teachers are accepted, valued, trusted, respected, and cared for; and high expectations are the norm (Khalifa, 2010). Additionally, CRLs foster a culturally affirming school environment for students, parents and families, and teachers and staff (Gardiner & Enomoto, 2006; Webb-Johnson, 2006; Webb-Johnson & Carter, 2007).

An example of how CRLs might foster such an environment is by identifying and remedying racialized gaps in any category, from school discipline to achievement results to how students are identified for special education. In the February 2020 edition of *School Administrator*, Muhammad Khalifa explains that in order to promote a culturally responsive and inclusive school culture, leaders must rely on community knowledge to shape and promote a schoolwide vision of equity and excellence, inclusivity, and cultural responsiveness. He urges leaders to understand that this vision should not be developed by educators alone: "Consider the history of how some underrepresented members of the community always have felt excluded. Such an approach would be more of the same. Rather, include community-based and student perspectives and histories at the time that you are crafting the vision" (Khalifa, 2020).

CRLs consider how they work with colleagues and community to develop, advocate, and act according to a shared school mission, vision, and core values for culturally responsive teaching and learning that supports all students in accessing and achieving rigorous standards. Again, the Culturally Responsive Leadership Framework (2022) in the "Additional Resources" section at the end of this chapter describes examples of actions for promoting a culturally responsive and inclusive school culture. (See page 6 of this framework.)

Pause and Reflect

1. To what extent do you and/or leaders you work with deliberately recruit, hire, and retain culturally responsive teachers?
2. What is the current level of practice in your district(s) and schools related to this characteristic of a culturally responsive leader?
3. What specific examples from your own or your colleagues' practices can you identify that are aligned to this characteristic?

Mentor and Model Culturally Responsive Teaching

As instructional leaders in schools, CRLs have the great responsibility of supporting the development of teaching effectiveness by managing the instructional program. Doing so includes building the capacity of teachers to enact culturally responsive practices (Madhlangobe & Gordon, 2012; National Policy Board for Educational Administration, 2015). CRLs not only model culturally responsive behaviors but also guide teachers and staff in conversations and critical interrogations of assumptions about race and culture and the impact of those assumptions on the classroom (Gooden & O'Doherty, 2015; Shields, 2010). CRLs implement strategies for developing cultural responsiveness in teachers who initially are not, and may even resist becoming, culturally responsive.

One practice, for example, highlighted in the *Principal's Guide to Building Culturally Responsive Schools* (NAESP Diversity Task Force, 2016), that a CRL might engage is to routinely conduct individual and building-wide self-assessments. Consider engaging in a "Who Am I?" exercise, in which a person writes down as many identity descriptors as possible to help identify his or her cultural, philosophical, and social identities and begin to understand the social contexts that guide individual belief systems. Developing positionality statements is another great practice to do with teachers to model and mentor cultural responsiveness.

Other practices include supporting teachers in identifying and implementing multicultural curriculum materials across all content areas and disciplines, expecting them to include development of their cultural competencies as an annual professional learning goal, and ensuring that professional learning experiences integrate opportunities for teachers to develop their cultural competencies. CRLs also have to be willing to encourage the departure of those teachers who recognize that this work is not for them.

Pause and Reflect

1. To what extent do you and/or leaders you work with mentor and model culturally responsive teaching?
2. What is the current level of practice in your district(s) and schools related to this characteristic of a culturally responsive leader?
3. What specific examples from your own or your colleagues' practices can you identify that are aligned to this characteristic?

Engage With Students, Families, and Communities in Culturally Responsive Ways

Research demonstrates that when families participate in their children's education, those children make academic gains (Carter, 2002; Dearing et al., 2006). The ability to engage students, families, and communities in culturally appropriate ways is an essential characteristic of CRLs. This ability includes understanding, addressing, and advocating for community-based issues. As one principal explained to me, engagement is not simply about having open-door policies; it's about forging relationships with students, families, and communities in spaces adjacent to the school.

Cultural and linguistic differences can play a big part in whether families become involved with school. Some are more easily addressed by CRLs than others. For example, language differences between the school and the student and his or her family may contribute to family members' discomfort discussing questions or concerns with educators because of their limited language skills. This may be addressed by expanding access to parents to interpreters or school/community liaisons who can facilitate communication between educators and family members and hiring more bilingual staff. More challenging for CRLs is building relationships and cultures based on trust and that ensure safety for students, families, and communities. Culturally based perceptions about school involvement may contribute to deficit beliefs by educators about families—that families do not care about their child's achievement in schools. Some communities may view educators as experts and feel uncomfortable questioning them as the "authority." Others may have anxiety about residency status that impacts their visible participation and presence in schools and with educators. CRLs address generalizations and assumptions about families and communities from different cultural backgrounds and support teachers to do the same, and work in intentional ways to expand and strengthen trust and safety for families and communities. Examples of actions include:

- Invite community members to supplement classroom instruction in the students' home language.
- Inform family members about classes and programs offered by community organizations (e.g., career planning, citizenship, computer literacy, health).
- Encourage community and business leaders to support and participate in school functions.
- Invite community members to participate in daily school activities such as involving them in instructional tasks, enlisting their help in the lunchroom, asking them to help with tutoring, and calling upon them to take part in special events.

CRLs see students and their families from an asset-based perspective and make efforts to build relationships with them both to help connect their lives to schooling and to connect schooling to their lives. They see the school as an integral part of the surrounding communities and therefore as contributing to the needs and health of communities.

Pause and Reflect

1. To what extent do you and/or leaders you work with engage with students, families, and communities in culturally responsive ways?
2. What is the current level of practice in your district(s) and schools related to this characteristic of a culturally responsive leader?
3. What specific examples from your own or your colleagues' practices can you identify that are aligned to this characteristic?

EXAMPLE OF A CULTURALLY RESPONSIVE LEADER

Cultivating the five characteristics of culturally responsive leaders takes time and practice. The following spotlight provides an example of how one culturally responsive leader modeled the foregoing recommendations.

Spotlight on Sharif El-Mekki: Every Child in Our Schools Is Our Own

Sharif El-Mekki is the director of the Center for Black Educator Development, launched in the summer of 2019 in Philadelphia and focused on direct and ongoing mentoring and coaching for Black teachers and cultural responsiveness for all teachers. Previously, he served for over a decade as a culturally responsive school leader in Philadelphia schools. The Education Trust recently published an in-depth feature on El-Mekki chronicling his career and commitments, aptly titled "Leading with Equity and Justice."

A core value for El-Mekki that he conveys explicitly to parents and families is that "it is an absolute privilege to serve your children." While leading at Mastery Charter School—Shoemaker Campus, a Title 1 school in a predominantly Black community with a student population that over the years has stayed about 98 percent Black—he never saw himself as separate from the parents and families of his students. Working from a servant-leader paradigm, he anchored his engagement in the aspirations of families and communities. He began each year by asking parents, "What are your goals for your child? What do you want me to do, start doing, or stop doing to help you meet your goals for your child?" He explained to me, "Every parent wants their child to do better than they did, to have more," so it would be misguided to assume they do not value education if they can't make every school meeting or event. "When I took on this responsibility, I made a promise to parents which requires me to listen and be responsive to their desires for their children."

For El-Mekki, being a culturally responsive leader also means hiring new teachers and building the capacity of existing teachers to be culturally responsive. In his words, "One of the promises I made to families was to get the best teachers possible for their children. The best teachers don't shy away from having conversations and doing the work related to interrogating race, class, and privilege. They understand the privilege that they have; whether it was White privilege, or male privilege, or college-educated Black person privilege; whatever it is, they are comfortable talking about this and exploring how race, class, and privilege play out in their classrooms, and how it will manifest in lesson plans."

During interviews with candidates, El-Mekki probed hard in order to screen out those whose stance, posture, and habits of practice did not demonstrate the characteristics of culturally responsive pedagogy and practice. He created and cultivated a learning culture at his school. In his words, "Through professional development, I also focused on race, class, and privilege and pushed teachers to investigate their beliefs and thinking, and created spaces for everyone to feel safe as they got uncomfortable. I always held them to high expectations when it came to their own growth, and especially in the service of our students. They had to be willing to be coached through things in this learning organization." And like many culturally responsive leaders, El-Mekki believes that the best teachers recognize the importance of "who you are as a person, how you see the humanity of other people."

El-Mekki's passion and commitment to recruiting and retaining more culturally responsive teachers, particularly Black males, led him to start a small support group of fewer than two dozen Black male teachers. The men met monthly to share success stories, solve problems, and build community. As word got out, the group grew quickly, so that in 2014 El-Mekki founded the Fellowship of Black Male Educators, an organization focused on recruiting, developing, and retaining Black male teachers.

Pause and Reflect

1. In the spotlight on Sharif El-Mekki, what characteristics of a culturally responsive school leader are evident?
2. What new behaviors or practices might you try in your own leadership context to be a culturally responsive leader?

CONCLUSION

As mentioned at the beginning of this chapter, teachers are the single most important factor in student achievement. Because of this, schools need teachers to be highly skilled, which includes being culturally responsive. All schools have significant cultural diversity, so all teachers can benefit from being culturally aware and competent. This competence begins with district and school leaders modeling cultural competence, as well as cultivating professional settings and safe learning environments that can sustain culturally responsive practices.

Take Action

1. How did the chapter's information, ideas, and activities align with or challenge your prior understanding?
2. Based on your reading, what actions or steps can you take moving forward?
3. What resources or information would be supportive to educators in your school or district and what role can you play in deepening their understanding, as well as professional practices?

ADDITIONAL RESOURCES

- *Principal's Guide to Building Culturally Responsive Schools* developed by the National Association of Elementary School Principals (NAESP) Diversity Task Force provides recommendations for and resources aligned to four leadership competencies that are meant to guide school leaders in their work to ensure equity for all students: advance culturally responsive leadership, diversify student and adult capacity to transform schools, utilize assets to ensure culturally responsive teaching and learning, and provide diverse opportunities for all students.

- *Creating a District Plan to Increase the Racial, Ethnic, and Linguistic Diversity of Your Educator Workforce: A Guidebook for Hiring and Selection.* Developed in collaboration with the Connecticut State Department of Education, the Northeast Comprehensive Center, and the Center for Great Teachers and Leaders, this book offers guidance, templates, tools, and a meaningful case story with a discussion guide that school leaders can use with staff.
- *The Culturally Responsive Curriculum Scorecard.* Includes a comprehensive set of rubrics for reviewing and evaluating the quality of cultural responsiveness within a district's existing curriculum resources and materials.
- *The Diversity Toolkit: Cultural Competence for Educators.* Offers a variety of information and resources for educators and leaders to use in supporting cultural competence in schools and classrooms.
- *Conducting a Cultural Competence Self-Assessment.* A self-assessment tool, developed by the SUNY/Downstate Medical Center (Brooklyn, NY), which can be used by district or school leaders for conducting an audit of their institution's cultural competence. (Although developed for a healthcare organization, this resource is easily transferable to an educational setting.)
- "Teachers, Race, and Student Achievement in a Randomized Experiment." A 2004 article by Thomas Dee in *The Review of Economics and Statistics* (vol. 86, no. 1, pp. 195–210).
- *Culturally Responsive School Leadership.* A 2018 book by Muhammad Khalifa, published by Harvard Education Press.
- *The Principal's Guide to Building Culturally Responsive Schools.* Developed by the National Association of Elementary School Principals in 2018.
- *Cultural Responsiveness, Biases, and Prejudices.* A February 2020 special edition of *School Administrator* from The American Association of School Administrators (AASA).
- *Portrait of a Culturally Responsive School.* Developed by the Leadership Academy, this guide includes definitions for key terms, indicators, and reflection questions. It can be used by school leaders as a baseline to create aspirational goals, an accountability tool to assess progress against goals, and a celebration tool to show quick wins.
- *Examining Biases for Cultural Competence.* Developed by CASEL as one part of a guide for schoolwide SEL, offers activities and resources that can be used by school leaders to help school staff to reflect on

their own biases to create safe, equitable, supportive, and inclusive environments for all students, staff, and families.

- *Culturally Responsive Leadership: A Framework for School and School System Leaders.* The Leadership Academy's (2022) framework identifies a set of research-based leadership behaviors that have shown to support creating more culturally responsive learning environments for every student.

REFERENCES

Brown, K. M. (2004). Leadership for social justice and equity: Weaving a transformative framework and pedagogy. *Educational Administration Quarterly, 40,* 77–108.

Carter, S. (2002). The Impact of Parent/Family Involvement of Student Outcomes: An Annotated Bibliography of Research from the Past Decade. Consortium for Appropriate Dispute Resolution in Special Education. 2002. Available online: https://oaklandliteracycoalition.org/wp-content/uploads/2016/12/Impact-Family-Involvement.pdf.

Dearing, E., Kreider, H., Simpkins, S., & Weiss, H. B. (2006). Family involvement in school and low-income children's literacy: Longitudinal associations between and within families. *Journal of Educational Psychology, 98*(4), 653–664.

Gardiner, M. E., & Enomoto, E. (2006). Urban school principals and their role as multicultural leaders. *Urban Education, 41,* 560–584.

Gay, G. (2010). *Culturally responsive teaching: Theory, research, and practice.* Teachers College Press.

Gilbert, N., Gran, J., Lewis, A., & Teodorescu, D. (2022). The shoulder tap: Educators of color on the leadership representation gap—and what we can do about it. https://newleaders.org/resources

Gooden, M. A., & Dantley, M. (2012). Centering race in a framework for leadership preparation. *Journal of Research on Leadership Education, 7,* 237–253.

Gooden, M. A., & O'Doherty, A. (2015). Do you see what I see? Fostering aspiring leaders' racial awareness. *Urban Education, 50,* 225–255.

Grissom, J. A., Egalite, A. J., & Lindsay, C. A. (February 2021). How principals affect students and schools: A systematic synthesis of two decades of research. *The Wallace Foundation.* https://www.wallacefoundation.org/knowledge-center/Documents/How-Principals-Affect-Students-and-Schools.pdf

Grissom, J. A., & Keiser, L. (2011). A supervisor like me: Race, representation, and the satisfaction and turnover decisions of public sector employees. *Journal of Policy Analysis and Management, 30*(3), 557–580. https://doi.org/10.1002/pam.20579

Jean-Marie, G., Normore, A. H., & Brooks, J. S. (2009). Leadership for social justice: Preparing twenty-first century school leaders for a new social order. *Journal of Research on Leadership Education, 4,* 1–31.

Johnson, L. S. (2006). "Making her community a better place to live": Culturally responsive urban school leadership in historical context. *Leadership and Policy in Schools*, *5*, 19–36.

Khalifa, M. (2010). Validating social and cultural capital of hyperghettoized at-risk students. *Education and Urban Society*, *42*, 620–646.

Khalifa, M. (2020). Promoting culturally responsive leadership practices: Shining a light on marginalized children with humanistic practices and data scrutiny. *School Administrator* [Special issue]. http://my.aasa.org/AASA/Resources/SAMag/2020/Feb20/Khalifa.aspx

Khalifa, M. A., Gooden, M. A., & Davis, J. E. (2016). Culturally responsive school leadership: A synthesis of the literature. *Review of Educational Research*, *86*(4), 1272–1311. https://doi.org/10.3102/0034654316630383

The Leadership Academy. (2022). *Culturally Responsive Leadership: A Framework for School & School System Leaders* [White paper]. https://www.leadershipacademy.org/resources/culturally-responsive-leadership-a-framework-for-school-school-system-leaders/

Leithwood, K., Louis, K. S., Anderson, S., & Wahlstrom, K. (2004). *How leadership influences student learning: Review of research*. Wallace Foundation.

Madhlangobe, L., & Gordon, S. P. (2012). Culturally responsive leadership in a diverse school: A case study of a high school leader. *NASSP Bulletin*, *96*, 177–202.

NAESP Diversity Task Force. (2016). *Principal's guide to building culturally responsive schools*. National Association of Elementary School Principals.

National Policy Board for Educational Administration. (2015). *Professional standards for educational leaders*. Author. http://npbea.org/psel/

Rice-Boothe, M. (2022, August 26). Culturally responsive leadership. *Edutopia*. https://www.edutopia.org/article/culturally-responsive-leadership/

Shields, C. M. (2010). Transformative leadership: Working for equity in diverse contexts. *Educational Administration Quarterly*, *46*, 558–589.

Skrla, L., Scheurich, J. J., Garcia, J., & Nolly, G. (2004). Equity audits: A practical leadership tool for developing equitable and excellent schools. *Educational Administration Quarterly*, *40*(1), 133–161. https://doi.org/10.1177/0013161X03259148

Warner, S. (2021). *Culturally responsive data literacy*. National Center for Systemic Improvement: WestEd https://ncsi.wested.org/wp-content/uploads/2021/03/NCSI-Culturally-Responsive-Data-Literacy.pdf

Webb-Johnson, G. C. (2006). To be young, gifted, emotionally challenged and Black: A principal's role in providing a culturally responsive context. *Voices in Urban Education*, *12*, 20–27.

Webb-Johnson, G. C., & Carter, N. (2007). Culturally responsive urban school leadership: Partnering to improve outcomes for African American learners. *National Journal of Urban Education and Practice*, *1*, 77–99.

CHAPTER 3

Is an Equity Audit in Your Future?

Shandy Hauk and Joyce Kaser

This chapter is based upon work supported by the National Science Foundation (NSF) under Grant Nos. DGE 1445522, DUE 1504551, and DUE 1625215. Any opinions, findings, and conclusions or recommendations expressed are those of the authors and do not necessarily reflect the views of the NSF.

Pause and Reflect Before Reading

Consider and record your response to the following prompts. For each statement, decide whether it is true or false.*

- The more people see the need for some action, the more likely they are to support it.
- Gathering data on performance will usually be sufficient for determining disparities.
- There is a relatively short learning curve for mastering the art of conducting an equity audit.
- It is possible to conduct an equity audit without having a vision of equity for your school or district.
- There are effective strategies for dealing with resistance to an equity audit.
- The equity audit process includes a cycle of developing and implementing a plan that responds to audit findings.

*The authors' answers to the T/F questions are T, F, F, F, T, T.

INTRODUCTION

A close read of the federal Every Student Succeeds Act (ESSA) reveals that it provides more openings for addressing equity in our nation's schools than previous legislation. As Cook-Harvey and her colleagues (2016) describe in their analysis and Ayscue and colleagues (2022) examined in pandemic-era state educational planning, a number of provisions within ESSA can be leveraged to improve equity for individuals who have been traditionally underserved within U.S. education systems. However, for schools and districts to determine how to leverage ESSA to improve equity, it is beneficial first for them to undertake a thoughtful analysis of their existing systems. This analysis may involve conducting an equity audit. Some leaders and educators may not be familiar with equity audits, including what they are and their potential benefits. The purpose of this report is to provide an introduction to equity audits. In addition to defining an equity audit and the advantages it can afford, this chapter offers six suggestions for how to conduct a successful equity audit. These suggestions come from the authors' research- and practice-based knowledge and experiences in examining equity in a variety of educational contexts with partners across the country.

WHAT IS EQUITY?

Explicitly, at this moment in the elementary, secondary, and post-secondary educational research and practice communities in the United States, there is not a well-defined, crisp, and shared definition of equity (National Academies, 2019). Given this absence, for the purposes of communication, one might start with the Merriam-Webster dictionary and say, equity is fairness. This starting point begs the question: Who decides what is fair? It is also important to distinguish between equity and equality: equality is everyone having the same thing while equity is based on a person's current situation and future goals, and it means people have what they need to grow from the one to the other in a given context (e.g., social, political, economic environments). In some sense, too, equity can be partially defined by its complement: inequity. If equity is evidenced by the absence of disparities, so that membership in a group that has been historically disadvantaged is in no way correlated to access to opportunities, attainment of educational outcomes, or achievement of life goals, then monitoring change in disparity is a way to measure progress toward equity (by measuring reduction in inequity).

The word "equity" is often used near words such as "diversity" and "inclusion." To be clear, diversity is quantitative; it is a measure of the variation of particular characteristics of interest across people or groups. Inclusion in a group or in a structure may, like diversity, provide a metric related to equity in that inclusion "involves an authentic and empowered participation" (Annie E. Casey Foundation, 2014, p. 5). Though inclusion may be necessary, it is not sufficient for a situation or process to be equitable. In addition to focusing on fairness, some might say equity includes "impartiality." However, achieving fairness may require partiality in some decisions in order to effectively address inequities. Hence, the need for an equity audit.

WHAT IS AN EQUITY AUDIT?

Simply put, an equity audit is a study of the fairness of an institution's policies, programs, and practices. A key reason to conduct an equity audit is to identify areas of inequity, where groups of students are being underserved, so that actions and steps can be taken to prioritize improvement in these areas. In general, an equity audit will analyze policies, programs, and practices, specifically in terms of how they directly or indirectly impact students or staff relative to race, ethnicity, gender, national origin, color, (dis)ability, age, sexual orientation, sexual identity, religion, and/or other socioculturally significant factors.

An equity audit may be extensive in scope or narrower. Looking at an entire school's or district's policies, programs, and practices can be a major undertaking. Focusing more narrowly on analyzing specific school functions, such as transportation, registration, graduation, or professional development, can be more manageable. For instance, one component of a transportation study might be to examine the availability, cost, and length of a bus ride to and from school for students, based on their race or ethnicity. Another example might be a study of graduation requirements that examines relationships among, and possible disparities correlated to, graduation rate and student race, ethnicity, gender, or (dis)ability. Or a staff-focused study might examine the experience of teachers and other instructional staff in relation to the schools to which they are assigned.

The intended outcomes of an equity audit are typically to report on areas of inequities and equities in a school's or district's policies, programs, and practices with specific demographic details. For example, a transportation-focused equity audit might reveal that Black students have a bus ride of 45 minutes on average while White students' average ride is 25 minutes.

WHY CONDUCT AN EQUITY AUDIT?

The need for an equity audit can originate in many ways. It may start simply from local self-awareness of a potential inequity or may originate from a need to comply with federal law, such as when the U.S. Office for Civil Rights has issued a finding requiring response and a district needs data to determine how pervasive the problem may be. Moreover, in any period of political uncertainty, a school or other organization may simply want to clarify local equity goals, resources, and priorities. A significant body of research has indicated that when organizations like schools and districts prioritize improvement for specific groups of students, all students can benefit (e.g., Allexsaht-Snider & Sherick, 2020; Darling-Hammond & Cook-Harvey, 2018; Wang & Sheikh-Khalil, 2021).

Pause and Reflect

- Are you feeling validated by what you are reading? If so, what values are being reinforced?
- Are you feeling challenged by anything you just read? If so, what is it you find challenging and why?

IMPORTANT CONSIDERATIONS

Leaders who are preparing to conduct an equity audit will want to communicate to interested individuals and groups about why the audit is being conducted, how information from the audit can be useful, and how they can become involved. Among the known benefits of equity audits are that they do the following:

- Result in data that serve as a common base for understanding what constitutes equity and inequity in an education system.
- Provide the basis for decision-making around priorities for improvement.
- Allow for measuring improvement over time and spotting inequities in a timely manner.
- Protect a school or district from unwarranted charges of discrimination.

Some individuals and groups involved in the education community may not perceive any inequities and may feel threatened by an inquiry into possible imbalances. By their nature, equity audits are fraught with potential for conflict because of the attention they bring to societal, organizational, and personal values and how those values are enacted. School personnel may have no clear sense of the range of inequities that can exist in schools. They may also see an audit as unnecessary and a diversion of resources.

In some schools and districts, equity may never have been acknowledged as an area of current or potential concern. Little or no demographically disaggregated data on students or staff may be available. Or, perhaps data have been gathered and supplied to an external agency, but there has been no local examination of the data. In either case, there may be an "it's not my problem" attitude in the school or district. All these factors—and others—can interfere with and generate resistance to an audit. Thus, it is important at the outset for leaders to communicate why the audit is being conducted, what the benefits will be, and how related decisions for change might be made. Given all of this, what follows are suggestions for smoothly conducting an equity audit.

Suggestion 1: Include a Diverse Base of Individuals and Groups

To get useful and accurate data, it is critical to involve representatives from groups affected by the policies, programs, and practices being studied in the audit. Without involvement from a diverse group of partners, the process can be seen as the majority examining the minority (or the powerful examining the disempowered) and can convey a message that the minority (or disempowered subgroup) is "the problem." A broadly based group will both provide pertinent insight and be more likely to send a message that everyone is in the process together. An authentic, inclusive equity audit might be introduced as follows: "We're conducting this audit to provide data that will tell us the extent of our inequities and guide us in resolving them."

Unless people can see the need for an equity audit, they are not likely to be supportive and may actively work against its data-gathering activities. This may include people who are involved but who do not, at first, acknowledge the importance of examining student experience and staff performance in light of race, ethnicity, gender, (dis)ability, and similar factors associated with social, political, economic, and educational disparities. Leaders can scaffold participation of interested and affected individuals and groups by offering opportunities to learn the language of equity around concepts such as bias and stereotyping, institutional racism and sexism, and the differences and commonalities between equality and equity. Supports might include having a third party provide workshops or webinars on how to be open to examining one's own views and how to understand the variety in perspectives that others may have, appreciate the benefits that diversity can bring, and build skills in noticing and dealing with differences.

Pause and Reflect

- Are you feeling validated by what you are reading? If so, what values are being reinforced?
- Are you feeling challenged by anything you just read? If so, what is it you find challenging and why?

Suggestion 2: Design the Audit to Be Systemic

Equity is important throughout an entire organization's policies, programs, and practices, affecting staff as well as students. Because inequities may be pervasive, an audit needs to take a comprehensive view. That means examining all inputs and outputs—for example, examining student access to educational programs, the programs themselves, and the results of such programs.

As another example, an equity study focused on the completion rates of students taking Algebra I would look at the policy (such as a requirement that all students take Algebra I in the 8th grade), the algebra curriculum, students' class assignments, supports for students, and the qualifications and instructional assignments of the algebra teachers. A systemic equity audit can bring to light patterns of inequities that may be in schools' procedures and assumptions. One of the purposes of an equity audit is to identify patterns. Then, partners involved in the process can use the highlighted patterns to discuss and generate a pool of potential responses to the identified patterns. Systemic change is complex, and having a framework for understanding it can be useful (e.g., considering patterns in terms of people, power, structures, and symbols; Reinholz & Andrews, 2020; Reinholz & Apkarian, 2018).

Two caveats here: (1) A simultaneous examination of many aspects of policies, programs, and practices is not the same thing as being systemic. An effective audit dives deep into each aspect to get at the connections across areas in order to uncover the issues that a school or district may need to address. (2) It is essential to disaggregate data. Examining and comparing conditions across subgroups can bring to light nuances of similarity and difference that would otherwise be missed by examining data in broad groupings that have not been disaggregated.

Pause and Reflect

- Are you feeling validated by what you are reading? If so, what values are being reinforced?
- Are you feeling challenged by anything you just read? If so, what is it you find challenging and why?

Suggestion 3: Seek Experienced Equity Experts

Leading an equity audit is not a task for a novice. Whether an audit will be conducted by a school's or district's own staff or by external consultants, the people who lead the effort need to be skilled in conducting audits—especially equity audits. Certainly, junior and senior staff can be team members, but the group leaders will need to have experience conducting audits.

In addition, at least one of the people leading the audit needs to have skills in evaluation. The appropriate evaluation expert will know how to design an equity study, gather and interpret data, present results, and orchestrate team conversations that result in viable recommendations for change.

Audit leaders also need to be interculturally competent, which means being aware of their own cultural orientations, the perspectives of different involved and affected partner groups, and strategies for working within and across professional and personal cultures. They also need to be seen as trustworthy by all involved, including those who may be in the minority.

Pause and Reflect

- Are you feeling validated by what you are reading? If so, what values are being reinforced?
- Are you feeling challenged by anything you just read? If so, what is it you find challenging and why?

Suggestion 4: Ask and Answer Questions That Clarify the Vision of Equity for the Audit

Having piles of data is likely to be overwhelming without a vision or goal for equitable policies, programs, and practices. From a bird's eye view, one might say that equity exists when every student has "the greatest opportunity to learn, enhanced by the resources and supports necessary to achieve competence, excellence, independence, responsibility, and self-sufficiency for school and for life" (Skrla et al., 2009, p. 14). But what does that look like? How do we know it when we see (or do not see) it? How do we sustain conditions that interrupt inequity and support equity in a particular district or school context? An equity audit is founded on an initial statement or vision of equity.

A first step can be to search online for what other schools, districts, and states have developed in terms of mission, vision, and goals for equity. These examples can then be used to shape or focus the local vision and the audit goals. For example, in a school-level audit, how is equity measured for the school's mathematics program? If the expectation for evidence of an equitable mathematics program is that the average mathematics achievement score for the school's students is within an identified range of the district average, then a clear specification is available. Yet, a broader vision of equity might lead to questions that can create greater clarity: What about class size? Test scores for each different subgroup of students? What inequities might those data reveal? Do the answers change how the group that is conducting the audit will define equity? Answering questions about what is considered evidence of equity will clarify the overall vision for equity.

A school leader might well comment, "Nice to have a vision, but what if we don't already have one? Are we doomed?" No, not at all. A useful vision of equity is dynamic. Schools can develop one as they move along. There will be some moving forward and moving back as leaders and staff review the relevant data and examine priorities and resources. At some point, however, districts and schools definitely need to set a vision for high-priority areas in order to guide what actions to take in response to any issues raised by equity audits.

Pause and Reflect

- Are you feeling validated by what you are reading? If so, what values are being reinforced?
- Are you feeling challenged by anything you just read? If so, what is it you find challenging and why?

Suggestion 5: Be Prepared for Resistance

Equity audits can require a significant investment in resources—human and material. Thus, it is worthwhile to anticipate potential challenges and make plans in advance to address them. If a change is to be impactful, it will generate questions. Not all questioning is resistance! Wanting to understand before committing to change can be a good thing, especially for equity changes. In preparing for questions and possible resistance to an equity audit, effective leaders take into account their school's or district's institutional culture about change. Perhaps change is seen as disruptive and negative, something to be avoided. Questions, reluctance, nonresponse, and other forms of resistance can be a barometer of the potential impact of the change. Knowing the source and type of potential resistance can help leaders respond positively rather than defensively or fearfully. Leaders can let the push-back be an indicator of what staff, students, and community members are thinking and feeling about equity or related social justice issues.

There are two major ways of decreasing resistance to change: increasing the difficulty of not supporting the change (e.g., by documenting thoroughly the need for change) and decreasing the difficulty related to trying the new way (e.g., by determining the concerns of the resisters and responding with appropriate actions). By using one—or both—of these strategies, leaders can reduce resistance.

Pause and Reflect

- Are you feeling validated by what you are reading? If so, what values are being reinforced?
- Are you feeling challenged by anything you just read? If so, what is it you find challenging and why?

Suggestion 6: Develop and Implement an Equity Audit Response Plan

Developing, implementing, and revising an equity audit response plan is an ongoing process with feedback loops built in that will last a number of years. As with any dynamic planning process, the order in which the components are developed can vary, depending on local conditions. However, at the least, the plan will include sections for (1) a commitment statement about the purpose of the audit and the importance of using the results, (2) findings, (3) priorities for responding to the findings, (4) timeline and specific actions that address identified inequities, and (5) how and when monitoring of progress will be done.

Leaders are well-advised to consider whether the school or district is prepared to engage in such a planning process. If so, it will be informed by the equity audit. Creating a nonresponsive plan, one that ignores pertinent data, can get leaders into trouble quickly. The commitment to follow through needs to be made at the beginning of the equity audit process, revisited, and confirmed along the way. Changes to an initial response plan are inevitable, but leaders will lose credibility and accountability by abandoning a plan before it has even had a chance to be implemented.

Pause and Reflect

- Are you feeling validated by what you are reading? If so, what values are being reinforced?
- Are you feeling challenged by anything you just read? If so, what is it you find challenging and why?

CONCLUSION

Following the foregoing suggestions can make the task of leading an equity audit for district and school leaders a bit less anxiety-inducing and lead to a more successful outcome. Such an audit can provide solid evidence of the state of equity in a school or district, something that can serve students, and all others who are involved and affected as partners, as well.

ADDITIONAL RESOURCES AND SUGGESTED READINGS

- *Leading Every Day: Actions for Effective Leadership,* 3rd edition, by Joyce Kaser, Susan Mundry, Katherine E. Stiles, & Susan Loucks-Horsley (Corwin, 2013). See the book's "Leading Change" section. https://wested.org/resources/leading-every-day-actions-for-effective-leadership-third-edition/
- Radd, S. I., Generett, G. G., Gooden, M. A., & Theoharis, G. (2021). *Five practices for equity-focused school leadership.* ASCD.
- The federally funded Equity Assistance Centers provide a range of services to school districts across the country. All four centers have a variety of materials on equity audits. The materials are available at no charge to education institutions. https://www2.ed.gov/programs/equitycenters/contacts.html
- "Setting Strategic Direction: Vision, Strategy, & Tactics," by Stever Robbins (2017). This article lays out a path to developing a vision. http://www.steverrobbins.com/?s=Setting+Strategic+Direction
- Publications from the American Evaluation Association are excellent resources for guiding equity audits: "Guiding Principles for Evaluators" (2004, http://www.eval.org/p/cm/ld/ fid=51), "Statement on Cultural Competence in Evaluation" (2011, http://www.eval.org/ccstatement), and "Essential Competencies for Evaluators" [Draft] (being developed as of this writing; for more information see http://aea365.org/blog/tag/evaluator-competencies/).

REFERENCES

Allexsaht-Snider, M., & Sherick, H. M. (2020). Effects of the whole-school improvement model on elementary school students' achievement and behavioral outcomes. *Educational Researcher, 49*(8), 599–610.

Annie E. Casey Foundation. (2014). Race, equity, and inclusion action guide. http://www.aecf.org/m/resourcedoc/AECF_EmbracingEquity7Steps-2014.pdf

Ayscue, J. B., D. Fusarelli, L., & Uzzell, E. M. (2022). Equity and early implementation of the every student succeeds act in state-designed plans during COVID. *Educational Policy.* https://doi.org/10.1177/08959048221130994

Cook-Harvey, C. M., Darling-Hammond, L., Lam, L., Mercer, C., & Roc, M. (2016). Equity and ESSA: Leveraging educational opportunity through the Every Student Succeeds Act. *Learning Policy Institute.*

Darling-Hammond, L., & Cook-Harvey, C. M. (2018). Educating the whole child: Improving school climate to support student success. *Learning Policy Institute.*

Kaser, J., Mundry, S., Stiles, K. E., & Loucks-Horsley, S. (Eds.). (2013). *Leading every day: Actions for effective leadership.* Corwin Press.

National Academies of Sciences, Engineering, and Medicine. (2019). *Monitoring educational equity*. National Academies Press.

Reinholz, D. L., & Andrews, T. C. (2020). Change theory and theory of change: What's the difference anyway? *International Journal of STEM Education, 7*(1), 1–12.

Reinholz, D. L., & Apkarian, N. (2018). Four frames for systemic change in STEM departments. *International Journal of STEM Education, 5*(1), 1–10.

Skrla, L., McKenzie, K. B., & Scheurich, J. (Eds.). (2009). *Using equity audits to create equitable and excellent schools*. Corwin.

Wang, M. T., & Sheikh-Khalil, S. (2021). Promoting equity in education: How inclusive school environments benefit academically disadvantaged students and their more advantaged peers. *Journal of Educational Psychology, 113*(2), 238–256.

CHAPTER 4

Planning and Implementing a Special Education Program Review

Nancy Hurley, Kristin Reedy, and Dona Meinders

Pause and Reflect Before Reading

- Why would a district conduct a review of its special education program?
- What could be the benefits of conducting periodic reviews of a district's special education program?
- What do you think a special education review would include?

INTRODUCTION

As most education leaders know, special education programs are an essential component of a district's education system, and as such they should be periodically reviewed. Effective educational programs ensure that the individual needs of every student are routinely being met. This requires providing students with disabilities access to the same educational opportunities as their nondisabled peers and often includes accommodations like assistive technologies, specialized instruction, and/or curricular modifications. Strong special education programs also provide the necessary emotional and social support that students with disabilities need to succeed. Thus, given the importance and complexity of a district's special education program, these programs should be periodically reviewed or evaluated to ensure the program is effectively targeting supports to meet the needs of all students. Such reviews can identify areas of strength and weakness, as well as provide opportunities to make adjustments and improvements.

This chapter presents guidance for district educational leaders who are considering implementing a review of their special education programs and services. It begins by exploring why education leaders should consider conducting a review. This is followed by key considerations for planning a review, as well as suggestions on what data to collect and how to analyze it. At the end of the chapter, there are a handful of activities to help administrators and district teams work through the various steps of a successful process.

Before proceeding further, it is important to mention two key points. First, a program review can either be conducted externally, in collaboration with an external evaluator, or internally, by a designated group of district staff that collaboratively evaluates the program. Whether conducted by external reviewers or internal staff, any evaluation plan should be individualized based on the needs of the district and the particular questions the district needs to address. Second, the review process works best when it is approached collaboratively. Collaborative evaluation involves engaging teams of educators in a dynamic inquiry process focused on assessing the effectiveness of local programs and initiatives. Whether the district contracts with an external evaluator or conducts the review "in house," a collaborative approach is one that involves a diverse and representative range of interested individuals and groups in all phases of the process. Such an approach is most likely to yield results that are actionable by the district and that will have the support of the diverse audiences who will be impacted by the resulting plans for improvement.

WHY CONDUCT A LOCAL SPECIAL EDUCATION PROGRAM REVIEW?

A district might decide to engage in a local review of its special education programs and services for a number of reasons. The most common reason is to improve the effectiveness and efficiency of the district's special education offerings in order to improve academic results and functional outcomes for children with disabilities and their families who are served by the district. Findings from a review will provide insights into how education leaders can make adjustments to the existing program of services to better customize and target supports to meet students' needs. Possible outcomes could include increased capacity to diagnose and respond to students' learning needs, enhanced opportunities to provide professional learning to staff, and a stronger culture focused on student learning.

There may also be other specific issues and concerns that precipitate the district's interest in reviewing its continuum of special education programs and services. For instance, there may be concerns about low achievement for students with disabilities and/or concerns about the achievement gap between students with disabilities and their peers without disabilities. There may be specific groups of students who are struggling and may need improved or additional support. There may be a large number of students who are placed in highly restrictive programs outside the district. There may be an unusually high number of students identified as eligible for special education overall, or an unusually high number of students classified within particular categories of disability. Parents may be dissatisfied with the services that their children currently receive. Community members may be concerned about costs of special education programs and services and want to know if there are better or more cost-effective ways of providing special education services while maintaining high program quality. There may be new leaders in the district who may want to have an overall examination of the special education program and services, or the leadership might be looking for more collaboration and alignment between general and special education.

District leadership might also be concerned with the disruptions and challenges which occurred from the COVID-19 pandemic and still persist today. The responses to the pandemic, which included a move to virtual instruction for extended periods of time, have impacted the learning of all students. For students with disabilities, especially students with intellectual and developmental disabilities, the shift to remote instruction was particularly disruptive (Root et al., 2023). Examining these challenges and the systemic issues that have been created may help to identify long-term solutions for improving the outcomes for students receiving special education services. Whatever the reason for conducting the program review, it should ideally be a valuable, collaborative process that ultimately provides the district with an objective report of the strengths, needs, and recommendations for improvement for the district's special education programs and services.

Pause and Reflect

- To what extent would your district benefit from a special education review?
- When was the last time your district engaged in a review of its special education program?
- If your district were to begin planning a special education review, who would you include in the process and why?

PLANNING THE SPECIAL EDUCATION PROGRAM REVIEW

In order to have an effective special education program review, it is important to carefully plan the various components of the review. Key planning consideration include the following:

- Deciding whether to have the evaluation conducted externally or internally
- Developing a multidimensional evaluation design

- Mapping the overall plan for implementing the evaluation (i.e., tasks, timelines, and persons responsible)
- Designing the overarching evaluation questions
- Determining the approach to collecting and analyzing the data

Deciding Whether to Use an External or Internal Evaluator

Once the district has decided to conduct a review of its special education program, it will need to decide whether the evaluation will be conducted by an external contractor (which could be either an individual or an organization) or by internal staff. There are several questions to consider when deciding between an external and an internal approach. For instance, leaders may wish to consider the following:

- Will it be important to the credibility of the review to have an external, objective source conduct the evaluation?
- What is the climate/culture of the district, and how might that affect the success of an external versus an internal evaluation?
- Does the district have the internal capacity to take on the activities involved in an evaluation of this magnitude?
- How will accountability for completing the evaluation be monitored? Will it be easier to monitor and enforce accountability with external or internal staff?
- Does the staff have the knowledge and ability to include a focus on equity, inclusion, and diversity?
- Will staff and families feel comfortable expressing their opinions without fear of retribution from internal staff?

Considering these sorts of questions at the start of the process will help the district determine which approach will be most efficient and effective, given the district's particular context and capacity.

Designing a Multidimensional Evaluation

When planning the special education program review, it is ideal to use a multiple-methods design that captures the perspectives of diverse individuals, groups, providers, and recipients of special education services in the school district. A multiple-methods approach is based on the understanding that multiple sources of data and the perceptions and contributions of a diverse variety of individuals and key stakeholder groups must be used to inform judgments that are made about the comprehensiveness, cost effectiveness, and overall quality of the district's special education programs and services (Brackett & Hurley, 2004). In addition to capturing multiple perspectives, it is ideal to use both quantitative data (e.g., surveys, checklists, district budgets) and qualitative data (e.g., interviews, focus group notes, survey open ended questions).

Understanding the Evaluation Process and Developing the Evaluation Plan

The process for the special education program review may also differ depending on whether the district decides to have the review conducted externally or internally. If an external evaluator is used, typically there will be an initial meeting between the district team and the external evaluator during which they will collaboratively develop the evaluation plan. When creating this evaluation plan, the district team and external evaluator will discuss the scope of the evaluation, overarching evaluation questions, potential sources of data, timeline for data gathering activities, and instrumentation and protocol development. Once agreement on these components has been reached, the external evaluator will proceed with the process of setting up the review and developing the protocols (e.g., interview and focus group questions, online survey questions and process, observation checklists).

Typically, an important component of the external review is a multi-day onsite visit, during which school and classroom observations and a few selected interviews will be conducted. Due to increased familiarity with virtual meetings, staff and families may now feel more comfortable with online meetings, so most focus groups and interviews could be successfully conducted virtually. This provides the participants and evaluators more flexibility in arranging the meetings and allows for less upheaval for participants (arranging for locations to hold meetings, driving to a central meeting location, arranging for childcare, etc.). Most records and district information (e.g., procedural handbooks, previous reviews or other reports, collective bargaining agreements) are now available in electronic formats and can be shared with evaluators via email or through secure data storage sites. It will be important to ensure that the external evaluator has a data security plan in place to protect the data provided by the district.

Another component often included in the program review process is a review of individualized education programs (IEPs) for educational benefit. A sample of IEPs is selected by staff that is representative of the various types of programs and services that the district has to offer. The reviews are then conducted through online IEP systems, and the IEPs will not be downloaded to the external evaluator's data storage systems.

It is important to designate a district contact person to work with the external evaluator to set up the onsite visits and virtual data collection processes and meet with the external evaluator on a regular basis to ensure that the process is progressing according to the plan.

With an internal review process, the evaluation plan should be developed during an initial meeting of the district evaluation team. At this time, the team will come to agreement on which aspects of the district's special education program (e.g., particular initiatives and/or services) to evaluate, and what level of effort will be manageable for the team to undertake. It is important to be realistic about the scope of review that will be possible, given the resources that are available. Although the district evaluation team may come up with four or five overarching evaluation questions, starting with a single overarching question or one specific program can help the team avoid an overly ambitious approach. There are also several self-assessment tools that are based on evidenced-based practices which an internal evaluation team might choose to use to assist in identifying and prioritizing key areas in which to begin the evaluation process. Links to several of these tools are included in the "Additional Resources" section at the end of the chapter.

Throughout the entire process, local educators and other invested individuals and groups will work together to design the data gathering methods, collect and organize the data, reflect on the findings, and determine the implications for program improvement. This kind of collaborative work enriches school and district learning communities and builds capacity, as local educators, to continuously assess progress that informs program improvement and helps the district develop an ongoing culture of evaluation.

Developing the Overarching Evaluation Questions

When the evaluation plan is being developed, an essential component is identifying the questions that will guide the data gathering. What does the district want to know and learn as a result of the review? Based on the answer(s) to that question, the review's evaluation questions and sub-questions can be organized around the main categories of inquiry that have been identified by the district. These questions should then be matched with correlating data collection methods to enable the team to gather the necessary information to answer the questions (see the "Locating and Collecting the Data" section later in the chapter for more information on collecting data for the special education program review).

As part of the planning process, it will be important to make sure the data collection includes a focus on equity of race, culture, and ability levels across all levels of the process. This can be done by including questions on issues of equity and inclusion throughout the process such as the following:

- Does the district include a disproportionate number of students of color in special education?
- Is the knowledge base of staff adequate in addressing and including culturally responsive practices and strategies to support diverse learners?

- Do the district's hiring practices reflect and focus on inclusion of a diverse workforce?

Questions such as these should be included in the research design from the planning stages and should be a focus throughout all phases of the review process. Some examples of overarching questions include the following.

- How, and to what extent, is the district's continuum of special education services adequately serving students with disabilities?
- What are the district's methods for finding and placing children into special education services? To what extent are these methods effective?
- What are the district's current professional development offerings related to special education? Do they meet the needs of all staff?
- To what extent are the roles and responsibilities of staff throughout the district clearly communicated and understood by all?
- To what degree are special education programs and services resulting in educational benefits to students with disabilities?
- How, and to what extent, are students who receive special education services able to access the general education curriculum?
- In what ways are parents and community members aware of, engaged in, and satisfied with the district's special education services?
- How, and to what extent, are fiscal and other resources being used efficiently and effectively?

Pause and Reflect

- To what extent would your district benefit from a special education review?
- When was the last time your district engaged in a review of its special education program?
- If your district were to begin planning a special education review, who would you include in the process and why?

IMPLEMENTING THE SPECIAL EDUCATION PROGRAM REVIEW

Once the evaluation team has developed the evaluation plan—including the evaluation design, overarching evaluation questions, and data collection strategies—the special education program review is set to begin. The first step is to start collecting data. The second is analyzing it.

Locating and Collecting the Data

The activities in this step will be similar whether the district is working with an external evaluator or conducting the review with internal staff and resources.

Following the initial meeting to develop the evaluation plan, the evaluation team will begin by collecting and reviewing all relevant sources of data. If the review is being conducted internally, the internal evaluation team will need to determine who is responsible for each data-gathering activity and commence these activities according to the district's timeline. Data collection activities might include the following.

- Interviewing key administrators and staff
- Conducting focus groups with teachers, staff, students, and parents
- Visiting schools and conducting classroom observations
- Reviewing relevant records and documents
- Administering an online survey for instructional staff
- Administering an online survey for parents
- Reviewing IEPs for educational benefit

Reviewing Documents and Extant Data

In addition to the data collection activities listed previously, the external evaluator or the district's evaluation team typically conducts an online scan of publicly available data, documents, and information on the state department of education and district/school websites. After conducting that scan, they may ask the district to provide any relevant information they were unable to locate or that is not available online. Within this document review process, the evaluator may want to identify and collect available data on an appropriate set of similar districts for comparison purposes.

Documents to use in the special education program review may include:

- Descriptions of programs and services
- Documented policies and procedures
- District strategic or improvement plans
- Compliance monitoring reports
- Professional development plans

Extant data to use in the special education program review may include:

- State and district assessment results for all students and for students with disabilities
- Child count data for students with disabilities, disaggregated by disability category, race/ethnicity, placement, etc.

- Least restrictive environment (LRE) data for students with disabilities
- Discipline data
- Graduation/completion rates
- Dropout rates
- Staffing information by category and student-to-staff ratio
- Comparisons with other similar districts in the state or with national data

Analyzing the Data

For the data that is quantitative (e.g., number of dropouts, number of discipline events, percentages of demographics, number of graduates), analysis should be conducted through descriptive data analysis methods (which includes measures such as means, ranges, and numbers of valid cases of one variable).

Qualitative data (e.g., surveys, interviews, focus group notes) should be analyzed through basic content analysis (which involves categorizing major emerging themes, trends, and/or patterns). Effective and timely analysis is dependent on the quality, consistency, and accessibility of district- and school-level data.

Ultimately, the evaluation team (whether external or internal) will analyze the data, based on the specific evaluation questions, to determine the strengths and weaknesses of the district's special education programs and services. Then, based on the findings from the program review, the district should bring together relevant stakeholders to discuss and document a set of recommendations and/or improvement plans. In order to achieve the most buy-in and positive impact, it is important to share the findings broadly and to actively involve all key individuals and groups in the process of developing recommendations for improvement.

CONCLUSION

Program evaluation is a responsibility of the administrators who are charged with implementing educational services for all students. Conducting the program evaluation is essential for determining program quality, planning program improvement, documenting the effectiveness of improvement efforts, and justifying and supporting ongoing implementation.

A review of the effectiveness and efficiency of the district's special education programs and services is an important aspect of the ongoing assessment of how district resources are being spent, how the students receiving special education services are faring, and what all invested parties think about the services provided. Whether a district decides to engage the services of an external evaluator or conduct an internal collaborative evaluation, the information gathered from a well-designed program review should provide the data and recommendations to guide program improvement going forward, influence budget and priority decisions, and ultimately improve the quality of education for students with disabilities.

Take Action

- How did the chapter's information, ideas, and activities align with or challenge your prior understanding?
- Based on your reading, what actions or steps can you take moving forward?

ADDITIONAL RESOURCES

Literature

- Havelock, R. G., & Hamilton, J. L. (2004). *Guiding change in special education.* Corwin Press.
- Levenson, N. (2009). A win-win approach to raising achievement while reducing special education cost. District Management Council. https://dmj.dmgroupk12.com/articles/a-win-win-approach-to -reducing-special-education-costs.
- Levenson, N. (2012). Boosting the quality and efficiency of special education. Thomas B. Fordham Institute. http://www.edexcellence .net.
- Sanders, J. R. (2000). *Evaluating school programs* (2nd ed.). Corwin Press.
- WestEd. (2021). Anti-racist evaluation strategies: A guide for evaluation teams. https://www.wested.org/resources/anti-racist -evaluation-strategies/

Self-Assessment Tools

- California Department of Education, California Collaborative for Educational Excellence, & WestEd. (2020). *Serving students with disabilities: A resource for assessing the basic components of your special education infrastructure.* WestEd. https://ccee-ca.org/resources/serving -students-with-disabilities-the-basic-components-tool/
- Grabill, D., & Rhim, L. M. (2017). Assessing and improving special education: A program review tool for schools and districts engaged

in rapid school improvement. The Center on School Turnaround. WestEd. https://www.wested.org/resources/assessing-and-improving -special-education/

- Illinois State Board of Education. (n.d.). Critical components tool for special education programs. https://illinoiscriticalcomponents.com /tool
- Lammert, J. D., Heinemeier, S., Schaaf, J. M., Fiore, T. A., & Howell, B. (2016). Evaluating special education programs: Resource toolkit. Westat. https://osepideasthatwork.org/sites/default/files/Evaluating %20Special%20Education%20Programs%20Resource%20Toolkit _Section%20508_12.pdf
- Hanover Research. (2023). Step-by-step guide to program evaluation. https://www.hanoverresearch.com/reports-and-briefs/k-12-program -evaluations-guide/?org=k-12-education
- WestEd. (2021). Anti-racist evaluation strategies: A guide for evaluation teams. https://www.wested.org/resources/anti-racist -evaluation-strategies/

Suggested Activities

The following activities may help educational leaders think through the steps involved in planning and implementing the district's review of its special education programs and services.

Activity 1—Convening Groups Interested in Participating in the Review Process

1. Convene a stakeholder group of individuals who bring diverse perspectives, have a stake in what happens for children with disabilities in your district, and represent both general and special education.
2. Ask each individual to read this chapter and to respond in writing to the following question: Is there a particular reason or impetus for initiating a review at this particular time?
   a. Interest in improving academic results and functional outcomes for students with disabilities?
   b. Interest in improving special education programs and services?
   c. Pressing political or budgetary reason?
   d. Changes in central office leadership?
   e. Pressure or criticism from an internal or external stakeholder group?
   f. Budget constraints, cuts, or unanticipated cost increases?
   g. Poor achievement test results?
   h. State requirement?

3. As a group, share perspectives on the chapter and participants' responses to these initial questions.

Activity 2—Deciding Whether to Use an External Evaluator

1. Given the foregoing activities, ask your group or team to discuss whether the district has the internal resources to conduct the evaluation or program review on its own or whether it makes more sense to contract with an external evaluator (which could be either a consultant or an organization).
2. Consider the following issues when deciding between an internally or externally conducted evaluation:
   a. Purpose/impetus for conducting the review (e.g., state requirement, School Board directive, internal interest in improving services and programs for students with disabilities).
   b. Time frame: How quickly do you need the data, and which approach is likely to be quicker?
   c. Cost of internal staff time versus a contract with an external evaluator
   d. Staff capacity to conduct a program evaluation.
   e. District culture/climate
      i.   What is the likelihood of staff buy-in to an external versus an internal review?
      ii. How open to evaluation are teachers/staff?
      iii. Is there disagreement or strong criticism of the program from within or from parents/community members?
      iv. Do teachers/staff commonly collaborate or tend to work in isolation?
      v.   How strong is the need for an external/objective perspective?

Activity 3—Generating Questions for Evaluating the District's Special Education Program

1. In a large group or small group breakouts, brainstorm a list of questions that stakeholders would like to see addressed as part of a review of your district's special education program.
2. Write down the questions that you would consider critical to answer in a review of your district's special education program. When compiling your list, consider the information you gleaned from participants' discussion of the chapter, from your own knowledge of special education programs in the district, and from data that you may already have collected.

3. Compile all proposed questions, categorize them, and distill them down into four or five overarching evaluation questions that would form the basis of the special education program review. (Some categories of questions might include cost efficiency of current programs/services, achievement results of students with disabilities, professional development needs, or staffing requirements).
4. If the district chooses to conduct an internal review, form a small (four or five member) evaluation team that will lead or guide the program review. If the district decides to use an external evaluator, this team and/or the director of special education would work collaboratively with the external evaluator as needed.

Activity 4—Identifying Sources and Collection Strategies

1. Generate a list of data sources that are currently available in your district (e.g., child count data for all the children receiving special education services, information on all your district programs and staffing, budget and spending for all special education programs and services).
2. Generate a list of any new or additional data you might need to collect in order to answer the overarching evaluation questions. For example, you might want to know more about parent perceptions of the special education services their children are receiving.
   a. Indicate the source for each type of data. For example, you might administer surveys or elicit targeted feedback from general and special education teachers, paraprofessionals, administrators, students, guidance counselors, and/or parents.
3. Now that you have a sense of what additional data you need to collect, generate a list of some potential methods for collecting that data.
   a. Consider both qualitative and quantitative strategies.
   b. Consider multiple sources of data. Consider what data gathering tools (e.g., surveys, interview protocols, observation checklists) you might need to develop.

REFERENCES

Brackett, A., & Hurley, N. (2004). *Collaborative evaluation led by local educators: A practical print- and web-based guide*. WestEd. https://www.wested.org/wp-content/uploads/2016/11/1374814340li0401-3.pdf

Root, J. R., Lindström, E. R., Gilley, D., & Chen, R. (2023). Impact of COVID-19 pandemic on instructional experiences of students with intellectual and

developmental disability. *The Journal of Special Education*, 1–9. https://www.ncbi
.nlm.nih.gov/pmc/articles/PMC9895282/pdf/10.1177_00224669231151914
.pdf.

ADDITIONAL ACKNOWLEDGEMENTS

This chapter was originally authored by Kristin Reedy and Nancy Hurley. The
chapter was updated by Dona Meinders.

Part II

TALENT DEVELOPMENT

The Talent Development domain of the Four Domains of Rapid School Improvement emphasizes the important role school and district leaders play in cultivating and enhancing the knowledge and skills of all staff. It places an emphasis on sustaining growth of staff and the importance of continuously building their capacity to equitably support all students. Based on the research behind the Four Domains framework, three key practices that leaders can focus on to drive improvements in the Talent Development domain include (1) recruiting, developing, retaining, and sustaining staff; (2) targeting professional learning opportunities; and (3) setting clear performance expectations.

When considered in concert, all three practices are essential to driving improvement efforts in schools and district. To borrow a phrase from Jim Collins, it is essential the school and district leaders get "the right people on the bus."[1] Once on the bus, educational leaders must work to retain their high qualified staff. This includes providing ongoing professional learning support, as well as communicating clear expectations to all so that everyone is working in concert and moving in the same direction on behalf of students.

All three chapters in this section provide guidance to help educational leaders sustain and retain their high-quality staff. Chapter 5, "Supporting Educator Wellbeing: Strategies for Self-Care," explores the importance of prioritizing the wellness of staff. Much as passengers on airplanes are reminded to put their oxygen masks on first in an emergency, it is important for educators to take care of themselves in order to be at the best for their students. This chapter provides a plethora of tips and strategies for leaders to consider and share with staff.

---

1 Collins, J. (2009). *Good to great: Lessons for the social sector*. Bridgespan.

Chapter 6, "Strengthening Staff Motivation and Morale," briefly explores research on motivation and engagement and applies this to help educational leaders understand how to motivate staff to engage in improvement efforts. As most educational leaders come to quickly learn, getting all staff on board and working together to support substantive improvement initiatives is no easy task. To that end, this chapter provides a useful framework with key practices and strategies that leaders can use to optimize engagement when the work gets challenging.

Finally, Chapter 7, "Achieving the Promise of Professional Learning Communities," explores the potential professional learning communities (PLCs) have to support teacher and staff learning. This chapter begins with defining PLCs and describing their benefits when implemented well. It also provides educational leaders with guidance on the types of work PLCs should engage in and what to look for from high functioning PLCs. The chapter concludes with suggestions on what school and district leaders can do to build and/or optimize their systems of PLCs.

As they read the chapters in this section, readers are encouraged to consider the following questions before and as they engage with the content.

- To what extent do you believe educators and educational staff in your school or district are routinely attending to their own social and emotional well-being? To what extent has your school or district developed systems and practices designed to promote the well-being of staff?
- What substantive improvement efforts has your school or district recently engaged in? To what extent were all relevant stakeholders excited and motivated to engage in this work? What steps were taken to foster buy-in and build positive morale?
- What opportunities do staff, and particularly teachers, have to support their own professional learning? How frequently do staff get together in PLCs or other kinds of teams to support each other around their professional development? To what extent does your school or district have a culture of learning among staff?

CHAPTER 5

Supporting Educator Wellbeing
Strategies for Self-Care

Christina Pate

Before Reading

• What were you told or taught about self-care?
• What do you know about self-care?
• What do you do for self-care?

INTRODUCTION

Have you recently felt stressed and/or overworked? If so, you are not alone. Americans in general tend to idealize and glamorize being overworked, busy, and stressed. In fact, research shows that we associate it with prestige and status (Bellezza et al., 2017). Unfortunately, we don't show up as our best selves when we're stressed. Additionally, we know that stress and burnout are substantial concerns and lead to poor educator retention, teacher–student relationships, and various student and school outcomes (see Mahfouz et al., 2019; Skovholt & Trotter-Mathison, 2016; Sorenson, 2007), true even pre-pandemic. Additionally, according to reports from RAND (Steiner et al., 2022a; Woo & Steiner, 2022), this has worsened since the pandemic—especially for secondary principals of color, for female principals, for principals serving high-poverty schools, for principals serving schools with high enrollment of students of color, and for principals who are operating 100 percent remote instruction. Therefore, in order to best support others, educators—with the help of educational leaders—must learn how to support themselves first. In fact, across helping professions in general, it can be argued that self-care is an ethical imperative. Given all of this, this chapter provides guidance to education leaders in charge of supporting their education staff. It offers practical information and guidance on self-care in our ever-challenging times.

It builds on a growing research base about educator well-being and self-care (Greenberg et al., 2016; Steiner et al., 2022a, 2022b, 2022c; Von der Embse et al., 2019; Woo et al., 2022).

WHAT IS SELF-CARE AND WHY DOES IT MATTER?

When discussing self-care in education, it is important to clarify what it is and what it is not as there are a range of common misperceptions about it. First, while there are a lot of definitions of self-care, most generally include the following characteristics (Martínez et al., 2021; Oxford, n.d.):

- Providing adequate attention to your own physical and psychological health and wellness
- Taking an active role to preserve, protect, or improve your own health and well-being

Similarly, it is important to define what is not considered to be self-care. In short, self-care does not include the following:

- Something we force ourselves to do
- Something we don't enjoy
- Something that "takes" from us
- Something we give the same energy and time as our work

Many educators dismiss self-care because we think it refers to spa treatments and beach vacations. While both of those activities are certainly ways to relax, they are not examples of what is typically considered self-care. In short, self-care refers to the manageable ways we routinely sustain and improve our physical and psychological health. In our work with educators, we often hear people say they don't have time for self-care; we believe these are the people who often need it the most.

Pause and Reflect

- Do you tend to idealize or glamorize being busy or overworked? Or do you get reinforced or rewarded for doing so?
- Do you notice the stress-related outcomes among yourself, your staff, and/or your students?
- Are you, individually, modeling busyness or balance?
- Is your school/district's climate and culture busy or balanced? Healthy or unhealthy?

THE SCIENCE OF WELL-BEING

At appropriate levels, stress is good for our bodies and minds. There is a continuum of stress responses that range from positive to tolerable to toxic (Center on the Developing Child, 2007; Shonkoff et al., 2009, 2012). A reasonable amount of stress helps us get out of bed in the morning and contributes to life. Most stress is healthy until we reach about 75–80 percent of our body's physical capacity (Nixon, 1982). When we reach this point, we feel so good because we're functioning at peak capacity. In this state, we easily become prone to believing that if we take on more, we'll feel even better and be more productive. How many times do you hear people say they perform their best when under pressure? They are most likely referring to times when they were at their peak. However, when we are at our peak, it does not take much to go too far. Just one more thing, issue, interaction, and so on could be what puts someone over the edge and outside of their window of tolerance (see Siegel, 1999, 2010).

When we go past our peak level of stress, we have ignored our mind and body cues, and we enter a fatigue zone. This eventually leads to exhaustion and burnout. When we move beyond our peak, we don't show up as our best selves. We fall back into bad habits and rely more heavily on our biases, faulty thinking, and deficit mindsets. It's here when we become less self-aware, we become more impatient, and we become more reactive. This leads us down the road to dysregulation. This is why it is so important to self-regulate—to regularly get still and check in with our body and mind to notice what is happening and to listen to ourselves.

Understanding how brains and bodies influence mindsets, moods, behaviors, relationships, and decision-making can help us remain at peak stress and avoid becoming dysregulated. One simple framework that helps explain how this all works is neuroscientist Bruce Perry's 3 Rs: Regulate, Relate, and Reason (Perry, 2006; Perry, n.d.). According to Perry's framework, in order to effectively learn, work, and thrive, a person must first feel physically and emotionally safe, calm, and settled ("regulate"). If they are well-regulated, they should then feel socially and emotionally connected with others who are attuned to each other's needs ("relate"). Only when a person is well-regulated and in relation with others can they feel optimally ready and able to engage with learning, working, and leading ("reason").

The bottom line is this: When educators show up healthy and present, they have positive interactions with their students and colleagues, and that leads to improved student and school outcomes of all kinds, both academic and nonacademic. Essentially, adult well-being is a prerequisite to the student and school outcomes we're all striving for. So, what can educational leaders do about this?

Pause and Reflect

The following questions are adapted from Pate, Tilley-Gyado, and Betz (2022).

- *Regulate:* How do you help yourself and others get grounded and centered first and then connected in safe and supportive relationships before engaging in challenging work? How do you learn to recognize the signs in your mind and body that indicate you're stressed or about to react?
- *Relate:* How do you and others support each other in preventing or responding early to distress and dysregulation?
- *Reason:* How do you create cultures of care that allow people agency over their own minds, bodies, and behaviors in the workplace and that offer culturally appropriate and timely supports when needed?

STRATEGIES THAT SUPPORT SELF-CARE

The following are simple strategies and practices that educational leaders can try and can encourage others to try as well to support self-care and well-being. They are divided into three categories: mindsets and behaviors, relationships, and systems. Multiple strategies and suggestions are shared within each.

As you explore the suggestions, keep in mind that this list is not exhaustive nor prescriptive. Rather, it is an invitation and a foundation upon which to build and strengthen self-care practices. We encourage leaders to model these with staff, colleagues, and students in an effort to normalize well-being practices and institutionalize a culture of care.

It is important to note that the strategies provided subsequently are shared as examples of general support. It is normal to have a low mood or some anxiety sometimes. But intense, persistent, or prolonged feelings of helplessness, hopelessness, despair, or anxiety are not. It's ok to not be ok, but seeking professional help that is culturally appropriate and responsive is important if fear or hopelessness is significantly disrupting daily functioning. Also, be on the lookout for signs of distress in colleagues. These can show up as outbursts, withdrawal, task avoidance, or absenteeism, so let them know where they can find support or help connect them to support.

Mindsets and Behaviors

Create a "new normal"—a culture of well-being. Many educators are not always prepared personally or professionally to manage the increasing stressors associated with education and leadership and to support school communities facing insurmountable odds in our current times. The following suggestions encourage them to take time to reflect on the current culture of your context.

Be realistic and gentle with yourself. Set a new baseline. As you're reimagining and redesigning your paradigm of well-being and care, be gentle and realistic with yourself and your staff. While educators and leaders want to provide effective and meaningful instruction, don't expect them to have mastered all of the skills necessary to support themselves and students in nonacademic ways. Remember, these nonacademic skills are prerequisites to the student outcomes we're seeking. Thus, allow time and space for you and your staff to figure out your "new normal": to learn some of these mindset and behavior shifts and to grapple with healing and change. Additionally, provide supports for you and your staff to focus on these critical nonacademic aspects of your work. Give yourself and them permission for trial and lots and lots of error. Iterate, but also be patient, prioritize, and let some things go.

Reduce the workload for yourself, your staff, and your students. Experiencing a lot of stress and change has diminished everyone's mental capacity to handle the load. Allow educators to reduce their loads. Encourage them to implement the same lessons as normal, but in smaller amounts. (Of course, your school/district may have existing protocols around pacing and workload as well.) For example, if teachers normally assign five word problems, consider encouraging them to cut that to two or three, reducing the mental and emotional burden on themselves, their students, and families supporting these students. Collect information from staff about the number of meetings, committees, and other extra responsibilities they are assigned. Find areas of overlap and duplication and find ways to consolidate, minimizing staff time. Engaging parents or other community volunteers to work events, recess duty, or bus duty can also decrease the workload for staff. Analyze data collection activities (surveys, assessments, referrals, etc.) and programs/initiatives to identify areas of overlap and redundancy (and either consolidate or remove them). This can also decrease the workload for staff.

Shift the focus from academic content to positive, healthy relationships. As teachers reduce some of their students' workloads, encourage them to prioritize positive interactions with students and families, as well as to routinely connect with them on a personal, and not exclusively academic, level. What matters most is how students *feel* as they are learning. Just like adults, students need to feel physically and emotionally calm and settled (regulated) and socially connected in safe and supportive ways in order to effectively engage in learning. Additionally, many educators are concerned about increased levels of disengagement among students and families. Focusing on relationship-building is one of the most effective ways to offset this disengagement and to increase positive teacher–student relationships and student academic outcomes.

Foster self-awareness. Being aware of and accepting one's own thoughts and feelings, and adjusting and acting accordingly, is essential these days. However, getting stuck in feelings is all too easy if you are worried about myriad of stressors personally and professionally, as well as the well-being of your family and community. Remind staff that experiencing feelings is essential, as long as the feelings do not become overwhelming. The following points are helpful for managing significant challenges and high amounts of stress so they do not become too much to manage.

Get calm. Notice what's happening in the mind and body, release looping or obsessive thoughts, and focus on your breath. Studies show that somatic and mindfulness practices can reduce emotional reactivity and support decision-making (Chiesa & Serretti, 2010; Gu et al., 2015; Roemer et al., 2015; Shapiro et al., 2012). Additionally, deep (belly) breathing, rhythmic breathing, and mindful breathing techniques can support physiological regulation. (See Pate et al., 2022 for examples.) Physical exercise, sitting or walking in nature, or talking with a good friend can also help. Bottom line: Encourage staff to do what works for them. Think about strategies that have been helpful in the past and try applying those first.

Become aware of the stories you're telling yourself. Encourage yourself and others to consider whether the way they think and talk about their current circumstances is realistic or primarily fear-based. If individuals find that their thoughts are mostly rooted in fear and that they are having trouble staying calm or focused, they should allow and accept their feelings and give themselves permission to not force or push things. For example, if you have a live interaction scheduled with a staff member, or a student or family, consider ways to reschedule or reconnect when your mind is feeling steadier and more stable.

Know that emotions (like a virus) can be contagious—both positively and negatively. Help yourself and others do their best to keep fear and panic at bay and to support healing and well-being by modeling calm behavior and emoting positively and optimistically. For example, when you are feeling overwhelmed, try to pause, take a breath, notice the thoughts in your mind and the sensations in your body, and give yourself a moment (or more) to relax your mind and body before responding or deciding. Encourage others to do the same. How you feel and how you appear in interactions will have a significant influence on how your staff, families, and students feel and how they approach their lives and work.

Monitor the amount (and type) of information you take in. Remind yourself and others to be critical consumers of information, including what is received from family, friends, colleagues, and the media. To help avoid feeling like life is out of your control, control what and how much information you seek and consume. When you do consume, focus on facts. Consult reliable and up-to-date sources. Limit the amount of time spent talking about stressful events and circumstances with family, friends, and colleagues. Limit social media to fact-based, reliable sources and uplifting content. Limit the amount of time spent reading, listening to, or watching the news and other information sources.

Set boundaries with yourself, others, and media on negative topics. Being bombarded with negative information and news tends to increase stress levels. Commiserating often with colleagues is actually a form of co-dysregulation (rather than the supportive counterpart of co-regulation). Thus, it is important to monitor what you allow yourself to be exposed to. A key strategy is to create times during the day when the focus is on positive and uplifting news, stories, and conversations. A particularly important time for doing so is bedtime. For example, if a family member is watching the news before bed, you might say, "Watching this before bed makes falling asleep difficult for me. Can we watch something else?" On social media, follow accounts that support healthy and safe lifestyles, personal and collective growth, and those that leave you feeling empowered; minimize or remove those that leave you feeling activated, dysregulated, or disempowered.

Take a solution-focused approach. If you or others find yourselves overly focused on problems or getting into "analysis paralysis," be sure to take time to search for and brainstorm solutions. You might do so through conversations or by individually considering alternative solutions, challenging previously held beliefs, considering perspectives outside yourself or the immediate group, or reframing issues (e.g., shifting negative framing to positive framing).

Shift from pessimism to optimism. Often it is normal to think of what *cannot* be done before thinking of what *can* be accomplished. However, try not to get stuck in those negative first thoughts. Immediately redirect your focus to moving forward. Take perspective and be patient with yourself— have confidence that you can figure out what to do. Focus on what you like and want, rather than on what you do not like or want. These simple shifts can have a profound impact on your well-being and can shift how others respond to you. Practicing gratitude can also shift your perspective from pessimistic to optimistic. Taking some time to express appreciation and gratitude can help yourself and others through challenging times. You might do so through personal journaling (e.g., each morning upon waking or each evening before sleeping, writing three things you're grateful for), writing gratitude letters (to friends, colleagues, family, students), speaking your appreciation (calling friends, colleagues, families, students), posting on social media, and so on.

Practice reframing. When faced with challenging new situations, distinguish the positive aspects from the negative. For example, as shown in the following examples, you might make a two-column list and in one column list all the negative aspects of your circumstance. Then, in the other column, reframe each point to identify something positive about your circumstance. Some call this positive reframing a "silver lining" or "blessing in disguise."

Table 5.1. Reframing Negative Perceptions

"Negative" Thought/ Perception	"Positive" or "Neutral" Thought/Perception
This community connection meeting every Monday takes 30 minutes of my planning time. Ugh I don't have time for this!	Although this community connection meeting every Monday takes 30 minutes of my time, it affords me the opportunity to connect with my colleagues about light, fun things that happened over the weekend that have nothing to do with work. This is what my brain and body need to be ready for work. It also helps me build positive trusting relationships with my staff—so I'm willing to take the time.
I totally forgot to include two of our key staff's input in our last budget and programming conversation. Ugh. Now I've ruined it! They will never trust me again. I feel so humiliated.	While I'm disappointed that I forgot to include some of my staff's input in that budget and programming conversation, this is an opportunity for me to apologize, to model humility and accountability, and to make amends. This demonstrates that I'm human and I'm willing to make things right when I make a mistake. It also models restorative approaches instead of punitive ones which we're implementing for students and staff right now.

Demonstrate compassion for yourself and others. Refraining from judging or criticizing others during stressful times can be difficult, particularly in regard to those who have responses much different from yours. Connect with others through active listening, seeking to understand as well as to be understood, and strengthening feelings of concern for others—not just for those suffering from trauma or grief, but for those suffering from stress, fear, anxiety, or low mood as well. Also, be kind to yourself. Try not to judge or shame yourself. Treat yourself the way you would a dear friend. Remember that everyone (yourself included) is doing the best they can with what they know, what they have, and where they are in life. Depending on the day or the moment, your or your colleagues' windows of tolerance may be wider or narrower—and that's okay.

Practice openness, flexibility, adaptability, and humor. The only constant in our ever-evolving world is change. At one time or another, everyone has needed to demonstrate flexibility and adaptiveness, perhaps to deal with sick children or schedule changes. The same kinds of skills—shifting mindsets, perspectives, and actions when unexpected events arise—are more important now than ever. Even finding humor amid the stress can be a healthy coping mechanism. Mindsets that are critical for remaining calm, thinking clearly, and making conscious choices (rather than succumbing to being overwhelmed or chronically anxious) can be developed and improved in various ways, such as the following:

Take physical and mental breaks. These include breaks from screens of all kinds—computers, phones, televisions, and so on. Breaks can also include moving from one room to another (if possible; otherwise, shifting your position in a room) or moving from indoors to outdoors (or simply finding a natural light source or opening a window).

Find opportunities for humor and laughter. Doing so may include having light or fun conversations with colleagues or friends, or watching funny movies, videos, television shows, and so on.

Engage in mind–body activities. Try mindfulness practices, jogging, yoga, exercise, listening or dancing to music, taking a walk outdoors, or other relaxing or invigorating activities; even 15 minutes a day can be regenerative.

Relationships

In addition to practicing healthy mindsets and personal behaviors, fostering healthy relationships supports strong well-being. Healthy relationships can be bolstered by focusing on fostering connectedness and belonging.

Be intentional about connecting with colleagues. Connecting with colleagues can provide a social and emotional context for your work. As facilitating learning in current times can be challenging, intentional connection with friends and colleagues who understand your circumstances can help now more than ever. We often default to thinking that we do not have enough time. However, putting time for positive connections in your calendar is essential in order to effectively educate and lead.

Initiate positive contact with students and families. Whether or not you have direct access to students and families, you can send letters or create and mail postcards, make phone calls, send messages, create online hubs for connecting, or offer "community hours" during which they can check in with you about nonacademic topics.

Set healthy physical, social, and work boundaries. Poor self-care is often a *symptom* of poor boundaries (Tawwab, 2021). Oftentimes, when we lack boundaries with ourselves (e.g., having expectations on exercise, sleep, diet, etc.), when we lack boundaries with others (e.g., people pleasing, appeasing, over-giving, going against our values), and when we lack boundaries with our work (e.g., time, tasks), we end up unable to care for ourselves as well as unable to care for others—even though we often fool ourselves into thinking we are. Having healthy boundaries means knowing what your limits are and clearly communicating what you will and will not allow, as well as what you need. Establishing clear and healthy boundaries can support health and wellness for all.

Find a place where you can be alone. Seek some time alone at least once per day, even if only for a brief time. This allows you to check in with yourself, notice and name any thoughts or feelings (physical or emotional) that are coming up, and practice self-regulation and identifying what you need moving forward. If you don't have a room or office, this place could be the yard or sidewalk, bathroom, or vehicle. If you are taking care of children alone, find times when you can claim some solitude, such as during their naptime or after their bedtime.

Communicate when you need space or connection. Some people need more connection and interaction—physically, socially, or mentally—while others need more quiet time and solitude. It's important to understand what you need and clearly communicate that to others. Create a norm that conveys that all members of your household and work community need space, and that communicating that need is normal and healthy. You may need to create a word, phrase, or signal to indicate when you need space, and ask that it be honored any time that prompt is used. Equally important is to communicate when you need more connection. Ask others if there are ways to connect that respect their needs and boundaries.

Set boundaries around physical touch or social contact. Doing so can be challenging with family members, but find ways to create physical boundaries that respect each other's need to protect one's health, safety, or well-being (physical or psychological). For example, your neighbor, family, member, or colleague may think a quick visit is okay, but being a friend, family member, or colleague does not mean you have to allow their visiting. Determine what is right for you at that time. Practice saying "no."

Create communication norms and expectations. Create clear and consistent messaging to colleagues, students, and families. Elicit feedback from staff, students, and families and ensure that communication is reciprocal. Be clear about when you are and are not available, especially given that emails from colleagues, students, and parents can arrive at all hours. Don't feel compelled to reply to messages immediately. Even if you are working from home, you can still set official work hours.

Take more breaks. Adults need a break after 20 minutes of staring at a screen. Also, take time away from your computer for meals. Add break times in your schedule if you need to.

Create structure and let others know when you need help. Create schedules for clarity and stability for yourself and others. Identify times when you can focus on your work and other times when you can focus attention on other aspects of your life. Be gentle with yourself. Know when to reach out for help. Let your employer, your colleagues, and/or your family know if you're struggling to manage multiple responsibilities and see if there are opportunities for support. You are doing the best you can. Let people know when you're over your capacity or when you need support, and don't feel bad about it.

Recognize that everyone responds differently to stress. Accept your own feelings. Understand that others' thoughts, emotions, and reactions or responses are their responsibility, not yours. You can set healthy boundaries with others around what you will and will not allow. For example, you might say, "I know that you're anxious and afraid right now, but I need you to speak calmly and respectfully to me."

Respect others' decisions, but know what's right for you. There is often more than one solution to challenges and problems. In addition, sometimes what is best for one person or group of people is different from what is best for others. Thus, if you need to, you can set boundaries on conversations. For example, you might say, "Talking about this again is making me more anxious. Can we talk about something else?"

Altogether, when beginning to create healthy boundaries—start small and with low-risk situations—then you can build and tone that muscle over time. Bottom line: Your boundaries are valid. So are everyone else's. It's imperative that we also accept when others decide to set limits and also say "no."

Systems

While educator well-being is often framed in terms of self-care and individual strategies, this framing can inadvertently put the onus on individuals to heal and care for themselves, ignoring the significance of systems and structures in individual and collective well-being. While this chapter discusses many of those strategies for self-care, the strategies are often collective in nature or at least situated inside school communities and systems. Nonetheless, these short-term actions cannot replace your longer-term endeavors to make well-being efforts sustainable. This involves leadership, teaming, resources, and allocation (funding, training, time, staffing, ongoing supports), data, and participatory design approaches. Although approaches at the systems level is outside of the scope of this chapter, we encourage readers to see Pate et al. (2023) for additional information and strategies regarding the systems and structures needed to support educator well-being at individual and collective levels.

CONCLUSION

I hope that some of the concepts, strategies, and practices in this chapter have resonated with you. If so, select one or two at a time to practice. Embracing more may add to your stress. This list of strategies and practices is not exhaustive nor prescriptive. Rather, it is an invitation and a foundation upon which to build and strengthen your self-care practice in the context of community and systems. As you adopt and adapt any of these (or other) practices, you are encouraged to model these with your colleagues and students to normalize well-being practices and institutionalize a culture of care. Thus, not only is it important for us to shift our way of *doing*, but we must shift from a way of *doing* to a way of *being*—and *you* model the way. Overall, when we give ourselves permission to care for ourselves, we give others permission to do the same.

Reflect Further and Take Action

- How did the chapter's information, ideas, and activities align with or challenge your prior understanding?
- What is the current level of practice in your district(s) and school(s) in relation to the evidence-based practices described in the chapter?

- Based on your reading, what functions or steps would you like to take to promote self-care strategies for educators, particularly as they relate to the improvement plans of your school(s) or district(s), including the systems and structures that need to be in place to support self- and collective care?

REFERENCES

Bellezza, S., Paharia, N., & Keinan, A. (2017). Conspicuous consumption of time: When busyness and lack of leisure time become a status symbol. *Journal of Consumer Research, 44*(1), 118–138. https://doi.org/10.1093/jcr/ucw076

Center on the Developing Child. (2007). *InBrief: The impact of early adversity on child development.* Harvard University. https://developingchild.harvard.edu/resources/inbrief-the-impact-of-early-adversity-on-childrens-development/

Chiesa, A., & Serretti, A. (2010). A systematic review of neurobiological and clinical features of mindfulness meditations. *Psychological Medicine, 40*(8), 1239–1252.

Greenberg, M. T., Brown, J. L., & Abenavoli, R. M. (2016). *Teacher stress and health: Effects on teachers, students, and schools.* Edna Bennett Pierce Prevention Research Center, Pennsylvania State University. https://prevention.psu.edu/wp-content/uploads/2022/09/rwjf430428-TeacherStress.pdf.

Gu, J., Strauss, C., Bond, R., & Cavanagh, K. (2015). How do mindfulness-based cognitive therapy and mindfulness-based stress reduction improve mental health and wellbeing? A systematic review and meta-analysis of mediation studies. *Clinical Psychology Review, 37*, 1–12. https://doi.org/10.1016/j.cpr.2015.01.006

Mahfouz, J., Greenberg, M. T., & Rodriguez, A. (2019). *Principals social and emotional competence: A key factor for creating caring schools.* The Pennsylvania State University. https://www.researchgate.net/publication/337001604_Principals'_Social_and_Emotional_Competence_A_Key_Factor_for_Creating_Caring_Schools.

Martínez, N., Connelly, C. D., Pérez, A., & Calero, P. (2021). Self-care: A concept analysis. *International Journal of Nursing Sciences, 8*(4), 418–425. https://doi.org/10.1016/j.ijnss.2021.08.007

Nixon, P. G. (1982). Stress and the cardiovascular system. *The Practitioner, 226*(1371), 1589–1598.

Oxford. (n.d.) *Self-care.* Oxford English Dictionary Online. https://www.oed.com/

Pate, C. M., Pfister, T., & Ripma, T. (2023). *Creating a culture of care: A guide for education leaders to develop systems and structures that support educator well-being.* Center to Improve Social & Emotional Learning at WestEd. https://www.wested.org/resources/creating-a-culture-of-care/

Pate, C. M., Tilley-Gyado, T., & Betz, J. (2022). *Connecting the brain and body to support equity work: A toolkit for education leaders.* WestEd. https://www.wested.org/wp-content/uploads/2022/03/Brain-Body-Educ-Equity-Leaders_Brief.pdf

Perry, B. D. (n.d.). The 3 Rs: Reaching the learning brain. https://beaconhouse.org.uk/wp-content/uploads/2019/09/The-Three-Rs.pdf

Perry, B. D. (2006). The neurosequential model of therapeutics: Applying principles of neuroscience to clinical work with traumatized and maltreated children. In N. B. Webb (Ed.), *Working with traumatized youth in child welfare* (pp. 27–52). The Guilford Press.

Roemer, L., Williston, S. K., & Rollins, L. G. (2015). Mindfulness and emotion regulation. *Current Opinion in Psychology, 3*, 52–57.

Shapiro, S. L., Jazaieri, H., & Goldin, P. R. (2012). Mindfulness-based stress reduction effects on moral reasoning and decision making. *The Journal of Positive Psychology, 7*(6), 504–515.

Shonkoff, J. P., Boyce, W. T., & McEwen, B. S. (2009). Neuroscience, molecular biology, and the childhood roots of health disparities building a new framework for health promotion and disease prevention. *JAMA: Journal of the American Medical Association, 301*(21), 2252–2259. http://dx.doi.org/10.1001/jama.2009.754

Shonkoff, J. P., Garner, A. S., Siegel, B. S., Dobbins, M. I., Earls, Garner, A. S., M. F., McGuinn, L., Pascoe, J., & Wood, D. L. (2012). The lifelong effects of early childhood adversity and toxic stress. *Pediatrics, 129*(1), e232–e246. http://dx.doi.org/10.1542/peds.2011-2663

Siegel, D. (1999). *The developing mind: How relationships and the brain interact to shape who we are.* Guilford Press.

Siegel, D. (2010). *Mindsight: The new science of personal transformation.* Bantam Books.

Skovholt, T., & Trotter-Mathison, M. (2016). *The resilient practitioner: Burnout and compassion fatigue prevention and self-care strategies for the helping professions* (3rd ed.). Taylor and Francis, Inc.

Sorenson, R. D. (2007). Stress management in education: Warning signs and coping mechanisms. *Management in Education, 21*(3), 10–13.

Steiner, E. D., Doan, S., Woo, A., Gittens, A. D., Lawrence, R. A., Berdie, L., Wolfe, R. L., Greer, L., & Schwartz, H. L. (2022a). Restoring teacher and principal well-being is an essential step for rebuilding schools: Findings from the State of the American Teacher and State of the American Principal Surveys. *RAND Corporation.* https://www.rand.org/pubs/research_reports/RRA1108-4.html

Steiner, E. D., Greer, L., Berdie, L., Schwartz, H. L., Woo, A., Doan, S., Lawrence, R. A., L. Wolfe, R. L., & Gittens, A. D. (2022b). Prioritizing strategies to racially diversify the k–12 teacher workforce: Findings from the state of the American teacher and state of the American principal surveys. *RAND Corporation.* https://www.rand.org/pubs/research_reports/RRA1108-6.html

Steiner, E. D., Schwartz, H. L., & Diliberti, M. K. (2022c). Educators' poor morale matters, even if they don't quit. Here's why. *The Rand Blog.* https://www.rand.org/blog/2022/08/educators-poor-morale-matters-even-if-they-dont-quit.html.

Tawwab, N. G. (2021). *Set boundaries, find peace: A guide to reclaiming yourself.* Penguin.

Von der Embse, N., Ryan, S., Gibbs, T., & Mankin, A. (2019). Teacher stress interventions: A systematic review. *Psychology in the Schools, 56*(8), 1328–1343.

Woo, A., & Steiner, E. (2022). The well-being of secondary school principals one year into the COVID-19 pandemic. *RAND Corporation*. https://www.rand.org/pubs/research_reports/RRA827-6.html

Woo, A., Wolfe, R. L., Steiner, D., Doan, S., Lawrence, R. A., Berdie, L., Greer, L., Gittens, D., & Schwartz, H. L. (2022). Walking a fine line—Educators' views on politicized topics in schooling: Findings from the state of the American teacher and state of the American principal surveys. *RAND Corporation*. https://www.rand.org/pubs/research_reports/RRA1108-5.html

CHAPTER 6

Strengthening Staff Motivation and Morale

Michael Middleton and Kevin Perks

Pause and Reflect Before Reading

- What current tasks are teachers and/or other educational personnel most motivated to engage in, particularly as they relate to any district- or schoolwide improvement initiatives?
- What strategies are your school or district currently using to motivate staff and/or boost morale?
- What strategies are you familiar with that can strengthen staff motivation and/or boost morale to engage in improvement initiatives?

INTRODUCTION

"What about teachers and other staff?"

During a workshop on student motivation, a principal asked this question. After learning about a variety of practices and strategies designed to foster a positive culture of learning among students in classrooms, the principal wondered if similar approaches would help improve morale and motivation among teachers and staff. She continued: "What good is it to try and motivate students if we as educators are exhausted and unmotivated ourselves?" Since the pandemic, questions like this have only increased in our work with schools and districts across the country.

In our own work, we have continued to think about how to apply what we know about motivation to engage and energize educators, particularly within schools engaged in substantive improvement efforts. Although a great deal has been written about how to motivate students, less has been written on motivation as it relates to the adults who teach them. Nonetheless, one of our main objectives as educational leaders is to build and maintain teams of highly motivated and engaged school and district staff who directly serve students. This is especially true when leaders are engaging in continuous improvement efforts since teacher motivation is related to instructional strategies that lead to positive student outcomes (Woolfolk Hoy, 2021).

Data suggest that it is no easy task to build and sustain a staff that is highly motivated to continuously strengthen how they are working to improve outcomes for students. Although the data are not easy to analyze since the federal government does not keep track of the number of educators who leave the profession, one report found that across multiple states, attrition rates in 2021 were the highest they had been in recent years (Barnum, 2023). In another report on teacher attrition, the Alliance for Excellent Education (Haynes, 2014) estimates that high-poverty schools (many of which are in urban or rural settings) lose about one fifth of their teaching personnel on a yearly basis. The data are worse for teachers within their first five years in the profession. Forty to fifty percent leave teaching within that time frame. What can school and district leaders do to leverage the motivation of staff to create a positive climate where morale is high and teachers are excited and eager to work with students and colleagues?

This chapter offers practical approaches that can help school and district leaders boost motivation and morale among teachers and other personnel. The chapter briefly explores what is currently known about motivation and then describes four practices that educational leaders can use to leverage the motivation that already exists among their staff to support improvement work. The chapter concludes with an example of how leaders can combine all four practices together.

Pause and Reflect

- How would you describe the relationship between teacher motivation and student success?
- Based upon your responses to the previous questions, how would you define teacher motivation and morale?

WHAT IS MOTIVATION AND ITS RELATIONSHIP TO STAFF MORALE?

Over two or three decades, researchers' understanding of motivation has evolved (Kanfer et al., 2017). Motivation often refers to the internal and external factors that influence a person's behavior and help direct them toward specific goals or outcomes. It is a force that can initiate, sustain, and direct behavior. Motivation can be influenced by intrinsic factors such as personal interests, values, or a sense of achievement, or extrinsic factors like external rewards, such as money or recognition. In the field of education, one researcher (Sinclair, 2008) considers motivation through the lens of what attracts educators, particularly teachers, to the field, including how long they remain in the teaching profession and the extent to which they engage with others in their work. Moreover, Woolfolk Hoy (2021) reminds us of the importance of the school and district setting in teacher motivation and cautions that "Context often is overlooked in studies of teacher motivation, as if every teacher worked in and experienced similar physical, interpersonal, economic, and political contexts and as if teacher motivation is unaffected by work setting and situation."

Some of the earliest theories of motivation described it as a drive that came from an individual. You either had it or you didn't. A common metaphor for this type of motivation was the gas tank. If a person could "fill up" his or her gas tank, he or she would become more motivated. Subsequent theories of motivation considered motivation to be a product of the environment. Much like in a garden, if the right conditions were created, a person's motivation would increase or grow. In contrast, more recent theories suggest that while the self and environment play a role, motivation is more complicated (Nolen, 2020; Wigfield & Koenka, 2020). In addition, a range of research suggests that morale increases as motivation to engage in tasks and activities increases (Shikalepo, 2020).

According to some experts, the levels of motivation that individuals exhibit result from a dynamic interaction between individuals, the tasks they are engaged in, and the environment within which they are engaged (e.g., Hattie et al., 2020: Hickey & Zuiker, 2005). For example, although a person may be unmotivated to complete a specific task, he or she may become more motivated if his or her interests shift, the nature of the task is modified, the context is adjusted, or other people who are also involved in the work change. A metaphor that helps summarize such thinking is that of a river's current (Middleton & Perks, 2014). Although it ebbs and flows, there is always a current in a river—even if it is hidden below the surface. This metaphor conveys our enduring assumption that all teachers have motivation and are motivated for something. The task of district and school leaders, then, is to tap into teachers' motivational energy, harness it, and help staff keep it flowing to support their work and any continuous improvement efforts. With the right tools, planning, and belief that every teacher is capable of impacting student outcomes, educational leaders can harness teacher and staff motivation to create work and learning environments that exhibit greater engagement and increased morale.

HOW CAN LEADERS HARNESS MOTIVATION AMONG PERSONNEL?

The belief that motivation is a result of the dynamic interplay among individuals, the context, and the work being engaged in can provide educational leaders with a variety of ways to improve the motivational climate of a school. Following are four key practices that educational leaders can use to leverage the motivation among their staff. Each is described in brief detail with some suggested strategies for implementing them. These key practices include the following:

- Promote teacher and staff voice and decision-making
- Make tasks meaningful by connecting them to teaching and learning
- Support teachers' belief that they can succeed on challenging tasks and situations
- Provide opportunities for meaningful collaboration

Pause and Reflect

- Brainstorm strategies you or other educational leaders have used to increase motivation and morale in schools.
- Consider the four strategies mentioned previously and identify ways you or others have used them.
- Rank the four foregoing strategies from least familiar to most familiar.

INCREASE STAFF VOICE

One of the most robust findings from research on motivation is that individuals tend to feel more motivated and willing to engage in hard work when they perceive themselves as having autonomy (e.g., Farris-Berg & Diswager, 2012). In other words, individuals are more motivated when they perceive that they have a voice or the power to make decisions that impact what they do and how they work.

A common example of the impact of autonomy is with professional development for staff. In many schools and districts, teachers are given little to no voice in determining the types of staff development opportunities that would be the most valuable to them. In contrast, some effective school leaders create autonomy-supportive environments by actively encouraging teacher choice in professional development topics and activities. For example, in one school with high levels of motivation among staff, the principal annually asks staff to analyze student achievement data to determine areas of practice that could benefit from instructional improvements. After the staff generates a list, the principal develops a flexible approach to professional development that addresses many of the topics the staff had identified. Teachers have the opportunity to go to workshops, participate in book groups, or receive training from outside experts tailored to the topics they have identified. They are also given flexibility to focus on professional development activities before, during, or after school. For some topics, the staff may recognize that there are already experts on staff, so the principal also creates opportunities for staff to engage with and learn from their colleagues. Following are additional ways school and district leaders can increase voice and decision-making among staff.

Encourage Distributed Leadership

Distributed leadership is a common approach school and district leaders can embrace that involves sharing leadership responsibilities and decision-making across individuals and teams within or across schools (Spillane & Diamond, 2007). Rather than relying solely on a single leader to drive improvement efforts, distributed leadership recognizes that leadership is more effective when shared. Examples of ways leaders can implement distributed leadership include creating school and district leadership teams, as well as sharing challenges with staff and empowering them to generate plans and solutions. In one middle school we worked with, teachers organized into professional development communities based on local expertise and needs and worked in those groups for a school year to identify desired outcomes, develop and implement strategies, and evaluate impact. Their work was presented and celebrated at the end of the year in a school-wide gathering.

Provide Choice

Often there is more than one pathway or approach to solving challenging problems in schools. In many cases, complex challenges require multifaceted approaches to solutions. This often allows significant opportunities for giving choices to staff. For example, one large high school we worked with had over 40 percent of students reading more than two grades below grade level. The school leadership team developed a comprehensive approach to this problem that included providing literacy coaches to staff, offering books and other text resources for developing classroom libraries to support independent reading, as well as offering a range of professional learning opportunities for teachers. Teachers and staff had the option of choosing from these and a range of other supports designed to enhance literacy instruction and support across the school. As a result, all staff found one or more ways to improve their practices, and students' reading scores increased significantly.

Solicit Routine Feedback

Another way to promote staff voice is to create opportunities for staff to provide feedback about improvement initiatives. Most schools and districts we work with have improvement plans. The leaders who are most effective in implementing and monitoring these plans routinely ask for staff feedback about how things are going as a part of monitoring progress. Where this happens, requests for feedback are solicited in myriad ways and occur frequently. For example, after every meeting, staff can be given anonymous exit tickets to provide feedback. When plans are created, they can be shared with staff before implementation begins. School and district leaders can develop the habit of routinely asking teachers, other personnel, parents, and students about what is working well and what could be improved. It is critical that in subsequent meetings that school leaders identify specific changes they've made based on the feedback provided.

MAKE TASKS MEANINGFUL BY CONNECTING THEM TO TEACHING AND LEARNING

Individuals tend to be more motivated to engage in work they find meaningful (Eccles & Wigfield, 2002). Although there are myriad factors that make activities meaningful, common factors are *interest*, *value*, and *expectation of success*. An activity will be more meaningful if it connects to an individual's interests and/or has a connection to something he or she values. Teachers also need to believe that their actions will result in improvement or success. Educational leaders can increase the level of meaningfulness of teachers' work by striving to make sure most activities that a teacher engages in explicitly connect to teaching and learning. In other words, the more a task connects to what a teacher teaches (interest) or helps them improve teaching practice (value), the more likely the task is to be perceived as meaningful and the more likely the teacher will be motivated to engage in it.

There are a variety of actions educational leaders can take to increase the meaningfulness of the work staff engage in. The following are a few.

Routinely Assess Staff Responsibilities and Workloads

Another strategy to enhance meaningfulness is to routinely assess what staff are being asked to do. It is often the case that educators and school personnel have more to do than time permits and perceive some of those tasks as unrelated to student success. This is particularly true for teachers. Leaders can work with teachers to understand and prioritize responsibilities and to make sure that the primary tasks teachers are responsible for have strong connections to student learning.

Help Staff Establish Improvement Goals

A core tenet of teaching is that a person always has room to grow and improve. This is particularly true in the field of education where it is important for educators to model lifelong learning for students. Therefore, another strategy leaders can take is to encourage teachers and staff to focus evaluation and feedback on teachers' own learning and improvement goals. The most useful goals are ones that focus on growth that will improve outcomes for students, and school leaders can guide teachers in selecting goals most related to those outcomes. Additionally, it is important that these goals, once set, do not sit on a shelf, but are used to shape professional development and collaborative work time. To influence motivation, leaders and teachers should actively review their progress by establishing reflections and assessing learning and growth as routine in their school.

Communicate the Urgency of Improvement

In our experience it is quite commonplace for teachers and staff to not always fully understand the rationale for decisions that school and district leaders make. Often leaders believe that the reason for a change is apparent and intuitive, but this is often not the case. A common example is with the use of curriculum resources. On multiple occasions we have worked with districts and schools that decided to adopt new curriculum resources. In some cases, staff are not clear why the school or district is adopting new materials. When this happens, some staff become resentful and resistant to the change because they were familiar with the resources they were already using. In other cases, the school and district leaders used multiple methods of communication to explain why curriculum changes were being made. By working with their leadership team on a communication strategy, a school leader can effectively share their explanation for change, such as the lack of adequate resources available to all teachers, the inconsistent use of specific resources, and/or research and student achievement data showing existing resources are not as effective as newer materials. When leaders make it clear why they are doing what they are doing, particularly as it relates to supporting students, and when they do so frequently, the work becomes more meaningful to staff.

SUPPORT SUCCESS ON CHALLENGING TASKS

One of the more confusing elements of motivation is the role of challenge. Research and experience strongly suggest that challenge has the potential to be a very powerful motivator (Schunk & Pajares, 2005). For example, consider times when you were very motivated and deeply engaged in an activity or task. If you are reading this chapter in a group, pause to share and discuss your experiences together. It is likely that most, if not all, of the experiences had a significant element of challenge. The reason for this is that when we overcome a challenge, we feel as if we have done something meaningful. However, the difficult part of the challenge is that individuals need to also feel as if they have the capacity to succeed at the task. If a task is perceived to be too hard or even too easy, motivation can quickly wane. This is true at any all stages of a teachers' career.

Most of the tasks that educators engage in are inherently challenging due to the complex nature of teaching and learning. Unfortunately, at times teachers experience a lack of support or strategy to ensure success on challenging tasks. One example is with creating assessments. Educational leaders expect teachers to develop a variety of assessment strategies to measure student learning, including end-of-unit assessments, common assessments, or performance tasks. Often, these assessments are moderate- or high-stakes; however, most teachers have had minimal training on how to design valid and reliable assessments. Asking teachers to develop assessments without appropriate understanding or strategies puts them in an extremely difficult situation for supporting student learning and motivation while providing the required assessment data. Some actions educational leaders can take to improve motivation among teachers with regard to challenging tasks include:

- Allowing teachers to identify and share the more challenging aspects of their current work
- Providing teachers with the education and support to do what they are being asked to do
- Providing enough time for teachers to develop, practice, and receive feedback on their actions with an emphasis on continuous development.

Keep in mind that much of what works for school-aged students also works for adult learners. Just as it would not be good practice to ask students to do something complicated without giving them the opportunity to explore, instructing them in how to do it, and letting them practice in order to develop mastery, the same is the case for working with teachers as adult learners.

PROVIDE OPPORTUNITIES FOR MEANINGFUL COLLABORATION

A fourth practice that can have a positive impact on motivation and morale among teachers and other school personnel relates to the relationships and social connections that people make or strengthen through work (e.g., Deci & Ryan, 2002). Think about the most motivating activities you have previously participated in as an educator. Probably many of these were collaborative endeavors. While people can easily be motivated to engage in independent tasks, motivation often increases when there are added opportunities to work with others, particularly with people you like and care about. Teachers at times may feel isolated in their classrooms when, in fact, teaching can be highly collaborative and connected.

Given the role that relationships can play in accessing motivation and fostering a positive culture and climate, educational leaders should provide or promote opportunities that foster positive collaboration among staff members. However, relationships can be tricky. Once again, just as with students, simply putting educators together does not guarantee successful interactions. Thus, it is helpful to give individuals choices about which people they work with and on what tasks. In addition, collaboration is most successful when norms have been established, tasks are as clearly defined as possible, there is expert facilitation with clear protocols, and the work has structure that is appropriate to the task.

School leaders can take responsibility for and model positive, productive, collaborative professional relationships. By carefully structuring opportunities for professional collaboration, setting norms for positive interactions, and developing a culture that celebrates teamwork, a school leader can enhance the motivation of their teachers to engage in their school community.

Pause and Reflect

- Which of the four practices discussed previously resonate the most with you?
- Which of the four practices do you implement the least? What are concrete steps you can take as a leader to hone this practice?

AN INTEGRATIVE APPROACH

Many school and district leaders create innovative ways to tap into all four practices described previously. One of the most successful approaches we have seen is to provide teachers with routine opportunities to engage in collaborative professional development, such as professional learning communities (PLCs). Within this approach, school leaders establish routine times when teams of teachers can work together in small teams to improve their professional practice. In our experience, such collaboration tends to be at its strongest when leaders provide teams with a set of protocols and other resources that they can use to support a range of collaborative work. Additionally, it is important for leaders to make sure that each team has at least one member who has facilitation skills and is trained in leading teams. Effective protocols often include processes for planning or tuning units and lessons, designing or validating assessments, analyzing videos of instruction, or analyzing student work or data. Such collaborative professional development is very successful at leveraging into motivation and boosting morale because (1) it provides teachers with a wide range of choice, (2) it is highly meaningful and directly focused on instruction and learning, (3) it provides peer supports that help teachers manage the challenges of teaching, and (4) it strengthens interpersonal relationships among staff. In short, such highly collaborative work builds a positive culture by routinely engaging teachers in important tasks that improve their practice.

CONCLUSION

A high level of motivation is not just important for students; it is equally essential for teachers and all personnel who support student learning. Educational leaders must be deliberate in trying to build and maintain high levels of motivation among staff. When leaders are successful at doing this, schools become places where all individuals thrive and enjoy working. When these efforts are less successful, morale and achievement can suffer. A final suggestion for school leaders is to routinely review the four practices described in this chapter, particularly when they are developing or implementing any improvement initiative. When the work gets frantic, it is easy to just focus on "getting things done" and less on how they are getting done. The practices shared in the chapter are designed to help leaders be intentional so that most staff will be motivated to get on board with the important work of improvement on behalf of students.

Reflect Further and Take Action

- To what extent are you encouraging educators to make decisions that impact their work and learning?
- To what extent are you building meaningfulness by connecting work to teaching and learning?
- To what extent are you building capacity and supporting success on challenging tasks?
- To what extent are you providing opportunities for meaningful collaboration?

REFERENCES

Barnum, M. (2023, March 6). Teacher turnover hits new highs across the U.S. *Chalkbeat*. https://www.chalkbeat.org/2023/3/6/23624340/teacher-turnover-leaving-the-profession-quitting-higher-rate

Deci, E. L., & Ryan, R. M. (2002). Self-determination research: Reflections and future directions. In *Handbook of self-determination research* (pp. 431–441). University of Rochester Press.

Eccles, J. S., & Wigfield, A. (2002). Motivational beliefs, values, and goals. *Annual Review of Psychology, 53*, 1.

Farris-Berg, K., & Diswager, E. (2012). *Trusting teachers with school success*. Rowman and Littlefield.

Hattie, J., Hodis, F. A., & Kang, S. H. (2020). Theories of motivation: Integration and ways forward. *Contemporary Educational Psychology, 61*, 101865.

Haynes, M. (2014). *On the path to equity: Improving the effectiveness of beginning teachers*. Alliance for Excellent Education. Available from http://all4ed.org/reports-factsheets/path-to-equity/

Hickey, D. T., & Zuiker, S. J. (2005). Engaged participation: A sociocultural model of motivation with implications for educational assessment. *Educational Assessment, 10*(3), 277–305.

Kanfer, R., Frese, M., & Johnson, R. E. (2017). Motivation related to work: A century of progress. *Journal of Applied Psychology, 102*(3), 338.

Middleton, M., & Perks, K. (2014). *Motivation to learn: Transforming classroom culture to support student achievement*. Corwin Press.

Nolen, S. B. (2020). A situative turn in the conversation on motivation theories. *Contemporary Educational Psychology, 61*, 101866.

Schunk, D. H., & Pajares, F. (2005). Competence perceptions and academic functioning. In A. J. Elliot & C. S. Dweck (Eds.), *Handbook of competence and motivation* (pp. 85–104). Guilford Press.

Sinclair, C. (2008). Initial and changing student teacher motivation and commitment to teaching. *Asia-Pacific Journal of Teacher Education, 36*, 79–104.

Shikalepo, E. E. (2020). The role of motivational theories in shaping teacher motivation and performance: A review of related literature. *International Journal of Research and Innovation in Social Science (IJRISS), 4.*

Spillane, J. P., & Diamond, J. B. (Eds.). (2007). *Distributed leadership in practice.* Teachers College Press.

Wigfield, A., & Koenka, A. C. (2020). Where do we go from here in academic motivation theory and research? Some reflections and recommendations for future work. *Contemporary Educational Psychology, 61,* 101872.

Woolfolk Hoy, A. (2021). Teacher motivation, quality instruction, and student outcomes: Not a simple path. *Learning and Instruction, 76,* 101545. https://doi.org/10.1016/j.learninstruc.2021.101545

CHAPTER 7

Achieving the Promise of Professional Learning Communities (PLCs)

Kevin Perks

Pause and Reflect Before Reading

- How would you define PLCs and their purpose?
- How do you think PLCs benefit teachers and students?
- How robust are PLCs in your school and/or district?

INTRODUCTION

"I have learned more about teaching in my professional learning community than in any course I took in college!" This statement was made by a teacher who had been routinely engaging in a productive professional learning community (PLC) in her school. As many educational leaders know, PLCs are a collaborative approach to professional learning that many schools use to support educators in their schools and districts. PLCs are not the only approach to supporting collaborative learning among educational professionals, but in our experience, they are the most common. Other approaches include, but are not limited to, communities of practice (CoPs) (Wenger, 1999), professional learning teams (PLTs) (Johnson & Scull, 1999), and critical friends groups (CFGs) (Curry, 2008).

As the foregoing comment states quite directly, effective PLCs can be a powerful approach to supporting the continuous learning of in-service teachers. However, many schools that we have worked with struggle to achieve the full potential of PLCs, and many teachers we have met have yet to experience the powerful learning that can result when PLCs are well-designed and facilitated effectively. The purpose of this chapter is to provide school and district leaders with helpful insights and suggestions for designing and/or optimizing their systems of PLCs. We have organized this chapter around common questions we hear from educators about PLCs. These include the following:

- What are PLCs, and what is their purpose?
- What are the benefits?
- What kinds of work should be done in PLCs to achieve the intended outcomes?
- What factors contribute most to the success of a PLCs?
- What can school leaders do to support the effectiveness of PLCs?

DEFINITION AND PURPOSE

While there is no single definition of PLCs, in their review of the literature on them, Stoll and colleagues (2006) contend that, generally speaking, a PLC is a professional learning approach in which groups of educators meet routinely on the job to share and critically analyze their professional practices in a manner that is reflective, learning-centered, and growth-oriented. Ultimately, the purpose of a PLC is to support student learning and achievement by enhancing or improving teacher practices related to curriculum, instruction, and assessment. In their literature review, Lefstein and colleagues (2020) found that there is a great deal of variance in how teachers engage when working in collaborative contexts, but that a key factor that supports adult learning is generative discourse that has the potential to improve teaching practice.

In schools where professional learning for educators is robust, PLCs are often a vital component of a larger, multi-tiered system of professional learning for staff. Such multi-tiered systems often include (1) analysis of student data to target areas of teacher practice that, if improved, will most likely have a positive impact on student learning; (2) professional development opportunities on research- and evidence-based teaching practices; (3) well-established systems of instructional coaching with coaches who routinely meet one-on-one with teachers to support their growth and learning, and (4) systematic feedback loops where school leaders engage in frequent classroom visits and walk-throughs to provide formative feedback to teachers as they practice applying what they have learned from previous professional development opportunities. In short, within a robust and multi-tiered system of support for teachers, PLCs provide a collaborative context where teachers can work together to refine improvement goals for teaching, practice applying evidence-based practices learned during professional development, as well as respond to feedback received during coaching and classroom visits from school and district leaders.

A simple metaphor that helps describe how PLCs fit into a larger system of professional learning is viewing a school as a classroom of adult learners. For example, it has been well demonstrated that the gradual release of responsibility (GRR) model is a very effective approach to teaching complex knowledge and skills in classrooms (e.g., Fisher & Frey, 2021; Pearson et al., 2019). The GRR approach often begins with direct instruction. This is typically followed by guided-teacher support and opportunities for students to engage in collaborative practice in small groups. It concludes with independent practice.

Multi-tiered systems of professional learning mirror the GRR model. For example, professional development opportunities provide direct instruction, coaching provides guided support, and PLCs provide opportunities for collaborative practice where teachers can receive support from peers. Just as collaborative practice is essential in classrooms where students are the learners, PLCs are just as vital in adult learning contexts.

WHAT ARE THE POTENTIAL BENEFITS?

Why should leaders create routine opportunities for teachers and staff to engage in PLCs? Multiple studies and literature reviews have demonstrated that well-developed PLCs have strong potential to positively impact both teaching practice and student learning. Positive outcomes for teachers include improvements in instruction, enhanced perceptions of self-efficacy among teachers, a greater willingness to try new and innovative practices, and increases in student-centered practices (Servage, 2008; Stoll et al., 2006; Tam, 2015; Vescio et al., 2008). Other benefits include improved culture among teachers, as well as increased job satisfaction (Vescio et al., 2008; Zhang et al., 2023). Benefits for students include increases in motivation, achievement, and overall performance in school (Doğan & Adams, 2018; Vescio et al., 2008).

Pause and Reflect

- How did the foregoing descriptions align with your initial thinking?
- What characteristics do you think PLCs need to have to achieve their full potential?

THE WORK OF PLCS

A common question we are asked when helping school and district leaders improve their systems of PLCs is "what kinds of work should teachers be engaged in when working in a PLC?" Researcher John Hattie and cognitive psychologist Gregory Yates (2013) point out that learning is maximized when learners make their work visible to others and are open to receiving and incorporating new ideas and feedback. In our experience, this sums up the kind of work PLCs should engage in. In short, effective PLCs routinely create ongoing opportunities for teachers to make their practice visible by analyzing and giving feedback on artifacts of their professional work, such as lessons, units, assessments, examples of student work, or video clips of their instruction. Following are examples of the kinds of activities we recommend PLCs routinely engage in to reflect on, discuss, and improve their professional practice.

- **Design curriculum, instruction, and assessment resources:** Work together to design scope and sequences, units of study, lessons, or assessments.
- **Revise or "tune" curriculum and instruction resources:** Share copies of units or lessons and discuss feedback and suggestions for improvement.
- **Validate assessments and rubrics:** Assessment expert Rick Stiggins (2014) argues that assessment literacy is one of the largest professional knowledge gaps in education. Teachers can use PLCs to analyze and receive feedback on their assessments to help ensure that they are valid and reliable.
- **Analyze instruction in action:** Record, share, and use video clips of teaching to analyze a teacher's instructional practices. Free online resources such as VideoANT (https://ant.umn.edu) can easily be used to foster collaborative analysis of classroom instruction video.
- **Analyze student work and achievement data:** Analyze student work or data to identify strengths and areas of growth that can be used to inform future and ongoing instruction.

Hattie (2015) argues that one of the most important things school leaders can do is to support and develop teachers' expertise in engaging in the types of collaborative work described previously. But supporting a collaborative environment in which staff can safely and productively make their work visible to each other and exchange feedback can be difficult. Too often PLCs can become unproductive (Sims & Penny, 2014). The next section explores ways that school leaders can help PLCs be successful.

CHARACTERISTICS OF EFFECTIVE PLCS

According to a study by the Boston Consulting Group (2014), many teachers tend to think PLCs are ineffective. Dufour and Reeves (2015) suggest that such criticism might well be warranted in many cases because, when poorly implemented, PLCs can easily become "just another meeting" in which teachers discuss issues that do not have a direct impact on their professional practice or on student learning. If educational leaders are finding that the PLCs are not appearing to be effective, or if there does not appear to be a positive culture of adult learning emanating from PLCs, or if teachers are not routinely excited to engage in them, then it is likely time for a systems-level intervention to revitalize them. A simple heuristic that leaders can use to quickly assess their system of PLCs is to ask themselves if teachers are routinely walking out of a PLC better teachers than they walked in. If the answer is "no," then it is likely their PLCs would benefit from additional support. While there is no specific recipe or precise algorithm for a productive PLC, the following are some essential elements for school and district leaders to consider when determining where to focus support.

A Focus on Teacher Learning

If a PLC is to have a positive and substantive impact on teacher and student learning, the focus of collaborative time should remain squarely on sharing and receiving feedback and ideas that relate to curriculum, instruction, and assessment and that are oriented around teachers' improvement goals. PLCs are not the time to have meetings about logistics like planning field trips or scheduling parent conferences.

Consistent Membership

Members of a PLC must feel comfortable sharing artifacts of their professional practice with each other. As Hord (1997) points out, it can take time for teachers to develop the mutual trust necessary for effective collaboration in PLCs. Thus, productive PLCs must have consistent membership, enabling participants to become familiar and comfortable sharing their work and practices with each other.

Established Norms and Working Agreements

Having clear norms and working agreements makes any meeting more efficient and effective than it might otherwise be. When adhered to, they also help individuals feel safe enough to take risks and be innovative. Productive PLCs also have norms and agreements that help conversations be positive and transformative. Examples of useful norms include being fully present, being willing to put ideas on the table, and paying attention to self and others (Garmston & Wellman, 2013). Another set of agreements to consider as a starting point are Singleton's Four Agreements of Courageous Conversations

(2014). A variation of these includes the following: *stay engaged, speak your truth, be willing to experience discomfort,* and *expect and accept non-closure.* These can be effective because they recognize that for a teacher to put their work "on the table" for the scrutiny of their peers can be a scary and courageous act and that the most helpful feedback is that which is accurate and truthful. These agreements also help to keep equity at the center of conversations about teacher practice and student learning. Additionally, well-run PLCs frequently review norms at the beginning of each meeting, use them to get back on track when some participants might be heading off on a tangent, and refer to them again to debrief and reflect on their process at the end of each conversation.

Routine Meeting Time

If a PLC does not meet frequently or routinely, it will be difficult for participants to build the required trust and sense of community. Many schools that have productive PLCs provide time for teachers to get together at least once or twice a week. Meetings need to be long enough that members have adequate time to review teacher and student artifacts and to engage in a conversation that is rich enough to influence changes in teacher practice. We recommend that most PLCs dedicate at least 60 minutes for meeting. The reason for this is that it takes time for discussions to get deep enough to have the potential to transform teaching practice.

Structured Conversations

Often overlooked in the implementation of PLCs is the value of using tools and protocols to help focus conversations on sharing and analyzing teacher practice. Without this supportive structure, PLCs tend to spend more time on sharing work and less time on analyzing and discussing feedback. It is not uncommon for PLC participants to think they do not need protocols, but our experience has taught us that protocols are vital to ensuring that conversations become rigorous enough to improve professional practice.

Structured tools and protocols also help PLCs operate more efficiently, something that is especially important given the difficulty of making time for PLCs to routinely meet for sufficient periods of time. Most importantly, we have found—perhaps counterintuitively—that protocols are often necessary for conversations to be rigorous enough to generate transformative discourse. In sum, if PLCs are not able to foster generative discourse, it is not likely that the PLCs will achieve the purpose of helping teachers improve their practice (Lefstein et al., 2020).

Additional Characteristics of Effective PLCs

In addition to the characteristics described previously, there are additional elements for leaders to consider and support. The following list identifies actions that effective PLCs take on a routine basis.

- Determine agendas, clarify roles, and prepare materials in advance.
- Review roles and norms at the beginning of every meeting.
- Clarify the purpose or objective of the meeting at the outset.
- Use a structured process or protocol to guide the discussion.
- Provide time for members to review and analyze artifacts and materials before discussing.
- Make time to provide thoughtful feedback. Begin with praise and identification of effective examples of practice. Conclude with what PLC members have learned.
- Reflect on and adjust procedures at the end.

In regard to the foregoing list, effective PLC facilitators can also use it as a checklist to assess their PLC and identify ways to improve.

GUIDANCE FOR SCHOOL AND DISTRICT LEADERS

Fostering a well-run PLC takes deliberate preparation and planning. Based on our experiences, we suggest the following actions that school and district leaders can take to create PLCs and/or ensure that they remain high-functioning.

Create and Communicate a Clear Vision and Plan for Collaborative Work

For any PLC to have a positive impact on teacher and student learning, participants must have a shared understanding of the PLC's purpose, particularly the importance of focusing on learning for both teachers and students. Hord (1997) describes this as establishing shared values and a common vision. One way of getting PLC members on the same page is for school leaders to work collaboratively with teachers to clearly define, and document in writing, the vision and purpose of PLCs and to communicate this frequently.

Communicate Clear School Guidelines That Define Roles and Expectations for All Staff

In schools that have a strong system of PLCs, leaders have clearly defined and communicated the various roles of all involved. For themselves, they clearly communicate that they will participate in PLCs routinely and provide training and support as needed. For teacher leaders and instructional coaches who facilitate PLCs, school leaders make sure all staff now that the role of facilitators is to support the conversations in PLCs; their role is not to evaluate. Finally, it is important for leaders to communicate the purpose and importance of PLCs and expectations for all participants.

Create and Implement a Schedule of Routine Time for Teacher Teams to Collaborate

As noted previously, PLCs need to meet frequently enough so members can develop mutual trust and for long enough periods that members engage in substantive conversations about their professional practices. Schools can be very creative in how they find this time. For example, some leaders make sure the daily schedule creates time for PLCs to meet during the school day. Other leaders provide stipends for teachers to meet before or after school. Some principals dedicate existing staff or department meeting time to PLC work. Another strategy some districts have used is to build late starts or early releases into the school calendar to free up time when all teachers can meet when students are not at school.

Establish Common Resources That Support Effective Collaboration

As also noted earlier, to support practice-centered discussions, productive PLCs tend to use protocols or structured processes to guide the conversations and analysis of artifacts of teacher practice. Well written protocols typically provide time for teachers to clarify the purpose of the meeting, review norms, establish roles, become familiar with any artifacts, analyze, and offer feedback, as well as reflect and debrief on the success of the discussion. Following are a few online websites with protocols and other tools to support PLCs:

- The Center for Collaborative Education—http://www.cce.org
- The School Reform Initiative—http://www.schoolreforminitiative.org
- National School Reform Faculty—http://www.nsrfharmony.org

Provide One or More Trained Facilitators for Each PLC

Well-run PLCs usually have a facilitator who is comfortable leading his or her group. To develop a cadre of effective facilitators, administrators should provide opportunities for educators to receive training in facilitation skills. School leaders should also provide opportunities for PLC facilitators to meet routinely with each other to share resources and provide mutual support.

Provide Visible Leadership and Support

As mentioned previously about roles, an additional step school leaders can take to ensure the success of PLCs is to participate themselves, at least periodically, and to provide ongoing support as needs and questions arise. In many schools, leaders find it difficult to visit PLCs on a regular basis. However, in the absence of regular participation by school leaders, it is easy for PLCs to devolve into the types of meetings that will not influence teacher practice in positive ways (e.g., Sims & Penny, 2014).

CONCLUSION

To revisit the metaphor that described schools and classrooms of adult learners, we conclude re-emphasizing the important role that PLCs have within a broader system of talent development and teacher learning. Teaching is extremely challenging work, and as most educational leaders we know recognize, there is and should be no end to our continuous growth as professionals. This requires routinely engaging in professional learning and creating safe spaces where we can receive helpful feedback from our co-learners. This collaborative element to learning is essential in classrooms, and it is just as important for adults.

Finally, when considering the importance of PLCs in supporting teacher learning and growth, it is equally important to remember the essential role school and district leaders play in building and sustaining effective systems of collaboration like PLCs. Our collective experiences have convinced us that behind every effective system of PLCs are intentional and supportive school leaders. Similarly, school leaders also need the backing and guidance from district leaders to ensure that schools have the capacity to build and sustain effective teacher support systems.

Reflect Further and Take Action

- Consider the characteristic of effective PLCs described previously. Which are practiced most frequently in your school or district? Where are the greatest opportunities for improvement?
- Based on the information in this chapter, what are some immediate next steps you can take to enhance PLCs in your school or district?

REFERENCES

Boston Consulting Group. (2014). *Teachers know best: Teachers' views on professional development*. Bill and Melinda Gates Foundation.

Curry, M. (2008). Critical friends groups: The possibilities and limitations embedded in teacher professional communities aimed at instructional improvement and school reform. *Teachers College Record, 110*(4), 733–774.

Doğan, S., & Adams, A. (2018). Effect of professional learning communities on teachers and students: Reporting updated results and raising questions about research design. *School Effectiveness and School Improvement, 29*(4), 634–659.

Dufour, R., & Reeves, D. (2015, October 2). Professional learning communities still work (if done right). *Education Week*.

Fisher, D., & Frey, N. (2021). *Better learning through structured teaching: A framework for the gradual release of responsibility*. ASCD.

Garmston, R. J., & Wellman, B. M. (2013). *The adaptive school: A sourcebook for developing collaborative groups*. Rowman & Littlefield Publishers.

Hattie, J., & Yates, G. C. (2013). *Visible learning and the science of how we learn*. Routledge.

Hattie, J. (2015). *What works best in education: The politics of collaborative expertise*. Pearson.

Hord, S. M. (1997). *Professional learning communities: Communities of continuous inquiry and improvement*. Southwest Educational Development Laboratory.

Johnson, N. J., & Scull, J. (1999). The power of professional learning teams. *Improving Schools, 2*(1), 34–43.

Lefstein, A., Louie, N., Segal, A., & Becher, A. (2020). Taking stock of research on teacher collaborative discourse: Theory and method in a nascent field. *Teaching and Teacher Education, 88*, 102954.

Pearson, P. D., McVee, M. B., & Shanahan, L. E. (2019). In the beginning. In M. B. McVee, E. Ortlieb, J. Reichenberg, & P. D. Pearson (Eds.), *The gradual release of responsibility in literacy research and practice* (pp. 1–21). Emerald Group Publishing.

Servage, L. (2008). Critical and transformative practices in professional learning communities. *Teacher Education Quarterly*, 63–77.

Sims, R. L., & Penny, G. R. (2014). Examination of a failed professional learning community. *Journal of Education and Training Studies, 3*(1), 39–45.

Singleton, G. E. (2014). *Courageous conversations about race: A field guide for achieving equity in schools*. Corwin Press.

Stiggins, R. (2014). *Revolutionize assessment: Empower students, inspire learning*. Corwin Press.

Stoll, L., Bolam, R., McMahon, A., Wallace, M., & Thomas, S. (2006). Professional learning communities: A review of the literature. *Journal of Educational Change, 7*(4), 221–258.

Tam, A. C. F. (2015). The role of a professional learning community in teacher change: A perspective from beliefs and practices. *Teachers and Teaching, 21*(1), 22–43.

Vescio, V., Ross, D., & Adams, A. (2008). A review of research on the impact of professional learning communities on teaching practice and student learning. *Teaching and Teacher Education, 24*(1), 80–91.

Wenger, E. (1999). *Communities of practice: Learning, meaning, and identity.* Cambridge University Press.

Zhang, J., Yin, H., & Wang, T. (2023). Exploring the effects of professional learning communities on teacher's self-efficacy and job satisfaction in Shanghai, China. *Educational Studies, 49*(1), 17–34.

Part III

INSTRUCTIONAL TRANSFORMATION

Instructional Transformation is the third domain of the Four Domains of Rapid School Improvement, and it emphasizes the vital role school and district leaders play in enhancing teaching and learning practices within a school or district. School and district leaders play a critical role in this domain, as they have a key responsibility to ensure that instruction is optimized for student learning. Based on the research behind the Four Domains framework, three key practices that leaders can focus on to drive improvements in the Instructional Transformation domain include increasing capacity to (1) diagnose and respond to student learning needs, (2) provide rigorous and evidence-based instruction, and (3) remove barriers and provide opportunities for staff and students.

Taken together, all three practices work together to ensure that instruction is deliberately designed to target the specific needs of students, and that teachers are using research- and evidence-based strategies to optimize engagement and learning for all. To do this, it is essential that leaders support teachers and other educational personnel by helping to remove barriers that can impede high-quality teaching and learning and to increase opportunities that support it.

The chapters in Section 3 explore three areas of teaching and learning that can be confusing and/or challenging for school and district leaders to navigate. In Chapter 8, "Understanding How Social Emotional Learning, Culturally Responsive and Sustaining Education and Critical Race Theory Intersect," the authors explore and define three topics that have been receiving significant attention since the Covid-19 pandemic: social emotional learning, culturally responsive and sustaining education, and critical race theory. All three of these topics have influenced how schools and districts approach teaching and learning. There is also understandably significant confusion about each of these alone and how they relate to each other. This chapter helps to clarify confusion leaders may have and helps to prepare them for questions they are likely receive about them.

Another area of instruction that district and school leaders need to contend with is ensuring that teachers have high-quality curriculum materials that support effective instruction. Because curriculum is foundational to high-quality instruction, many districts have policies that require routine reviews of curriculum and curriculum resources every few years. To that end, Chapter 9, "Conducting a Targeted Curriculum Review," describes a comprehensive approach that school and district leaders can take implement thorough reviews of their various curricula. Readers will find this chapter to be an effective how-to guide for engaging in this complex and often time-consuming work.

Finally, Chapter 10, "Leading Formative Assessment to Improve Student Agency," defines and provides guidance to help district and school leaders build and enhance systems of formative assessment that can have a profound impact on optimizing and transforming instructional practice. As the chapter explains, formative assessment is often considered to be a type of quick assessment that teachers give in classrooms to check on student learning; however, at its most powerful, formative assessment is a practice where teachers routinely—and often collaboratively—review evidence of student learning to identify what they have learned and still need to learn, as well as what they may still be struggling with. By doing this, teachers are able to use student work and data to continuously inform instruction and tailor it to students' ever-evolving learning needs, particularly by using such information to remove barriers and identify new opportunities for learning. In this way, formative assessment becomes a powerful system that leverages all three of the practices at the heart of the Instructional Transformation domain.

When reading the chapters in this section, readers are encouraged to keep the following questions in mind as they engage with the material:

- To what extent have the topics of social and emotional learning, culturally responsive and sustaining education, and critical race theory come up in your work as a school leader? Why is each of these topics important in its own right, and how do these topics inform and influence teaching and learning? How do you think they intersect?
- How would you define the term "curriculum," and what is the state of the curricula in your school or district? To what extent do teachers

have shared resources across content, courses, and grade levels? What processes has your district or school recently engaged in to review curriculum in all areas?

- How would you define formative assessment? To what extent do teachers routinely use evidence of student work and learning to inform and modify instruction?

Understanding How Social Emotional Learning, Culturally Responsive and Sustaining Education, and Critical Race Theory Intersect

Andrea Browning and Saroja R. Warner

Pause and Reflect Before Reading

- How do you define social and emotional learning (SEL) and culturally responsive and sustaining education (CRSE)?
- What is your understanding of critical race theory (CRT), and how do you define it?
- What relationship do you see, if any, among all three concepts?
- Have you faced resistance or opposition to any or all of these concepts in your educational environment? If so, what have you learned from those experiences?

INTRODUCTION

Ensuring equity in education, whereby all student groups attain comparable positive outcomes, is an ongoing challenge, particularly for district and school leaders. While there is no single strategy for meeting this challenge, two broad approaches have gained traction among educational leaders who are committed to equity. One, referred to as social and emotional learning (SEL), focuses on supporting development of students' social and emotional intelligence, which research affirms can improve students' attitudes about self and others, social behavior, connection to school, and academic performance. Focusing on SEL can also lead to a reduction in students' behavioral referrals and emotional distress (Payton et al., 2008). While equity was not a focus in early iterations of SEL education, it has increasingly become so in recent years.

The other approach, culturally responsive and sustaining education (CRSE), focuses on affirming students' cultural identities and draws on their culture and lived experiences as assets to support their learning and strengthen positive sense of self. Research and evidence linking CRSE to positive student outcomes continues to accumulate (e.g., Bottiani et al., 2018; Dee & Penner, 2017). For instance, positive student–teacher relationships developed through CRSE are associated with better student academic and behavioral outcomes (Aronson & Laughter, 2016; Gay, 2018).

Despite the strong and positive value that SEL and CRSE provide, both have recently been called into question in some states and districts for their perceived connections to critical race theory (CRT), which is itself the subject of contentious political debate. This chapter explains each of these three concepts, how each contributes to addressing issues of equity, and how SEL and CRSE are distinct from the academic framework of CRT.

WHAT IS SOCIAL AND EMOTIONAL LEARNING?

SEL is not a new concept, and it is defined differently by many people. Broadly speaking, it refers to the process by which individuals develop and learn the mindsets, skills, and competencies (e.g., collaboration, persistence, empathy, emotional self-regulation) that help them successfully navigate the world and their place in it. The concept of SEL is based on a comprehensive notion of human development as taking place in and across four domains: physiological, cognitive, social, and emotional. Hundreds of social and emotional skills and competencies have been identified, although they tend to be interpreted and defined differently. To help address these divergent perspectives, the Harvard Taxonomy Project developed Explore SEL, an interactive tool to systematically explore SEL terms and crosswalk SEL frameworks (Jones et al., 2019).

In education, SEL programming—whether stand-alone or integrated into academic instruction and general classroom practice—is intended to accelerate and support students' development in the social and emotional domains listed previously. SEL is often thought of as the process by which one develops important life skills. In fact, mindsets, skills, and competencies in the social and emotional domains are sometimes thought of as nonacademic because they appear to be distinct from the cognitive skills needed for academic learning. Yet science shows that the four domains of human development are to some degree entwined, with health and well-being in one bolstering health and well-being in the others (Cantor et al., 2018). Moreover, research on high-quality SEL programming has documented improved academic outcomes; improved classroom behavior; increased ability to manage stress and depression; and better student attitudes about themselves, others, and school (Carneiro et al., 2007; Durlak et al., 2011). Equally important, having good social and emotional skills at an early age bodes well for later success. One longitudinal research study that followed all children born in a single week in Great Britain showed that children with good social skills at age 11 had better education outcomes, labor market outcomes, and social behaviors in adolescence and adulthood, compared to those whose early skills were not as strong (Carneiro et al., 2007).

The current political climate in the United States has hampered, and in some communities, shut down efforts to include SEL in classroom instruction. Historically, critics of SEL have maintained that the responsibility for a child's emotional development, attitudes, and values is the domain of families, not of schools. This concern is likely at the root of the current belief held by some critics that schools with an SEL focus are using SEL to indoctrinate students into a radical social or political agenda. For example, some detractors of SEL have accused it of being a "Trojan Horse" for CRT and LGBTQ-centered curriculum. Similarly, parents in some communities have pushed back against textbooks and other curricular materials that integrate SEL concepts into core academic areas, such as mathematics. Without an understanding of the science of social and emotional learning—that is, that the range of personal and interpersonal skills described as SEL develop *through* social interactions such as school-based learning—these arguments are likely to continue to bring into question the degree to which various political agendas are masquerading as SEL.

Pause and Reflect

- To what extent does my educational community understand the value of SEL in achieving students' academic achievement and success?
- Does my community see social and emotional learning as controversial? If so, what myths or misinformation may be contributing to that perspective?

WHAT IS CULTURALLY RESPONSIVE AND SUSTAINING EDUCATION?

CRSE is an approach to advancing learning and equity in education by creating culturally affirming and inclusive learning environments and experiences that support the attainment of comparably positive outcomes for all student groups. Central to CRSE is the practice of valuing students' cultural identities and lived experiences by substantively connecting those identities and experiences to the content and skills that students will learn and doing so in ways that counter cultural assimilation and instead support cultural pluralism.

CRSE is informed by an evolving cross-section of research, theories, and fields of study, including culturally relevant pedagogy, culturally responsive teaching, racial identity development, bilingualism, student agency, critical race theory, and social and emotional learning. Its intent is to affirm, sustain, and help strengthen students' identities, which research shows contributes to positive outcomes for all students (Hammond, 2015). CRSE recognizes cultural identities (including those based on race, ethnicity, language, gender, sexuality, and ability) as assets for teaching and learning, and as something to be built upon rather than ignored or diminished (Gay, 2013).

In particular, CRSE aims to build positive identities of students of color who have been disproportionately impacted by deficit perceptions and low expectations based on their race (Diamond et al., 2004). CRSE leverages the skills and knowledge that students bring in order to support the development of positive identities and academic and social and emotional learning. Building on students' prior knowledge and experiences when introducing new content can increase students' motivation for learning and effective information processing (Byrd, 2016; Hammond, 2015). Through CRSE's asset-focused orientation, students also learn to recognize, critique, and redress systemic bias and social inequalities (Ladson-Billings, 1994; 2014; Paris, 2012).

Similar to SEL, the current political climate and national debate in the United States around race, culture, and equity has also made it challenging for schools to prioritize culturally responsive teaching. Because of pushback and very public resistance in some communities to teaching narratives from nonwhite perspectives—for example, using resources from the 1619 project—many students haven't had access to learning that centers a range of cultural identities. Likewise, students in our schools today spent the past several years not just navigating challenges brought by the pandemic, but also navigating the nation's racial justice reckoning that was spurred by the death of George Floyd. Culturally responsive and sustaining educational environments are particularly essential right now to help young people reflect critically and make sense of the evolving world through their learning experiences.

Pause and Reflect

- How does this description of CRSE align with my own understanding of how to create culturally affirming and inclusive learning environments?
- To what extent do I see evidence of culturally responsive and sustaining teaching and learning in my own education environment or community?

- Does my community see CRSE as controversial? If so, what myths or misinformation may be contributing to that perspective?

WHAT IS CRITICAL RACE THEORY?

Critical race theory (CRT) is an academic theory and framework that identifies race as a social construct rather than a biological fact and attributes the prevalence of racism in American society not primarily to individual bias or prejudice but rather to its institutionalization in governmental systems, policies, and legal structures. In doing so, CRT challenges the long-held view, perpetuated at all levels of society, that America functions as a color-blind meritocracy.

CRT is not about criticizing or expressing disapproval of individuals or any particular racial group or gender. Rather, it is intended to provide a lens for carefully analyzing and examining systems, policies, and laws in order to better understand if and how they create, perpetuate, or possibly help dismantle racism. CRT's basic tenets originated in legal scholarship from the 1970s in the form of a framework for legal analysis (e.g., Bell, 1973/2008; Matsuda et al., 2018).

Critical race theorists recognized that the law can be complicit in maintaining an unjust social order and that, conversely, it can also be used to secure racial equality. By the 1990s, CRT was taken up in other fields as well, including education, where it has been used, for example, to examine and better understand existing policies or practices (and what underlies them), particularly those related to school discipline, intelligence, achievement testing, student tracking, and the relative inclusiveness of history and other curricula (Ladson-Billings, 2003). CRT has also been one of a number of theories, frameworks, or research bodies from various fields that inform implementation of culturally responsive and sustaining education.

CRT argues that even though race is not a biological reality, it has undeniable significance as a social construct and has an impact particularly on students of color. Critical race theorists note that racism affects the experiences of people of color, including African Americans, Asian Americans, Indigenous populations, Latinx/Hispanics, and others who identify as or are perceived to be people of color. CRT also recognizes that the social construct of race intersects with other identities, including sexuality, gender identity, ability status, and national origin. Its theorists argue that understanding this "intersectionality" of race with other aspects of identity is critical to understanding the effects that systems and laws have on people of color.

Pause and Reflect

- To what extent does the description of CRT offered here align with my own understanding of CRT?
- Does my community see CRT as controversial? If so, what myths or misinformation may be contributing to that perspective?
- In my opinion, what role, if any, should CRT play in teaching and learning in my educational community?

WHAT IS THE RELATIONSHIP AMONG THESE THREE APPROACHES?

It is important for district and school leaders to understand that SEL programs and CRSE are two distinct education approaches intended to help build or reinforce positive student identity and support learning. The former does so by helping strengthen students' social and emotional skills, from emotional regulation to metacognition; the latter does so primarily by recognizing and valuing students' racial/ethnic identities and lived experiences, and by connecting coursework to those identities and experiences.

Both approaches recognize the importance of students having a positive sense of self—a healthy identity—and its influence on students' success in school, home, and community. Within this, a key difference between the two is that SEL historically has focused on identity broadly, whereas CRSE focuses particularly on the development of positive racial and ethnic identities, which is found to be important for students of all racial and ethnic groups (Umaña-Taylor et al., 2018). When educators acknowledge—rather than intentionally or unintentionally ignore—the roles that race and ethnicity play in identity development, they actively affirm the value of students' cultures. In doing so, they take an important step in creating a learning environment that is inclusive and feels welcoming and positive for all students—which is a goal for all educators whether they think of themselves as implementing SEL education, CRSE, or neither. Similarly, in teaching or promoting the social and emotional skill of metacognition—thinking about thinking and learning—an educator is naturally offering a way for students to do something that aligns closely with the goals of CRSE: to reflect on their personal views and consider how their respective cultures may influence their judgments, assumptions, and conclusions about people and the world.

Even so, SEL has not typically been used to directly address racism. Historically, its advocates have neither focused on students' racial or ethnic identity nor called out equity as a key goal. In fact, some scholars have noted that in some implementations, SEL education has reflected either a deficit-oriented approach to students of color that focuses on "fixing" them or a color-evasive approach that refers to diversity of students in general terms and is not explicit about the social and emotional implications of race, racism, and racial identity (Mahfouz & Anthony-Stevens, 2020). A recent meta-analysis found that most SEL programs assume that interventions are neutral on issues of race and culture (characterized by the researchers as "color-blind") and assume that SEL programs' values and strategies are universally relevant for all children (Jones et al., 2018). This finding suggests a collective need to ensure that all SEL programs are asset-oriented for all students (and especially students of color) and that schools provide identity-affirming ways for students to develop the SEL skills that are linked to improved academic and behavioral outcomes.

A shift in SEL orientation toward a greater focus on equity is already under way. Since its launch in 2018, the Center to Improve Social and Emotional Learning and School Safety (CISELSS) has provided resources and technical assistance to SEL educators throughout the country with a "recognition that inequitable experiences lead to inequitable outcomes" (CISELSS, 2019, p. 1). Thus, the center identifies equity, which "introduces the notion of where power resides in leadership and decision-making," as both a key goal and key content for SEL programs. In striving for equity, the center asserts, educators "must take a strengths-based approach to engaging with students, parents, and the community" (p. 2). In its first needs assessment, the center learned that getting help to ensure equity was, in fact, a top priority for the SEL practitioners it surveyed.

Over the last few years, education scholars and leaders have identified opportunities for achieving education equity by better aligning SEL education and CRSE and increasing the use of both approaches (Gregory & Fergus, 2017). Those working at the leading edge of culturally responsive SEL education contend that teaching students about critical consciousness and oppression is vital to students' social and emotional development. The Collaborative for Academic, Social, and Emotional Learning (CASEL), a long-standing standard bearer for SEL education, issued a 2018 paper focused on SEL's potential to help "mitigate the interrelated legacies of racial and class oppression in the U.S. and globally," noting that, to date, that "potential [had been] underrealized" (Jaegers et al., 2018, p. 1). Two years later, in 2020, CASEL updated its SEL definition to "emphasize the skills, knowledge, and mindsets needed to examine prejudices and biases, evaluate social norms and systemic inequities, and promote community well-being" (Neimi, 2020, para 10).

Dena Simmons, SEL scholar and founder of newly launched LiberateED, challenges the field to grow into a more "fearless SEL" approach (Simmons, 2019, para 9) that explicitly centers students' lives, addresses sociopolitical context, and considers the ability and willingness to speak about difficult topics to be a core life skill. Simmons sees SEL as a way to foster courageous conversations across differences in order to help students (and teachers) "confront injustice, hate, and inequity" (para 3).

Yet, even without an intentional effort to align or integrate SEL and CRSE, the development of some critical SEL competencies, such as social awareness, metacognition, and empathy, may lead students to apply their critical thinking skills to the world around them on their own initiative. With that inclination, they may be more likely to examine and question anything from how history is taught to how decisions are made about who gets accepted into what courses, as well as issues outside of school. Thus, it is essential for educators, particularly school and district leaders, to understand that teaching these social and emotional skills, and others like them, is not the same as what some critics refer to as "teaching" or "doing" CRT. In fact, CRT is not a curriculum or a set of skills to be taught. Rather it is one framework, or lens, for thinking critically about the important social, cultural, economic, and other issues, including power, that affect all citizens. Those individuals who have developed strong academic and social–emotional skills will be prepared to make their own decisions about what they perceive through that lens.

Pause and Reflect

- Why do SEL and CRSE get confused with CRT?
- In my role or in my community, to what extent have I encountered resistance (whether vocal or otherwise) to SEL and CRSE because of a perceived overlap with CRT?
- To what extent do I feel confident speaking to the overlap between SEL, CRSE, and CRT? What might I do to learn more and to be more confident speaking to these perceived connections?

BROADENING THE CONVERSATION

Principals and other instructional leaders are in an ideal position to help their communities navigate uncertainty about the role of SEL and CRSE in learning. By rejecting race evasive or so-called "color-blind" SEL, leaders can emphasize that SEL skills develop *because* of a student's social and cultural influences, not *despite* them. Likewise, leaders can help teachers and families better understand the power of SEL and CRSE in creating learning experiences that honor students' cultural assets and help students make powerful connections to their lived experiences.

Although leaders will likely continue to navigate a range of community perceptions about integrating topics of race, culture, or social justice into schooling, principals and other leaders can facilitate meaningful conversations with their communities that increase transparency about the benefits of SEL and CRSE. Leaders can also learn to recognize when opposition to "equity" or discourse around CRT is being used as a red herring for other resistance to change that comes from broadening learning experiences so that they are more inclusive for students. Finally, principals can commit to learning more about how teachers can integrate SEL and CRSE into their teaching and learning practices in ways that continually empower and engage students. When instruction is informed by culturally responsive and sustaining practices, including deliberate attention to social and emotional learning, our schools not only become more equitable, but also become places where students build justice-oriented civic engagement and positive social and cultural identities.

Reflect Further and Take Action

- How did the chapter's information, ideas, and activities align with or challenge my prior understanding?
- What is the current level of practice in my district(s) and schools related to the practices and approaches described in the chapter?
- Are there new strategies or approaches that I might try in my own leadership context?
- Based on my reading, how would I respond to critics who are conflating SEL, CRSE, and/or CRT?
- What resources or information would be supportive to educators in my school or district, and what role can I play in deepening our understanding, as well as our teaching and learning practices?

RESOURCES FOR EDUCATORS

Links to Useful Web-Based Resources

- "Communicating About Equity in a Racially Charged Environment: Practical Communication Tips for Schools and Districts Engaged in Equity Work," prepared by the Coalition of Oregon School Administrators and available by searching online for "COSA ODE Spring 22 Toolkit."
- "Winning Racial Justice in Our Schools: Resisting the Right Wing Attacks on Critical Race Theory": A resource created in 2021 by the New York University Metro Center's Education Justice Research and Organizing Collaborative (EJ-ROC) to help communities resist anti-CRT attacks and to continue to organize for antiracist, culturally responsive schools. https://futureforlearning.org/2021/08/26/winning-racial-justice-in-our-schools/.

- The Collaborative for Academic, Social and Emotional Learning (CASEL) is an education-focused nonprofit focused on making evidence-based social and emotional learning (SEL) an integral part of education from preschool through high school, online at www.casel.org.
  - » Also check out CASEL's interactive online feature of the core SEL competencies and associated framework: https://casel.org /fundamentals-of-sel/what-is-the-casel-framework/
  - » CASEL's recent work on transformative SEL is focused on utilizing SEL to transform inequitable settings and systems, and to promote justice-oriented civic engagement: https://casel.org /fundamentals-of-sel/how-does-sel-support-educational-equity -and-excellence/transformative-sel/
- For a scan of CRSE teaching standards, see "Culturally Responsive Teaching: A 50-State Survey of Teaching Standards," by the New America Foundation, which has also identified eight educator competencies for culturally responsive teaching: https://www .newamerica.org/education-policy/policy-papers/culturally -responsive-teaching-competencies/.

Selections From the Scholarship

- Crenshaw, Kimberlé W., Gotanda, Neil, Peller, Gary, & Thomas, Kendall. (1995). *Critical race theory: The key writings that formed the movement*, p. 101. Faculty Books. https://scholarship.law.columbia .edu/books/101
- Gay, Geneva. (2000). *Culturally responsive teaching: Theory, research, and practice*. Teachers College Press.
- Hernandez, M. G., Lopez, D. M., & Swier, R. (2022). *Dismantling disproportionality: A culturally responsive and sustaining approach*. Teachers College Press.
- Ladson-Billings, G. (1995). But that's just good teaching! The case for culturally relevant pedagogy. *Theory Into Practice, 34*(3), 159–165. https://doi.org/10.1080/00405849509543675
- Ladson-Billings, G., & Tate, W. (1995). Toward a critical race theory of education. *Teachers College Record, 97*(1), 47–68. Teachers College, Columbia University. https://www.unco.edu/education-behavioral -sciences/pdf/TowardaCRTEduca.pdf.
- Ladson-Billings, G. (1998). Just what is critical race theory and what's it doing in a nice field like education? *International Journal of Qualitative Studies in Education, 11*(1), 7–24. https://doi.org/10.1080 /095183998236863
- Paris, D. (2012). Culturally sustaining pedagogy. A needed change in stance, terminology, and practice. *Educational Researcher, 41*(3), 93–97.

REFERENCES

Aronson, B., & Laughter, J. (2016). The theory and practice of culturally relevant education: A synthesis of research across content areas. *Review of Educational Research, 86*(1), 163–206.

Bell, D. (2008). *Race, racism, and American law* (6th ed.). Little, Brown & Co. (Original work published 1973).

Bottiani, J. H., Larson, K. E., Debnam, K. J., Bischoff, C. M., & Bradshaw, C. P. (2018). Promoting educators' use of culturally responsive practices: A systematic review of inservice interventions. *Journal of Teacher Education, 69,* 4. https://journals.sagepub.com/doi/pdf/10.1177/0022487117722553

Byrd, C. M. (2016). Does culturally relevant teaching work? An examination from student perspectives. *Sage Open, 6*(3), 1–10.

Cantor, P., Osher, D., Berg, J., Steyer, L., & Rose, T. (2018). Malleability, plasticity, and individuality: How children learn and develop in context. *Applied Developmental Science, 23,* 1–31.

Carneiro, P., Crawford, C., & Goodman, A. (2007). The impact of early cognitive and non-cognitive skills on later outcomes. *Center for the Economics of Education.*

Center to Improve Social and Emotional Learning and School Safety (CISELSS). (2019). *Needs-driven areas of focus.* WestEd. https://selcenter.wested.org/wp-content/uploads/sites/3/2019/12/SEL-Center-Needs-Focused.pdf

Dee, T. S., & Penner, E. K. (2017). The causal effects of cultural relevance: Evidence from an ethnic studies curriculum. *American Educational Research Journal, 54*(1), 127–166.

Diamond, J. B., Randolph, A., & Spillane, J. P. (2004, March). Teachers' expectations and sense of responsibility for student learning: The importance of race, class, and organizational habitus. *Anthropology & Education Quarterly, 35*(1), 75–98.

Durlak, J. A., Weissberg, R. P., Dymnicki, A. B., Taylor, R. D., & Schellinger, K. B. (2011). The impact of enhancing students' social and emotional learning: A meta-analysis of school-based universal interventions. *Child Development, 82,* 405–432. https://casel.s3.us-east-2.amazonaws.com/meta-analysis-child-development-1.pdf

Gay, G. (2013). Teaching to and through cultural diversity. *Curriculum Inquiry, 43,* 48–70.

Gay, G. (2018). *Culturally responsive teaching: Theory, research, and practice* (3rd ed.). Teachers College Press.

Gregory, A., & Fergus, E. (2017). Social-emotional learning and equity in school discipline. *The Future of Children, 27,* 117–136.

Hammond, Z. (2015). *Culturally responsive teaching and the brain.* Corwin Press.

Jaegers, R., Rivas-Drake, D., & Borowski, T. (2018). Equity and social emotional learning: A cultural analysis [Frameworks Briefs: Special Issues Series]. *CASEL.* https://measuringsel.casel.org/wp-content/uploads/2018/11/Frameworks-Equity.pdf

Jones, S., Bailey, R., Brush, K., & Nelson, B. (2019). Introduction to the taxonomy project: Tools for selecting and aligning SEL frameworks. *Collaborative for*

Academic, Social, and Emotional Learning, 3, 1–13. https://measuringsel.casel.org/wp-content/uploads/2019/02/Frameworks-C.1.pdf

Jones, T. M., Fleming, C., & Gavin, A. (2018, May). Generalizability of social emotional learning programs to racially diverse students: A comprehensive literature review [Oral presentation]. Society for Prevention Research, Washington, DC.

Ladson-Billings, G. (1994). *Dreamkeepers: Successful teachers of African American children*. Jossey Bass.

Ladson-Billings, G. (Ed.). (2003). *Critical race theory perspectives on the social studies: The profession, policies, and curriculum*. Information Age.

Ladson-Billings, G. (2014). Culturally relevant pedagogy 2.0: a.k.a. the remix. *Harvard Educational Review, 84*, 74–84.

Mahfouz, J., & Anthony-Stevens, V. (2020). Why trouble SEL? The need for cultural relevance in SEL. *Occasional Paper Series*, (43). https://educate.bankstreet.edu/occasional-paper-series/vol2020/iss43/6/?utm_source=educate.bankstree

Matsuda, M. J., Lawrence, C. R., Delgado, R., & Crenshaw, K. (2018). *Words that wound: Critical race theory, assaultive speech, and the first amendment*. Taylor & Francis.

Neimi, K. (2020). CASEL is updating the most widely recognized definition of social-emotional learning. Here's why. [Online opinion]. *CASEL*. https://www.the74million.org/article/niemi-casel-is-updating-the-most-widely-recognized-definition-of-social-emotional-learning-heres-why/

Paris, D. (2012). Culturally sustaining pedagogy: A needed change in stance, terminology, and practice. *Educational Researcher, 41*, 93–97.

Payton, J., Weissberg, R. P., Durlak, J. A., Dymnicki, A. B., Taylor, R. D., Schellinger, K. B., & Pachan, M. (2008). The positive impact of social and emotional learning for kindergarten to eighth-grade students: Findings from three scientific reviews. *CASEL*.

Simmons, D. (2019, September). Why we can't afford whitewashed social-emotional learning. *ASCD, 61*(4). https://www.ascd.org/el/articles/why-we-cant-afford-whitewashed-social-emotional-learning

Umaña-Taylor, A. J., Kornienko, O., Douglass Bayless, S., & Updegraff, K. A. (2018). A universal intervention program increases ethnic-racial identity exploration and resolution to predict adolescent psychosocial functioning one year later. *Journal of Youth and Adolescence, 47*(1), 1–15. https://link.springer.com/article/10.1007%2Fs10964-017-0766-5

ADDITIONAL ACKNOWLEDGMENTS

This chapter was adapted from a WestEd paper written by Saroja Warner and Andrea Browning, titled "What are social and emotional learning and culturally responsive and sustaining education and what do they have to do with critical race theory? A primer." https://www.wested.org/wp-content/uploads/2021/09/SEL_CRSE_CRT-primer_Brief_Rd2-3.pdf.

CHAPTER 9

Conducting a Targeted Curriculum Review

Robert Rosenfeld

Pause and Reflect Before Reading

- What is a curriculum review, and when should you conduct one?
- What kinds of tasks are part of a curriculum review process?
- What is your experience leading or participating in a curriculum review or audit?

INTRODUCTION

Is student achievement in your school or district lower than expected or desired, or have there been decreases in achievement in the last few years? Did the pandemic lead to learning gaps that still seem insurmountable? Has there been significant turnover in teaching staff in a specific subject area recently? Do all teachers who teach the same grade level or course provide consistent and equitable instruction and assessment across classrooms? Based on your answers to these and similar questions, your district, school or department may benefit from engaging in a curriculum review.

An increasing body of research continues to show that one of the most efficient and effective ways to support student achievement is to ensure that all students have access to a high-quality, content-rich, and standards-aligned curriculum (Steiner, 2017; Chiefs for Change, 2017). In addition, many state departments of education are emphasizing that all schools and districts adopt high quality curriculum materials. Some states are even provided curated lists of materials that meet their expectations and standards (e.g., Oregon Department of Education, 2023). These and other findings suggest that many districts and schools could benefit from reviewing their existing curricula to ensure high quality, alignment to standards, and access to rigorous evidence-based instruction. This chapter provides district and school leaders with a framework for establishing and implementing a curriculum review process that will fit their specific needs.

WHAT IS AN ALIGNED AND HIGH-QUALITY CURRICULUM?

A common misconception encountered by school improvement facilitators is the belief that a curriculum is primarily the collection of resources used to teach a specific course or subject. This definition is limited, and it is helpful to think about a curriculum more broadly as having three facets that are aligned to standards: the *intended* curriculum, the *lived* curriculum, and the *learned* curriculum (e.g., Kurz et al., 2010; see Figure 9.1).

The **intended** curriculum refers to *what* students are expected to learn as defined by the standards, as well as the print and digital materials used to support instruction and assessment. The **lived** curriculum refers to *how* the intended curriculum is delivered and assessed, how students experience it, and how well it removes barriers and provides opportunities to learn. The **learned** curriculum refers to *how much of* and *how well* the intended curriculum is learned and achieved. When a curriculum is well-aligned, all three facets are tightly connected to the standards and to each other.

When it is high quality, a curriculum is also more than well-aligned; each facet is also strong in its own right. First, the intended curriculum must be firmly grounded in the standards and contain a robust set of common print and digital resources that all teachers know how to use to design instruction

Figure 9.1. Facets of an Aligned Curriculum

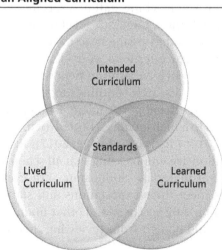

and assessment for students. Characteristics of a strong lived curriculum include consistent instruction across classrooms that is driven by standards, evidence-based practices, learning tasks for students that are rigorous and engaging, and a valid and reliable system of assessment. Overall, what ultimately defines the strength of a curriculum is student learning and achievement, that is, how well students demonstrate their mastery of the standards and expectations established through the intended curriculum.

Pause and Reflect

- How well do these three facets of curriculum, "intended, lived, learned," match your concept of an aligned and high-quality curriculum?
- What specific examples from your own district, school, or classroom are aligned to each of these three facets?
- What factors may be contributing to the three facets not currently being as well aligned as they could be?

WHEN TO CONDUCT A CURRICULUM REVIEW

The following questions, though not exhaustive, are intended to provide an initial gauge to help educational leaders determine whether a specific curriculum may be in need of a review. For the most part, the questions focus on the integrity of each facet of the curriculum for a specific course, grade level, or subject. To complete this quick inventory, think about a specific content area and answer each question with a "yes," "possibly," or "no."

- Have there been recent changes to the standards?
- Do some teachers lack a solid understanding of the standards?
- Have there been policy changes that would impact the curriculum?
- Have curriculum resources become outdated and/or potentially misaligned to the current standards?
- Is there significant potential for teachers in the same content and/or grade level to implement a different curriculum or use different curriculum resources?
- Are teachers struggling to consistently use rigorous evidence-based practices aligned to the curriculum?
- Are significant numbers or particular groups of students struggling to achieve on grade level in the content area?
- Has there been significant teacher turnover recently in the content area?

When you have answered each of the questions, go back and review your responses. The more questions to which you answered "yes" or "possibly," the more likely that it may be time to conduct a curriculum review. And, the more questions that were answered affirmatively, the greater the depth of the review that is needed. If your school or district will be conducting a review, the next step is to determine the specific questions that will guide the review.

DEVELOPING QUESTIONS TO GUIDE A CURRICULUM REVIEW

Once district or school leaders believe that a specific curriculum needs to be reviewed, it is recommended that they quickly establish a curriculum review team to begin planning. Many schools and districts may not have the time or resources to do a comprehensive review of a curriculum, which would include a thorough analysis of the intended, lived, and learned curriculum. Therefore, it is helpful to be strategic and determine what specifically is best to target for review. This determination begins by identifying what questions will frame the review.

A curriculum review is essentially a study of an existing curriculum and, as such, requires research questions to guide it. The following are sample questions that can guide the design and implementation of a review process that will fit the district's, school's, department's, or grade level's needs. The questions are organized according to the three different facets of a curriculum described earlier.

1. To what extent does the **intended** curriculum demonstrate the following?
   a. Alignment to the content of the standards as well as the pedagogical approaches built into the standards
   b. Consistent access to high-quality instructional resources that help teachers design instruction
   c. Consistent access to high-quality assessment resources that help teachers design and/or implement assessment that is engaging and rigorous
2. To what extent does the **lived** curriculum demonstrate the following?
   a. High-quality, rigorous, evidence-based instruction
   b. Consistent use of common resources across classrooms
   c. Active student engagement
   d. Formative assessment practices and feedback for students
   e. Opportunities to learn for diverse students

3. To what extent does the **learned** curriculum demonstrate the following?
   a. Consistently high levels of achievement for all students
   b. Consistently high levels of achievement for all subgroups
   c. Low equity gap scores across all subgroups

The foregoing questions are not exhaustive and are only intended to provide examples of the kinds of questions that can frame a curriculum review and assist in designing such a review. District leaders are encouraged to choose from this suggested list and/or identify other key questions that will drive the review. If time and/or budgets are tight, the curriculum review team may need to prioritize which questions to address. Perhaps a review needs to focus on the instructional and assessment resources. Or, a review may need to examine the extent to which recently purchased resources are being used consistently and well. Or, the review may focus on equity. Once the curriculum review team decides on the focus questions, it can use these questions to develop a sequence of activities for gathering and analyzing the appropriate data needed to find the answers.

Pause and Reflect

- Which questions resonate most for you?
- What are some additional questions you might consider asking?

BUILDING A SCOPE AND SEQUENCE OF CURRICULUM DATA TO REVIEW

After guiding questions have been developed, the curriculum review team should work with internal leaders and/or outside partners to build a review plan. A complete curriculum review should engage stakeholders in analyses of data that will provide answers to the guiding questions. Based on my experience helping school and district partners conduct curriculum reviews, I recommend considering the common data analysis tasks described in the following paragraphs for building a curriculum review scope of work. Most curriculum reviews will include some or all of these tasks.

ANALYSES OF ACHIEVEMENT DATA

As with many educational endeavors, starting at the end and working backward can be a wise way to proceed. Therefore, one of the first tasks that might be conducted to launch a curriculum review is an analysis of student learning and achievement data to evaluate the quality of the learned curriculum. This process begins with determining what data are available and putting the data into sets to be analyzed by the data teams. Examples of data that schools tend to review include results of state summative and interim assessments; end-of-course exams; results from the SAT, PSAT, and ACT data; as well as other local or curriculum-embedded assessments that are in use.

Once data sets have been established, teams should analyze the data to determine where students tend to excel and where they tend to struggle. These analyses are often conducted for all students by grade level, as well as for all subgroups. Once data teams identify patterns of strengths and challenges, they should also attempt to connect the trends to specific standards or clusters of standards. The purpose of connecting patterns in achievement data to standards is to use this information to review existing resources. For example, if students tend to struggle with specific standards, data teams will be able to see if existing instructional resources sufficiently prioritize these standards throughout their materials.

Both the National School Reform Faculty and the School Reform Initiative have websites that provide a variety of data analysis protocols and other resources to support collaboration. The National School Reform Faculty offers a variety of protocols that data teams may find useful, including protocols for analyzing data and student work. The School Reform Initiative also offers a robust list of protocols, many of which have instructions in Spanish and Portuguese. (See "Resources" at the end of this chapter for links to both websites.)

ANALYSES OF INSTRUCTIONAL RESOURCES

In order to determine the quality of the intended curriculum, data teams need to analyze the resources that teachers use to design instruction. This process begins with auditing what is available at each grade level and/or in each school. Sometimes the same program is used across multiple schools, and sometimes teachers use different digital and print resources from classroom to classroom. A successful audit will culminate in a list or map of print and digital resources that are available, whether each resource is available to all teachers and students, along with a description of who tends to use which of these resources and to what degree.

Next, the data team needs to analyze these resources to ensure that they fit the school's or the district's curriculum needs. In many cases, the amount of resource material to review can be daunting. Thus, reviewers should decide which resources to review and what factors to focus on assessing. For example, reviewers should analyze how well the existing resources provide support for the teaching standards that were identified as being the standards on which students struggle the most (based on the analyses of achievement data). There may be other factors that are important to review as well, such as culturally relevant pedagogy, scaffolding for English Learners, or support for social and emotional learning.

Once review team members know what they want to look for when reviewing existing resources, they may benefit from tools and other resources for guiding and recording their analyses. Fortunately, there are many resources freely available that data teams can use. One excellent resource is edreports.org. Edreports.org is an independent, nonprofit organization that conducts and provides comprehensive reviews of K–12 instructional materials. There is also a variety of rubrics and tools that data teams can use and that provide models for how to review curriculum and instructional materials. Examples include the Instructional Materials Evaluation Tool from Achievethecore.org, the Equip rubrics from Achieve.org, and the New York State STEM Quality Learning Rubric from StemX.us. (See "Resources to Conduct Curriculum Reviews" at the end of this chapter for links to these resources.)

ANALYSES OF COMMON ASSESSMENTS

Other resources that data teams can analyze to gain insights into all three facets of the curriculum are the common summative and interim assessments that are administered. Typically, teachers in a subject or course administer assessments to measure what students have learned. These assessments must be aligned to standards and should validly assess the knowledge and skills intended in the standards. Common assessments should also be used consistently across multiple classrooms. Some examples of common assessments that are frequently used by teachers are end-of-unit assessments, summative tasks, and curriculum-embedded performance measures.

Tightly aligning assessments to the standards and ensuring that the assessments accurately measure the specific knowledge and skills in the standards may sound straightforward but rarely is. To gauge the alignment and validity of assessments, data teams can use an assessment validation protocol. Such protocols help teams analyze the extent to which any given assessment accurately measures the specific constructs within the standards that are being assessed. An example of an assessment validation protocol and a description of how to use it can be found on the School Reform Initiative website. (See "Resources to Conduct Curriculum Reviews" at the end of this chapter for a link.)

ANALYSES OF THE LIVED CURRICULUM

While analyses of instruction and assessment resources will provide some insights into the lived curriculum, they are not able to fully capture what students actually experience during teaching. To determine the true quality of the lived curriculum, data teams can engage in classroom observations. As when preparing to analyze instructional resources, data teams that are planning to conduct classroom observations need to determine what to look for in advance. When making this determination or when choosing observation protocols, team members should keep in mind that understanding students' perspectives is central to fully understanding the lived curriculum. Therefore, the use of student-focused observation protocols, either instead of or in addition to teacher-focused observations, is essential. The goal is to see through students' eyes to gain an understanding of how students view instructional activities and the curriculum as a whole. Analyzing student work is another method to get a sense of the lived curriculum through the students' eyes and to determine how well student learning relates to key knowledge and skills in the standards. A variety of observation tools, rubrics, and student work review protocols can be found online; however, it is important to adapt any such tools to fit the school's or district's curriculum, pedagogical philosophies, instructional strategies, or other local context. Throughout the process of reviewing the lived curriculum, teams need to be aware of the importance of keeping data anonymous to help ensure integrity of the process.

ANALYSES OF STAKEHOLDER SURVEYS ABOUT THE CURRICULUM

Finally, surveys are excellent tools for capturing the perceptions of stakeholders who have valuable insights into the quality of a curriculum (e.g., Weber, 2010). Perception data are important because they help answer many of the questions about the quality of a curriculum—from how well-aligned the resources and standards are, to how effective the teaching is, to beliefs about what type of learning is most valued. Focus groups and empathy interviews can be used instead of surveys or in addition to surveys. The benefit of focus groups and interviews is that they allow reviewers to probe more deeply into specific responses; however, they may take more time and be more costly than using surveys for stakeholder input. Key stakeholders to include in curriculum-review surveys, focus groups, or interviews are students, teachers, administrators, other school staff, and parents.

The following are some examples of the types of questions to ask stakeholders:

- What are the strengths of the curriculum?
- What are the challenges or weaknesses of the curriculum?
- How familiar are you with the standards for the curriculum?
- What standards are the most challenging to teach (or learn)? Why?
- Are curriculum resources easy to use?
- Are learning activities engaging for students?

- Are assessments accurate and fair?
- Do teachers use the curriculum to guide decisions about instruction and assessment?
- If you had a child enrolled in this school district, would you be satisfied with the curriculum?
- What changes would you make to improve the curriculum?

When analyzing perception data, teams need to look for patterns and trends that point to strengths and weaknesses of the curriculum.

CONCLUSION

Conducting a thoughtful and thorough curriculum review can be a lengthy process. Even expedited reviews require substantial collaboration and commitment. Because most school subjects require periodic review of the curriculum, it is recommended that every district and/or school establish a fixed set of procedures for conducting curriculum reviews, as well as a schedule for when they will review each of their curricula so that they can be proactive rather than reactive. Ideally, a curriculum should be reviewed before student learning and achievement decline, and gaining insights into all facets of the curriculum—including intended, lived, and learned—should contribute to ongoing improvements in teaching, student learning, and equitable achievement.

Reflect Further and Take Action

- How did the chapter's information, ideas, and activities align with or challenge your prior understanding?
- Based on your reading, what actions or steps will you take moving forward?
- What resources, information, or processes would be supportive to educators in your school or district, and what role can you play in motivating them to engage in a curriculum review?

RESOURCES TO SUPPORT CURRICULUM REVIEWS

- EdReports—EdReports provides rating on widely used curriculum resources and materials. https://www.edreports.org/
- Instructional Materials Evaluation Tool (IMET)—The IMET rubrics from Achieve the Core can be used to evaluate curriculum resources. https://achievethecore.org/aligned/intro-to-the-imet/

- Equip Rubrics—The Equip rubrics can be used to evaluate lessons and units in math and English language arts. https://www.achieve .org/our-initiatives/equip/all-equip-resources/rubrics-and-feedback -forms
- The School Reform Initiative (SRI)—SRI, now housed at the Center for Leadership and Educational Equity, contains a large library of protocols that can support many facets of curriculum reviews. https://www.schoolreforminitiative.org/
- The National School Reform Faculty—This organization also has a library of resources and protocols that can support many facets of curriculum reviews. https://nsrfharmony.org/

REFERENCES

Chiefs for Change. (2017). *Hiding in plain sight: Leveraging curriculum to improve student learning.* Author.

Kurz, A., Elliott, S. N., Wehby, J. H., & Smithson, J. L. (2010). Alignment of the intended, planned, and enacted curriculum in general and special education and its relation to student achievement. *The Journal of Special Education, 44*(3), 131–145.

Oregon Department of Education. (2023). Instructional materials toolkit: Oregon Department of Education. https://www.oregon.gov/ode/educator-resources /teachingcontent/instructional-materials/Pages/Instructional-Materials-Toolkit .aspx

Steiner, D. (2017). Curriculum research: What we know and where we need to go. *Standards Work,* 1–13.

Weber, S. (2010). Twenty-one questions to ask about curriculum. *ASCD Blog.* https:// www.ascd.org/blogs/21-questions-to-ask-about-curriculum-development.

CHAPTER 10

Leading Formative Assessment to Improve Student Agency

Nancy Gerzon

Pause and Reflect Before Reading

- What is your current understanding of formative assessment and how would you define it? Can you give an example?
- How do you think formative assessment connects to student agency, and why do you think the relationship is important?
- To what extent do you think formative assessment is practiced in your local educational context?

INTRODUCTION

A common hope for many, if not all, school and district leaders is to effectively prepare all students to be self-directed and lifelong learners with the capacity to solve problems and challenges that may not even exist yet. A powerful approach to help students develop these skills is formative assessment practice, which enhances agency and strengthens the capacity of learners to develop control over and ultimately lead their own learning. The purpose of this chapter is to provide an overview of formative assessment practice (which is often misunderstood and misapplied by educators), explain how it strengthens student and teacher agency, and provide four practical strategies that educational leaders can use to strengthen formative assessment practice in their schools.

BACKGROUND

"What it means to be a learner is taking charge of my own learning. Like, being an agent of myself. But, it's just, instead of relying on someone else to tell me how I'm gonna do things, like I rely on myself to understand things and where it's that thing where you're not—it's kinda like your own teacher in a way. Or like, you have to self-reflect on yourself so you can better your own understanding."

—High school student

Student agency refers to the active engagement of students in determining their own learning processes and outcomes. Students with a high sense of agency create rather than respond to educational opportunities. In the classroom, they ask for a say in how problems are solved, seek to add relevance during learning, and communicate their interest in learning. When demonstrating agency, students act with intention by recommending goals or objectives, soliciting resources, identifying learning strategies, and seeking guidance when needed. Within a classroom learning culture that encourages students to make visible what they know and don't yet know, students develop the foundational skills and dispositions of agency.

Student agency is increasingly being recognized as essential to becoming college and career ready (Alliance for Excellent Education, 2011; Vaughn, 2020). In current college- and career-ready standards, students are expected to demonstrate deep knowledge within and across disciplines, apply that knowledge to novel situations, and use creative and critical approaches to problem solving. College- and career-ready standards also call on students to be able to communicate, collaborate, and manage their own learning (National Research Council, 2012).

To meet these expectations, schools and districts are looking closely at what teachers need to know and be able to do in order to strengthen the student role in the learning process. Increasingly teachers are expected to use pedagogical approaches in which students develop the knowledge and skills to be self-directed learners (Shepard et al., 2020). Such approaches foster students' abilities to "define their own learning goals, ask questions, anticipate the structure of curriculum experiences, use metacognitive strategies when engaging with curriculum, and self-monitor" (Alton-Lee, 2003, p. 95).

Formative assessment is one pedagogical approach that strengthens the student role in learning (Heritage & Wiley, 2018; Andersson & Palm, 2017; Black & Wiliam, 2009). During formative assessment, students engage with daily routines and structures that help them internalize the learning outcomes, explore evidence of their own and their peers' learning, and conduct daily self-assessment to inform next steps in their learning. In formative assessment, students and teachers engage in partnership to move through each stage of the assessment process while learning is underway. Teachers apply new pedagogical techniques to make learning visible throughout the lesson so that students themselves can accurately assess and monitor their learning as it develops.

Since 2003, a team of WestEd staff has been leading professional learning focused on formative assessment in schools, districts, and state departments of education across the country. This chapter shares some of what we have learned about how to support leaders and teachers to successfully use formative assessment to improve student learning and agency. This chapter also highlights key lessons learned from school and district leaders who report improved student agency associated with implementing formative assessment.

DEFINING FORMATIVE ASSESSMENT

"I used to think formative assessment was only teacher-centered, that teachers would take the information, make decisions, . . . and decide what to do next. Now I am seeing students so much more involved in the process. They can guide their [own] learning, and they can give feedback."

—Elementary School Principal

The lack of a commonly accepted definition of formative assessment can present challenges in the early stages of school or district implementation. A first step for administrators is to ensure that faculty share a common definition of formative assessment that is aligned with research. Our team uses the following definition, published by Bronwyn Cowie and Beverly Bell (2001): *Formative assessment is the process used by teachers and students to notice, recognize, and respond to student learning in order to enhance that learning, during the learning.* By reflecting on the key phrases in this definition, as outlined subsequently, educators can begin to uncover essential characteristics of formative assessment practice, and how these might be similar or different to current learning and assessment practices in their school or district.

First, the definition calls out that **formative assessment is a process used by students and teachers**. While the word "assessment" typically conjures an image of a written test, formative assessment practice involves teachers and students working in partnership to assess how learning is developing within a lesson or series of lessons. Figure 10.1 shows how to enact this process through the formative assessment feedback loop (WestEd, 2018). The graphic integrates research about the essential characteristics of the formative assessment process (Black & Wiliam, 2009; Sadler, 1989) and specifies five core practices teachers and students can engage with during the formative assessment process.

Figure 10.1. The Formative Assessment Feedback Loop

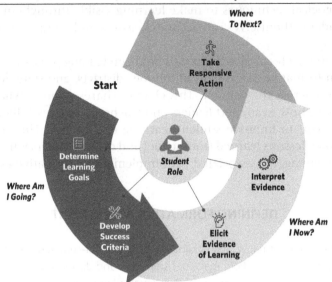

The formative assessment feedback loop outlines three guiding questions, which depict each stage of the process. To answer the first question, *Where am I going?*, teachers use learning goals and success criteria (typically co-constructed with students) to engage students in internalizing learning expectations. Teachers and students then consider the second question, *Where am I now?* During this stage of the process teachers use a variety of instructional routines that make learning visible and support students to engage with evidence themselves. For example, students may engage in peer review to assess their progress, using the lesson success criteria as an interpretive framework to make meaning of how they are progressing in the lesson. The question *Where to next?* guides the final stage of the process. To address this question, students and the teacher work in partnership to consider next steps based on students' individual progress during the lesson.

As soon as the formative assessment cycle has been completed for one learning goal, teachers and students may begin the cycle anew with the next learning goal. In this way, formative assessment supports a continuous cycle of learning for teachers and students.

The definition also states that the purpose of formative assessment is ***to notice, recognize, and respond to learning***. WestEd's Formative Insights team has led multiple online courses where we ask teachers to spend 10 minutes a day simply noticing learning. The vast majority of teachers have shared with us that until they were asked to do this, they *did not notice student learning.* Teachers have reported that they notice student behaviors, whether students are on task, and how far along students are in completing tasks, but not learning. In formative assessment the focus is on noticing and responding to evidence of learning, particularly how learning is developing during the lesson. To notice learning, teachers and students may focus on the qualities of partially formed ideas, emerging connections to previous learning, or how new learning adds to students' existing funds of knowledge.

> "Defining formative assessment was really important to our team. Partly because our district had, a few years ago, defined formative assessment differently. If I were to do this again, I would certainly work to invest time and energy so we were all on the same page in terms of what it means to assess formatively and how to use that information to help student learning."
>
> —High school assistant principal

Responding to learning as learning is happening is a radically new practice for many teachers. While traditional assessment models assess learning after learning has taken place, formative assessment requires that teachers develop strategies and approaches to respond based on evidence that is taking shape in the moment. Many teachers have reported that they've had to unlearn long-held instructional and assessment routines to be able to notice learning in the moment. Teachers may begin to focus, for example, on noticing students' developing understanding, or what successful learning looks like as students are on the path toward more sophisticated knowledge. Teachers report shifting from traditional dichotomous responses (got it/didn't get it, right/wrong) to responses in which they provide students with hints, clues, prompts, or questions that nudge learning along and help students see progress. For example, a simple strategy teachers can use to press for more evidence of student learning is to follow a student's response to a question with "tell me more."

In the final phrase of the Cowie and Bell definition, they clarify that the focus of formative assessment is **to enhance learning, during the learning**. Through the formative assessment process, teachers and students develop strategies to internalize learning outcomes, explore evidence of learning, and monitor their progress toward academic learning goals. Student learning is enhanced through rich opportunities to explore content independently, with their peers and with the teacher.

Pause and Reflect

- How does the explanation of formative assessment above compare to your previous understanding?
- To what extent is formative assessment, as described here, a common practice in the schools or districts you work with?

THE RELATIONSHIP BETWEEN FORMATIVE ASSESSMENT
AND STUDENT AGENCY

"My understanding of student agency has evolved over my years of teaching. When I first started teaching there was very much a mentality of you need to give the students everything they need. You need to spoon feed them, essentially. You can't rely on them to do any work outside of school. It all has to be done in class. And then over time as I became stronger and more effective in the classroom, I rejected that idea. I felt that students need to take ownership of their learning. We can ask them to do challenging but doable things inside and outside of class. And so for me, student agency is really about showing the kids and believing that the kids can do things on their own. That they can take control of their learning and be successful with it. And this year I've really seen that in action because they have the opportunity to get feedback from me and also from their peers in a variety of ways."

—Middle School Teacher

Learner agency is the set of skills, mindsets, and opportunities that enable learners to set purposeful goals for themselves, to take action in their learning to move toward those goals, and to reflect and adjust learning behaviors as they monitor their progress toward their goals. Learner agency requires an understanding of the learning process, a belief in one's abilities, opportunities to practice and demonstrate personal autonomy during learning, and the capacity to intentionally direct one's efforts to meet specific goals.

Leaders benefit from having a precise definition of agency, one that clearly distinguishes the differences between agency and other types of learning behaviors. Varying misperceptions of agency may include, for example, being on time with assignments, showing up for class, correcting work based on feedback, or being motivated to get a good grade. Agency can also be confused with students having "voice and choice" to choose from a range of activities during lessons.

Students who demonstrate the skills of learner agency internalize the expected learning outcomes, understand the evidence of their current learning to accurately assess progress toward those outcomes, and plan to move their learning forward. In this way, students with agency are metacognitive (they are aware of their thinking), have skills to support self-regulation (they can determine and take next steps in learning), and show confidence and motivation to move their learning forward.

The power of formative assessment lies in its ability to strengthen students' metacognition (awareness of one's own thinking) and self-regulation (knowledge and skills to select next steps in learning) to improve academic outcomes, increase motivation and confidence, and deepen academic inquiry. Effective formative assessment also strengthens collective efficacy through the use of sociocultural learning practices in which student knowledge is situated as a source of expertise and used as a way to explore and better understand the learning goals.

As compared to traditional approaches to instruction, an important shift in formative assessment is the explicit attention to teaching agency skills as integral to disciplinary learning. The routines of formative assessment are not just strategies that teachers use to engage students in learning. Rather, when supported by explicit instruction and modeling on their use, these routines are the vehicle through which students deepen agency.

While agency is sometimes thought of as an individual character trait—either someone has agency or does not—the skills of agency can and must be taught. In formative assessment, students learn to notice, interpret, and use evidence through daily routines that include the following:

- Co-constructing success criteria
- Using success criteria to gauge the status of their learning
- Listening to how peers understand new content during learning tasks and academic discourse
- Giving and receiving peer feedback
- Conducting self-assessment
- Exploring next steps with peers and the teacher

During the early stages of formative assessment implementation, teachers are learning these practices themselves. Over time, teachers learn to engage students in these practices. To do so, teachers model, explicitly teach, and provide feedback to students on their use. In classrooms where these practices are in routine use, students have multiple opportunities to explore and share evidence of new learning, to receive feedback from peers and the teacher, and to self-assess.

Pause and Reflect

- How does the concept of agency described here compare your initial thinking?
- In your own words, explain why agency is so important and how effective formative assessment practices can strengthen it.

FOUR STRATEGIES FOR LEADERS TO PROMOTE STUDENT AGENCY

Effective leadership of formative assessment leads to more complete implementation of formative assessment practices, and it supports implementation of changes in the roles of both teachers and students, in ways that more fully activate students to have ownership for their own learning (Moss et al., 2013; Swaffield, 2016). While there is more research to be done to clarify exactly which leadership activities have the most leverage, the following four leadership strategies highlight lessons learned during my team's work with school and district leaders, offering ideas on how to put these practices into use. These four leadership strategies focus on ways leaders can support and engage faculty and students in this work.

Leadership Strategy 1: Develop a Compelling Rationale for and a Shared Understanding of Formative Assessment Implementation

A leader's first task in formative assessment implementation is to establish a compelling vision that includes how both teacher and student roles will change as a result of this work. To establish a vision, leaders benefit from taking time to explore what formative assessment will look like in their own context and how student roles, in particular, will shift. Educators are motivated by strategies that more actively engage students in learning, but this engagement takes time to accomplish. Until teachers begin to see changes in their own roles and the students' roles, leaders must continually frame and reframe the purpose and goals of this work.

> "My definition of formative assessment is it's student-centered learning, students becoming knowledgeable in understanding their own continuum of learning, and then being able to set goals, make a plan of action, and set criteria for success, but also be able to recognize where they are in that continuum of learning. The teachers' responsibility is to provide explicit instruction to students on how to learn. . . . It's not just providing [the students] with steps. It's to teach them how to recognize where they are."
>
> —Middle School Principal

> "When I walk into a classroom and I really look for students that are empowered to own their own learning… I look for students taking the learning goal and really being able to tell the teacher or being asked by the teacher what would it mean if I'm successful today, and then being able to reflect on their own work to see whether or not they've met those goals. I'm looking for classrooms where there's lots of dialogue . . . where students can bounce ideas off of each other, and the teacher and they do that freely—they do that because that's the best way to learn."
>
> —High School Principal

In the early stages of formative assessment implementation, leaders are responsible for establishing a shared definition of formative assessment at their site, particularly if there are previous definitions that do not include the research-based elements of formative assessment.

Leaders can encourage their teachers to consider how their definitions are similar to, or different from, the Cowie and Bell definition. If there is any confusion or disagreement about what formative assessment is, it is beneficial to resolve these issues early so that all leaders, teachers, and students share a clear understanding and have shared expectations.

Putting the Strategy into Practice: Conduct an Assessment Inventory. A simple way to begin building a shared vision and understanding of formative assessment is to clarify and resolve potential misconceptions. With your faculty or school leadership team, create a list of the assessments currently in use at your school or district, and then discuss and make notes on each one to clarify how it aligns with the definition and research on formative assessment. As you review the list together, pay close attention to assessments that are entitled "formative" and how these may or may not share characteristics outlined in the research. Once done, clarify what the results mean and how you might address any inconsistencies that arose during this assessment inventory process.

Leadership Strategy 2: Support Teachers to Look for, and Monitor, Changes That Lead to Greater Student Agency

Above all, formative assessment is about what students are doing—what students' learning goals are, the gap between students' current understanding and their goals, and what teachers and students can do to support students in reaching their goals. As your school or district begins implementing formative assessment, keep the spotlight on the student role in learning.

Leaders can support this shift toward student agency by monitoring how students are responding to formative assessment implementation. As students learn to engage with learning goals, success criteria, and feedback, they are better able to answer the questions, "What are you learning right now?" and "What comes next?" A student's reasoned responses to these questions highlight the formative assessment process in action.

Putting the Strategy into Practice: Monitor Changes in Student Learning Practices. Here is a sample of survey items that my team has developed to understand students' perceptions of agency. These items are aligned with research on metacognition, self-regulation, self-efficacy, and learner autonomy. This survey tool is helpful for teachers to consider how students experience learning, and to monitor changes in student perceptions at key stages of formative assessment implementation.

- I use information about where I am in my learning to assess my learning progress.
- I share and clarify information with others about where I am in my own learning.
- I adapt my learning plan when needed to meet my goals.
- I actively seek out opportunities to receive peer feedback on my work.
- I actively seek out opportunities to receive feedback from my teachers on my work.
- I use the feedback I am provided to deepen my thinking about my learning.
- I use strategies that help me continue learning even when the learning is challenging.
- I talk with my teacher and peers to develop strategies to meet my learning goals.
- I believe in myself and my ability to learn.
- I take initiative in learning new content when I don't know something.
- I make connections to things I already know in my classroom.
- I advocate for my continued learning.

Leadership Strategy 3: Help Teachers to Identify Instructional Practices That Promote Student Agency, and to Eliminate Those That Might Hinder Its Development

Encourage teachers to elicit evidence of student learning in the course of daily instruction. As the school culture shifts toward more responsibility by students for their learning, leaders can expect to see classrooms that are more active, include more public dialogue, and include more shared sense-making (Birenbaum, 2011). As students take more ownership of learning, both the teacher roles and the student roles change. Encourage teachers to shift practices rather than simply pile on new practices without examining and replacing the old.

"I think that was a really big 'aha moment' for teachers to not have to grade everything and to know that we can get valuable information from practices that are put in place without having some kind of grade attached."

—High school principal

Leaders can have explicit conversations with teachers about how to simplify instructional and assessment practices. One indication of a shift in teacher practice is in the amount of assessment evidence collected and graded. Evidence collected and not used to support instruction wastes instructional time. In formative assessment, teachers should know where each student is on the learning progression, or what progress each student is making toward the standard. Evidence is collected only when teachers need to know something more in order to help students move forward. Encourage teachers to use their professional judgment about when, and from whom, to collect evidence. Conversations about grading often arise as teachers question how to incorporate and make time for ungraded observational evidence. In addition, a key concept in formative assessment is that new evidence of learning replaces older evidence of learning, and this shift can have an impact on traditional gradebook routines. However, shifting these practices supports students' ownership in their learning by helping students realize that learning does not end when a test is given, and that there are many opportunities to demonstrate learning.

Putting the Strategy into Practice: Revisit Grading Practices. Grading and reporting practices often require review and revision as schools move toward improving instructional practices to promote student agency. The following discussion prompts can guide the review of grading practices and can support significant changes that lead to more effective collection and use of student evidence by both teachers and students.

- To what extent do faculty grade students for only their work products? What can be done to ensure students receive grades only for their work products, and not for effort, attendance, or late work?
- What strategies are teachers using to actively involve students in the collection, interpretation, and communication of the students' own evidence of achievement? How can these kinds of strategies be used more widely?
- To what extent are students evaluated only on their most recent work, which shows their best understanding of new content? How might grading practices need to shift to ensure all students are evaluated on only the work products that show their best understandings?

Leadership Strategy 4: Support All Stakeholders to Model an Effective Culture of Learning

Developing student agency takes place in the context of a classroom culture in which all students feel respected and see that their contribution to the learning community is valued. In a learning culture, all students are engaged to explore, make meaning, take risks, and use feedback. When the culture reflects these characteristics, students feel confident about revealing their learning status in front of peers and their teacher, and in giving and receiving peer feedback.

> When we talk about learning culture in a classroom, we are talking about the conversations, the discourse that's happening between students and the focus of all of their interactions around academics. "That has been the biggest shift, because when teachers are able to focus and build a learning culture and not just a nice, fun, kind climate, you see a different kind of student emerge. . . . We see students emerge as scholars. We see them bloom into scientists and mathematicians that we didn't see before we had very intentional conversations about what is discourse in a classroom, what is, what does peer feedback look like and how is that helpful?"
>
> —Elementary school principal

A core learning from my team's work in formative assessment is that a learning culture begins with adults. When adults show students that the adults, too, are continuously learning, that they are taking risks and getting feedback from their peers to help them improve, then a learning culture is more readily embraced by students.

A school culture that promotes learning for all has greater activity, more public dialogue, and many opportunities for shared sensemaking. One strategy that leaders employ is to demonstrate that they, too, are learning formative assessment alongside their teachers.

Leaders who take on the idea of learning together endeavor to develop shared understanding about each of the stages of formative assessment implementation and, in particular, to clarify what this implementation means in their own context. This modeling by leaders has a powerful benefit to establishing the kind of culture that drives formative assessment implementation and student agency.

Putting the Strategy into Practice: Develop a Culture of Learning. While there are many ways to model an effective learning culture, teacher teams have reported to WestEd trainers that several concepts have significant leverage when used by both teachers and students. Working with faculty teams, consider the following five high-leverage ideas and how to enhance these ideas in your schools:

- Teachers model careful listening to student ideas, and students listen to each other and build on each other's thinking.
- Students feel comfortable revealing their thinking in front of the teacher and their peers.

- Teachers model that mistakes are sources of new learning, and students also use their mistakes as learning resources.
- Teachers provide descriptive feedback to students, and students are given time and opportunity to act on that feedback to advance their learning.
- Students know that they—in collaboration with their peers and the teacher—are responsible for their own learning and the learning of their classmates.

CONCLUSION

Formative assessment transforms teaching and learning by allowing teachers to collect information about student learning in the moment and by empowering students to develop the knowledge, skills, and dispositions to take charge of their own learning. The process thrives in schools led by leaders who deeply understand formative assessment research and practice, maintain a focus on what students are doing, and help shape teachers improve instructional practices over time. The four leadership strategies offer lessons learned from school leaders who have successfully engaged their teachers to increase student agency through formative assessment implementation.

Reflect Further and Take Action

- Consider the four strategies described in the chapter and describe the extent to which the schools and districts you are familiar with have used any or all of them.
- What are some immediate next steps you could take as an educational leader to strengthen formative assessment practices in schools and/or districts you work with or support?

REFERENCES

Alliance for Excellent Education. (2011). *A time for deeper learning: Preparing students for a changing world.* Author. https://all4ed.org/wp-content/uploads/2013/06/DeeperLearning.pdf

Alton-Lee, A. (2003). *Quality teaching for diverse students in schooling: Best evidence synthesis.* Medium Term Strategy Policy Division, New Zealand Ministry of Education.

Andersson, C., & Palm, T. (2017). Characteristics of improved formative assessment practice. *Education Inquiry, 8*(2), 104–122.

Bell, B., & Cowie, B. (2001). *Formative assessment and science education.* Kluwer.

Birenbaum, M., Kimron, H., & Shilton, H. (2011). Nested contexts that shape assessment for learning: School-based professional learning community and classroom culture. *Studies in Educational Evaluation, 37*, 35–48. http://dx.doi.org/10.1016/j.stueduc.2011.04.001

Black, P., & Wiliam, D. (2009). Developing the theory of formative assessment. *Educational Assessment, Evaluation and Accountability, 21*(1), 5.

Heritage, M., & Wiley, C. (2018). Reaping the benefits of assessment for learning: Achievement, identity and equity. *ZDM: The International Journal on Mathematics Education, 50*, 729–741. https://doi.org/10.1007/s11858-018-0943-3

Moss, C. M., Brookhart, S. M., & Long, B. A. (2013). Administrators' roles in helping teachers use formative assessment information. *Applied Measurement in Education, 26*(3), 205–218.

National Research Council. (2012). *Education for life and work: Developing transferable knowledge and skills in the twenty-first century.* Committee on Defining Deeper Learning and Twenty-first Century Skills of the Board on Testing and Assessment and Board on Science Education, Division of Behavioral and Social Sciences and Education. The National Academies Press.

Sadler, D. R. (1989). Formative assessment and the design of instructional systems. *Instructional Science, 18*, 119–144.

Shepard, L. A., Diaz-Bilello, E., Penuel, W. R., & Marion, S. (2020). *Classroom assessment principles to support teaching and learning.* Center for Assessment, Design, Research and Evaluation, University of Colorado.

Swaffield, S. (2016). Multilevel leadership for assessment for learning, and the potential of critical friendship. In G. Johnson & N. Dempster (Eds.), *Leadership in Diverse Learning Contexts* (pp. 93–108). Springer.

Vaughn, M. (2020). What is student agency and why is it needed now more than ever? *Theory Into Practice, 59*(2), 109–118.

WestEd. (2018). *Student agency in learning: A digital professional learning experience for teachers.* WestEd.

Part IV

CULTURE SHIFT

Culture Shift is the fourth domain of the Four Domains of Rapid School Improvement. This domain emphasizes how important it is to have an overall culture and climate within a school or district that is intently focused on improving positive outcomes and learning for all students. School and district leaders play a crucial role in this domain, as they are responsible for creating an environment that supports positive relationships, collaboration, and a shared sense of purpose. However, the Culture Shift domain also recognizes the importance of engaging stakeholders in improvement work as leaders cannot transform schools alone.

The three research-based practices emphasized within the Four Domains framework around culture shift that school and district leaders are encouraged to prioritize include the following: build a strong community intensely focused on student learning, solicit and act upon stakeholder input, and engage students and families in pursuing education goals. These three practices work well together to ensure that educational leaders do not try to go it alone and work assiduously to involve stakeholders in all facets of improvement.

The chapters in Section 4 were selected to help school and district leaders cultivate a positive and inclusive climate that is able to build a strong culture of learning and improvement across a school or district. Chapter 11, "School Climate Essentials: A Call to Action" can serve as a primer for educational leaders to help them build and sustain safe, supportive, and equitable learning environments for all students. To that end, the chapter describes many helpful practices and strategies that school and district leaders will find extremely valuable.

Chapter 12, "Foundations of Trauma-Informed Practice in Education," takes many of the topics and themes in Chapter 11 and goes deeper. This chapter helps readers understand the nature of trauma and its prevalence among students and staff. Because of this, it is important for educators to understand and be able to apply trauma-informed practices in their work and teaching. The chapter demonstrates how one need not be a trauma expert in order to be able to apply trauma-informed practices that are responsive to the needs of everyone.

As mentioned previously in the description of the Culture Shift domain, a core practice around culture shift is engaging students and families in pursuing educational goals. Despite the profound impact that effective family engagement can have on student learning, many schools and districts struggle to develop robust systems and practices designed to routinely engage families in educational efforts on behalf of students. Therefore, Chapter 13, "Building on Family and Community Strengths," provides practical support and guidance to educational leaders to help them enhance their systems and practices in this area.

The final chapter in Section 4 is perhaps one of the most important in the book. It addresses a topic that is unfortunately controversial across the country today and is having a significant impact on schools and on particular groups of students. Chapter 14, "Deepening Understanding to Support Transgender Youth," provides a deep look at the frightening statistics related to our population of transgender youth and the challenges they and their families routinely face in schools and society. The chapter helps clarify many of the key terms and phrases related to the LGBTQ+ community that educational leaders need to be well-versed in. It also explores the shifting policy landscape as it relates to transgender students across the country, and will assist readers in understanding the various challenges educational leaders, as well as school board and community leaders, face and provides guidance in addressing them.

As readers dive into the chapters in this section and begin to read, they are encouraged to consider the following questions.

- What specific actions has your district or school taken to foster a safe, supportive, and equitable learning environment for all students? Where are the greatest opportunities for growth in this area?
- How would you define trauma, and what percentage of students and staff do you think suffer from trauma that has an impact on their work and learning? What do you think are defining characteristics of trauma-informed educational practice, and how familiar do you think staff in your educational context are with them?
- In what ways does your school or district routinely engage with families outside of parent and teacher conferences? Why do you think family engagement is important to supporting student learning and driving improvement efforts?
- What are the current policies in your district that relate to transgender youth? What are your current state's policies? What impact do you think these have on the transgender students in your community and the challenges they face?

CHAPTER 11

School Climate Essentials

A Call to Action

Shazia Hashmi, Rebeca Cerna, and Alexis Stern

Pause and Reflect Before Reading

- What strengths are you seeking to build upon, and what opportunities for growth are you seeking to address to support student success?
- What policies and structures have you or others identified as priorities to address the climate in your school(s) or district?
- What actions have you or others taken to strengthen the climate in your school(s) or district?

INTRODUCTION

A positive and equitable school climate is foundational to school and student success. Based on the latest findings from learning science, many schools and educational leaders have been embracing the need to support students' physiological, social, and emotional growth in addition to their cognitive development as a part of school climate improvement efforts. Social upheaval and growing disparities following the onset of the COVID-19 pandemic have increased this focus across the nation (Rosanbalm, 2021). Throughout this chapter, school climate is used to refer to the qualities of a school environment experienced by students and staff, encompassing relationships, teaching and learning practices, and organizational structures (National School Climate Center, n.d.). To ensure that all members of a school community can learn and thrive, educational leaders—including superintendents, principals, and instructional coaches—should collaborate to facilitate the conditions needed to sustain effective learning and teaching.

Research Overview: School Climate. A school's climate reflects its culture, defined as the shared norms, values, beliefs, and rituals that are informally developed over time and impact how members of a school community think, feel, and act in schools (Peterson & Deal, 1998). In schools with a positive climate and culture, there is a strong sense of community. In addition, students feel known, safe, and able to learn in a caring and supportive environment (Redding & Corbett, 2018). These schools also tend to implement a whole-person approach that supports well-being by drawing on the assets, needs, and aspirations of students and the adults who take care of them. Research demonstrates that such a supportive, positive environment increases motivation and achievement outcomes. A positive school climate also promotes strong interpersonal relationships between and among students and teachers, bolsters communication, and supports students' sense of belonging (Darling-Hammond & Cook-Harvey, 2018).

School culture norms also affect all aspects of students' experiences at school—both positively and negatively. For example, positive, consistent teacher–student relationships can be a protective factor, as students perform best when they feel highly supported (Darling-Hammond & Cook-Harvey, 2018). The presence of consistent, supportive adults can be particularly impactful in the lives of students of color who may face racism, discrimination, and prejudice in their daily social interactions. The presence of supportive adults can build resilience among students exposed to such systemic factors. Conversely, deficit thinking can influence teacher expectations for and interactions with Black and Latinx students, frequently resulting in reduced school engagement and achievement, as well as higher suspension rates among these students (Gregory et al., 2011; Woolley & Bowen, 2007).

Finally, as most district and school leaders already know, disparities in academic outcomes exist within schools and across school districts. Research on engagement, safety, and learning supports suggests that these gaps persist due to disparate access to quality school resources (Hanson et al., 2012; Murray, 2018). Such findings underscore the urgency of establishing conditions for equitable learning and development by ensuring that policies, procedures, resources, and instructional strategies across districts, schools, and classrooms support the well-being and growth of every student (García Coll et al., 1996).

HOW CAN LEADERS FOSTER A POSITIVE SCHOOL CLIMATE AND CULTURE?

Amid social, political, and cultural turmoil related to the COVID-19 pandemic, as well as the renewed scrutiny on racial inequity nationwide, historic federal, state, and local investments are being made in programs, services, and strategies that promote wellness and success for learners and their families. In allocating the resulting funding, educational leaders are presented with a unique opportunity to prioritize resources and create strategic plans that provide comprehensive supports for students' cognitive, physiological, social, and emotional well-being.

A variety of research and data indicate that schools and districts are most successful when leaders create policies, practices, and structures that ensure ongoing attention to and integration of school climate goals. Ideally, these goals support and facilitate all areas of student learning and development (Darling-Hammond & Cook-Harvey, 2018; U.S. Department of Education, Office of Safe and Healthy Students, 2016). For example, leaders may invest in the following strategies: professional learning for teachers, identity-affirming supports for students, initiatives to build community members' sense of safety at school, and nonpunitive school discipline approaches. Each of these areas warrants focus and investment on a par with its essential role in promoting positive student academic and social–emotional outcomes.

To ensure a safe, supportive, and equitable learning environment, we encourage leaders to ensure that their school climate improvement efforts are grounded in developing equitable supports, fostering community and family partnerships, promoting supportive relationships, establishing a schoolwide commitment and shared purpose, and implementing a continuous improvement approach to monitor change (see Figure 11.1). We have included

Figure 11.1. Essential Elements for Positive School Climate

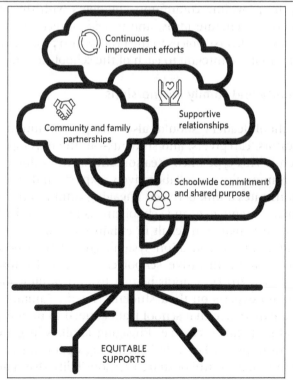

practical guidance that can help district and school leaders enact these essentials in the following sections.

Develop Equitable Supports

Equity is at the root of a positive school climate. An equitable school climate supports high expectations, safe and healthy environments, and positive and caring relationships between and among all students, staff, and families. District and school leaders can promote equity in their schools by ensuring policies and practices respond to the needs of all community members, creating safe school environments for diverse groups, understanding the strengths and needs of diverse groups and cultures, encouraging cultural awareness, and supporting the reflective practice of learning and unlearning past assumptions or practices.

One concrete strategy for ensuring that all students have equitable access to supports that meet their needs is to seek input from educators, students, and families and to include these and other community members in the process of identifying and addressing inequities. The process of gathering this input should be strengths-based, with a focus on recognizing and leveraging the social, cultural, and other assets of school communities rather than focusing only on needs and gaps (Walrond, 2021). This approach encourages distributive leadership by providing community members with the opportunity to contribute expertise, generate ideas, and provide direct feedback to leadership. The inclusion of diverse voices in the process also promotes transparency and trust, values that are integral to each of the school climate essentials.

Foster Community and Family Partnerships

District and school leaders should also engage community members—including educators, caregivers, and students—in the development of learning environments. This type of co-creation affirms the value of all members of the school community to collaboratively explore and discuss decisions. Research demonstrates a link between engaging communities and high student achievement, attendance, and school engagement (Bryk, 2010). Family partnerships, in particular, can result in enhanced community participation and understanding of the education system, greater trust between schools and communities, more inclusive school climates, and improved student outcomes (Ishimaru, 2014). Schools benefit from regarding all caregivers as equal partners and experts on their students' needs. Families offer insights from their lived experience that school leaders need to understand to create meaningful and sustainable change. Engaging families in genuine partnership allows them to play a key role in reducing opportunity gaps and ultimately contributes to a culture of shared responsibility (Ishimaru, 2014).

To foster such partnerships, school and district leaders should create opportunities for caregivers, educators, and other community members to hold leadership and decision-making roles in planning activities for school improvement, strategic visioning, budgeting, and more. Schools can also enlist students as active partners in creating safe and positive school environments through strategies such as youth participatory action research. This kind of student participation can promote engagement, strengthen teacher–student relationships and peer relationships, and give students a sense of ownership over school improvement (Voight, 2015).

Promote Supportive Relationships

The quality of relationships at school is one of the strongest predictors of both student academic achievement and teacher satisfaction (da Luz, 2015; Grayson & Alvarez, 2008; Hattie, 2009; Varga, 2017). Supportive relationships foster positive social interactions and establish an environment of trust. They provide the academic and social–emotional support that enables students to be open to new learning experiences. Caring relationships between and among students, staff, family members, and community partners also promote school connectedness. Students who feel connected at school report higher attendance rates; experience positive, supportive peer relationships; and have lower rates of emotional distress than peers who do not feel a sense of school connectedness (O'Malley & Amarillas, 2011b). Those same positive relationships keep staff motivated to be innovative, connected, and inspiring (O'Malley & Amarillas, 2011a).

To support quality relationships, district and school leaders can help to ensure that school and classroom practices create a sense of belonging and safety for all students (Darling-Hammond & Cook-Harvey, 2018). For example, creating dependable, supportive classroom routines for both managing classrooms and responding to student needs can deepen teacher–student relationships. Developing culturally responsive learning environments can also help ensure that all students feel valued, cared for, and affirmed in their identities (Darling-Hammond & Cook-Harvey, 2018).

Ensure Schoolwide Commitment and Shared Purpose

Building a positive school climate and culture is a continuous process that requires a commitment from the entire school community and ongoing attention from district and school leaders. That commitment develops when school leaders bring all community members together to determine shared beliefs and co-create common goals and agreements about roles, responsibilities, and expectations for each other. This process of co-creation has the benefit of bringing communities together around a shared sense of purpose.

The process also can promote transparency, consistency, and sustainability over time and despite staffing changes.

Developing partnerships across the school community can require a shift in staff mindsets about who should be involved, how they will work together, and how change toward a more positive, equitable school climate happens (Kania et al., 2014). For that shift to occur, staff must come together prepared to examine their current assumptions about their school community, including common beliefs that attribute educational disparities to the skills, knowledge, culture, values, or engagement of students and families. To support the mindset shifts that are needed for collective change, school leaders must consider what kinds of training and support staff may need (Ishimaru, 2014).

Pursue Continuous Improvement Efforts

School and district leaders who successfully foster and maintain a positive learning environment use data to help plan, implement, and monitor climate improvement efforts. Data on such indicators as student engagement, school safety, and learning supports can provide a critical window into student and staff perspectives on the school learning environment and on other aspects of school community members' daily experiences (Hanson et al., 2012). Given that different groups of students and staff can have disparate experiences of the same school environment, it is important to be intentional in collecting and disaggregating data by key student and staff demographics, such as race, ethnicity, gender, sexual orientation, and disability. Leaders who conduct these analyses are able to better position their schools to recognize and adapt to the assets and needs of the entire school community.

Many effective school leaders routinely host school climate data discussions with students, families, and other community members as part of their ongoing school improvement efforts. Such meetings are valuable opportunities to identify and discuss key questions, suggestions, and concerns. They also serve as way to promote a culture of transparency and growth, bolster engagement, and enhance schools' understanding of and responsiveness to community needs. Engaging students and families in ongoing efforts to interpret and make meaning from data ensures that schools design improvement activities *with* communities, not *for* them.

CONCLUSION

Research has established a clear connection between a positive school climate and a variety of positive student outcomes. By integrating the school climate essentials described in this chapter, school and district leaders can create learning conditions that support the ability of all students to achieve and thrive. Building a positive school climate—one that involves the entire school community and is rooted in equitable supports, with respectful and affirming relationships—can help ensure that every student has access to the resources and experiences that support an equitable learning environment.

RESOURCES

California Safe and Supportive Schools—Resource Library

This resource library is intended to help state and local education agency leaders as they develop practical strategies and programs to address student mental health needs and improve school climate. This library offers guidance documents, toolkits, briefs, research studies, and more that draw on current research in education, school psychology, and other related disciplines.

- https://ca-safe-supportive-schools.wested.org/resources/?fwp _related_pp_filter=california-center-for-school-climate

Beyond SEL: Stories of Well-Being, Connection, and Equity in Schools—Audiocasts

This audio gallery features real-world examples of schools and districts across the country that promote social and emotional well-being, connection, and equity for all students, educators, and families. These stories span the many conditions that educators must attend to as they foster whole-person learning and development—including the personal conditions that ensure individual health and well-being, the safe and supportive school environments and relationships that protect and enable learning, and the system-level community conditions within and beyond education that anchor and reinforce learners' development over time. https://beyondsel.wested.org/

National School Climate Center

The National School Climate Center (NSCC) is a nationally recognized organization that promotes safe, supportive, learning environments that nurture social and emotional, civic, and academic growth for all students through a variety of holistic offerings. https://schoolclimate.org/

National Center on Safe Supportive Learning Environments

The National Center on Safe Supportive Learning Environments offers information and technical assistance to states, districts, schools, institutions of higher learning, and communities focused on improving school climate and conditions for learning. https://safesupportivelearning.ed.gov/school-climate -improvement

Recommended Books

- Brasof, M., & Levitan, J. (Eds.). (2022). *Student voice research: Theory, methods, and innovations from the field*. Teachers College Press.
- Hammond, Z. (2014). *Culturally responsive teaching and the brain: Promoting authentic engagement and rigor among culturally and linguistically diverse students*. Corwin Press.
- Ishimaru, A. M. (2019). *Just schools: Building equitable collaborations with families and communities*. Teachers College Press.
- Mandinach, E. B., & Honey, M. (Eds.). (2008). *Data-driven school improvement: Linking data and learning*. Teachers College Press.
- Pacino, M. A., & Warren, S. R. (Eds.). (2022). *Building culturally responsive partnerships among schools, families, and communities*. Teachers College Press.
- Purkey, W. W., Novak, J. M., & Fretz, J. R. (2020). *Developing inviting schools: A beneficial framework for teaching and leading*. Teachers College Press.
- Wolter, D. L. (2021). *Restorative literacies: Creating a community of care in schools*. Teachers College Press.

Reflect Further and Take Action

- After reading this chapter, consider and reflect on the following prompts. If reading this chapter with others, record your responses prior to sharing and discussing with colleagues.
- How, and to what extent, does your school or district community currently incorporate the five climate essentials described in the chapter?
- What is your current process for designing, adapting, implementing, and monitoring school climate practices?
- Which policies, practices, and resources might you adapt to better meet the strengths, needs, and priorities of your school and/or district communities?
- What are some immediate next steps you can take to strengthen the climate in your school(s) or district?

REFERENCES

Bryk, A. S. (2010). Organizing schools for improvement. *Phi Delta Kappan, 91*(7), 23–30.

da Luz, F. (2015). *The relationship between teachers and students in the classroom: Communicative language teaching approach and cooperative learning strategy to improve learning* [Master's thesis, Bridgewater State University]. BSU Master's Theses and Projects. https://vc.bridgew.edu/theses/22/

Darling-Hammond, L., & Cook-Harvey, C. M. (2018). *Educating the whole child: Improving school climate to support student success.* Learning Policy Institute. https://files.eric.ed.gov/fulltext/ED606462.pdf

García Coll, C., Lamberty, G., Jenkins, R., McAdoo, H. P., Crnic, K., Wasic, B. H., & Vázquez García, H. (1996). An integrative model for the study of developmental competencies in minority children. *Child Development, 67*(5), 1891–1914.

Grayson, J. L., & Alvarez, H. K. (2008). School climate factors relating to teacher burnout: A mediator model. *Teaching and Teacher Education, 24,* 1349–1363.

Gregory, A., Cornell, D., & Fan, X. (2011). The relationship of school structure and support to suspension rates for Black and White high school students. *American Educational Research Journal, 48*(4), 904–934.

Hanson, T., Austin, G., & Li, J. (2012). *Racial/ethnic differences in student achievement, engagement, supports, and safety: Are they greater within schools or between schools in California?* (CHKS Factsheet #13). WestEd.

Hattie, J. A. C. (2009). *Visible learning: A synthesis of over 800 meta-analyses relating to achievement.* Routledge.

Ishimaru, A. (2014). Rewriting the rules of engagement: Elaborating a model of district-community collaboration. *Harvard Educational Review, 84*(2), 188–216.

Kania, J., Hanleybrown, F., & Splansky Juster, J. (2014). Essential mindset shifts for collective impact. *Stanford Social Innovation Review, 12*(4), A2–A5. https://doi.org/10.48558/VV1R-C414

Murray, K. E. (2018). The problem of intradistrict inequality. *Belmont Law Review, 5,* 85–102. https://papers.ssrn.com/sol3/papers.cfm?abstract_id=3240746

National School Climate Center. (n.d.). *What is school climate and why is it important?* https://schoolclimate.org/school-climate/

O'Malley, M. D., & Amarillas, A. (2011a). *What works brief #1: Caring relationships and high expectations.* WestEd. https://www.wested.org/resources/what-works-brief-1-caring-relationships-and-high-expectations/

O'Malley, M. D., & Amarillas, A. (2011b). *What works brief #4: School connectedness.* WestEd. https://www.wested.org/resources/what-works-brief-4-school-connectedness/#:~:text=Attend%20school%20more%20regularly,course%20of%20their%20young%20adult

Peterson, K. D., & Deal, T. E. (1998). How leaders influence the culture of schools. *Educational Leadership, 56,* 28–31.

Redding, R., & Corbett, J. (2018). *Shifting school culture to spark rapid improvement.* Center on School Turnaround, WestEd.

Rosanbalm, K. (2021). *Social and emotional learning during COVID-19 and beyond: Why it matters and how to support it.* Hunt Institute. https://hunt-institute.org/wp-content/uploads/2021/02/HI-Duke-Brief-SEL-Learning-During-COVID-19-Rosanbalm.pdf

U.S. Department of Education, Office of Safe and Healthy Students. (2016). *Quick guide on making school climate improvements.* https://safesupportivelearning.ed.gov/sites/default/files/NCSSLE_SCIRP_QuickGuide508%20gdc.pdf

Varga, M. (2017). *The effect of teacher-student relationships on the academic engagement of students.* https://mdsoar.org/bitstream/handle/11603/3893/VargaMeagan_paper.pdf?sequence=1&isAllowed=y

Voight, A. (2015). Student voice for school-climate improvement: A case study of an urban middle school. *Journal of Community & Applied Social Psychology, 25*(4), 310–326.

Walrond, N. (2021). *Serving the whole person: An alignment and coherence guide for local education agencies.* WestEd. https://www.wested.org/resources/whole-person-alignment-and-coherence-guide-for-local-education-agencies/

Woolley, M., & Bowen, G. L. (2007). In the context of risk: Supportive adults and the school engagement of middle school students. *Family Relations, 56*(1), 92–104. https://www.jstor.org/stable/4541650

ADDITIONAL ACKNOWLEDGMENTS

This chapter was adapted, with permission, from the brief *School Climate Essentials: A Call to Action.*

CHAPTER 12

Foundations of Trauma-Informed Practice in Education

Christina Pate, Nakanya Magby, and Jenny Betz

Pause and Reflect Before Reading

- How would you define the concepts of trauma?
- Given your definition for trauma, what do you know about trauma-informed practice? Can you provide examples of any strategies?
- What would you like to know about trauma-informed practice?

INTRODUCTION

Sometimes even the most effective educators may struggle to reach a student or even their colleague. Discerning the reasons can be challenging, especially if those reasons stem from the effects of chronic or toxic stress, adverse experiences, and/or trauma. Furthermore, the challenges of recognizing and responding to students' or staff's social, emotional, and mental health needs have been compounded post-pandemic.

In this chapter, you will deepen your understanding of trauma-informed practice by examining it on individual, collective, and systems levels. Information and strategies in this chapter build on a growing research base about the effects of stress and trauma (Bartlett & Sacks, 2019; Blodgett & Dorado, 2016; Centers for Disease Control and Prevention [CDC], 2020; Felitti et al., 1998; Maggi et al., 2010; Shonkoff et al., 2009; 2012; Van der Kolk, 2014) and how to attend to the needs of students and staff at personal, collective, and systems levels using a healing-centered approach (Ginwright, 2018). Throughout this chapter, you will have opportunities to consider how you might use trauma-informed practice to support students and staff in your care. Much of this chapter is derived from previous resources developed by WestEd (see Office of the California Surgeon General, 2023; Pate, 2020; Pate et al., 2022; 2023).

UNDERSTANDING STRESS, TRAUMA, RESILIENCE, AND HEALING

Educators play an important role in students' healthy development and well-being, and leaders play this role for staff. In this chapter, we examine important concepts such as stress, trauma, trauma-informed practices, healing, and resilience. Educational leaders may wonder if they are qualified to work with staff and students who have experienced trauma. Some staff (e.g., bus driver, cafeteria worker) may wonder how trauma-informed practice relates to them, while others may feel overwhelmed about the topic altogether. It is understandable that staff may have these thoughts and feelings. Nonetheless, trauma-informed practice does not require educators to be experts on trauma.

Trauma-informed practice is an approach to understanding and supporting people within a community. This may include, but is not limited to, people who have experienced trauma or stress. Educators may wonder why trauma-informed practices are used to respond to people who are stressed, since being stressed does not necessarily mean someone is traumatized. Trauma-informed practices can support the full range of responses that can result from everyday stressors to trauma.

STRESS AND STRESS RESPONSES

Stress is the brain and body's response to a stressor. Stressors are events or experiences that lead to a stress response. The ways our bodies respond to stressors are called stress responses. Stress responses can include, but are not limited to, heart rate changes; tense muscles; breathing changes; tingling; anger, frustration, or sadness; eating or sleep changes; difficulty concentrating; or social withdrawal.

Not all stress is bad, however. In fact, there are three levels or degrees of stress response—positive, tolerable, and toxic—and they range based on their potential to cause lasting disruption inside the brain and body (Shonkoff et al., 2009; 2012; The Center on the Developing Child, 2007). These three levels of stress are summarized as follows.

- **Positive stress response** is important for healthy development and can be helpful. For example, a positive stress response helps us get up and move in the morning. It can also be similar to feeling excited when planning an event or feeling a little nervous before starting a new job, or for students, before starting a new school year or when about to play in a sporting event. One might feel a brief increase in one's heart rate, which may be accompanied by a mild increase in stress hormone levels. An essential aspect of a positive stress response in children is the availability of a caring and responsive adult who helps the child cope with the stressor, which provides a protective effect that helps the stress response systems get back to baseline. The same is true for adults.

- **Tolerable stress response** is activated when someone is exposed to a less common experience that comes with greater adversity or threat. When experienced alongside support from an adult, the stress response system will return to baseline more quickly, and the long-term harm to health and learning is reduced. Examples of what might cause a tolerable stress response may include a contentious divorce, loss of a loved one, or a natural disaster.
- **Toxic stress response** is the prolonged activation of a stress response and happens when a person experiences stressors that are strong, frequent, or happen over long periods of time, and in the absence of protective factors, such as caring relationships and environmental supports to keep them safe and healthy and to help them cope and heal. When there is toxic stress, we experience physical symptoms and emotional distress over long periods of time.

Everyone experiences stress differently. When something scary, threatening, or upsetting happens, our stress response system is activated. The stress response happens immediately, often without our control. There are also four types of stress responses. The following outlines each type of stress response along with some common student behaviors which are symptoms of the stress response. These can be generalized to adult behaviors as well.

- **Fight:** Verbal or physical reaction which may appear as aggressive or violent such as yelling, screaming, arguing, cursing, making threats, kicking, hitting, biting, destroying property, throwing self on the floor.
- **Flight:** Nonverbal or physical reaction which may appear as withdrawal, avoidance, or leaving a situation. Running away, covering the face, pulling shirt or jacket over the head, crawling under a desk or table, keeping out of view of the adult, silencing in a conversation, looking away or avoiding eye contact; moving the self or chair/desk to get away from a person or situation.
- **Freeze:** Nonverbal or physical reaction which may appear as withdrawn, stuck, or shut down. Staying still, becoming numb, shutting down verbally and/or physically, withdrawing into the self, unresponsive to name being called or requests/commands/questions, excessive daydreaming, appearing tired or confused, going limp or fainting.

- **Fawn:** Verbal or physical reaction which may appear as overly compliant or appeasing. People-pleasing behaviors, trouble setting or maintaining healthy boundaries (physical or social), being overly helpful, apologizing when not at fault.

TRAUMA

As mentioned, not all stress is bad, and stress does not necessarily include trauma. However, some events or circumstances can be traumatizing. Trauma can be described as an experience of an event or series of events, or a circumstance or set of circumstances that is perceived by the body as harmful or life threatening and leaves a lasting effect on our health and well-being. (SAMHSA, 2014).

It is essential to understand that trauma is a person's *experience* of an event or circumstance, not the event or circumstance itself. For example, two people could be in the same car accident and one of them may be physically injured (aka traumatized) as a result of the event, while another person is not. The same is true for emotional or psychological trauma. One person's brain and body may experience the car accident as emotionally traumatizing, while the other person may not. Trauma is never a choice, and yet it impacts a person's well-being (SAMHSA, 2014). Thus, trauma is not an event that happens. Trauma is a person's experience of an event. It is the injury— physical or psychological—that results from the event or circumstance.

UNDERSTANDING THE BRAIN SCIENCE

Understanding brain science helps adults identify and respond to behaviors with compassion and understanding instead of disappointment or frustration. Whether we're teaching students or working with colleagues and staff, we can engender safe and supportive environments that improve our ability to teach and lead and improve our students' ability to engage and learn. One simple framework to consider is neuroscientist Bruce Perry's 3 Rs: Regulate, Relate, and Reason (Perry, 2006; n.d.). In order to effectively learn, work, and thrive, a person must first feel physically and emotionally safe, calm, and settled ("regulate"), then feel socially and emotionally connected through safe and supportive relationships that are attuned to the person's needs ("relate"), and only then can they feel ready and able to engage with learning, working, and leading ("reason").

If we try to jump straight into academic teaching, or straight into working or decision-making (or for students, straight into learning), we've completely bypassed what our brains need to get there. If staff and students are showing up dysregulated because they're stressed out and unsettled—which many are these days—or they're feeling disconnected from safe supportive relationships and environments, we won't effectively or sustainably reach the thinking brain. When unsettled, or "dysregulated," you are unlikely to relate to and connect with other people and, until you feel safe and supported, are limited in your capacity to connect with other people and will have a limited ability to access key thinking, learning, and leading strategies. While this understanding of stress has universal application, it becomes more salient within the bounds of educational work (Pate et al., 2022). Further, recognizing stress-related feelings and behaviors is essential for applying appropriately responsive and supportive strategies and supports.

BEHAVIOR IS COMMUNICATION

The stress responses and changes in the brain are what's happening inside a person's body. What we can observe are the person's actions and behaviors, which are an important manner of communication. When a person has become dysregulated, their behavior is communicating both that the person's stress response is activated and that they are outside of their ability to regulate. Notably, a person who has experienced chronic or toxic stress or trauma may have a decreased ability to regulate their stress responses. An adult may consider dysregulated behavior challenging. However, when we understand that behavior is communication, we are better able to respond to the person's needs and offer support rather than react to behavior that we feel is challenging which often ends up further dysregulating one or both people and may be punitive in nature.

If we consider behavior to be like an iceberg, what we see is the top of the iceberg. However, just under the surface and moving down quite deep, there are numerous factors that influence a person's behavior. Thus, it can be challenging to determine what is being communicated through a person's behavior. Taking time to pause and consider what might be influencing this person's behavior can help us respond rather than react as well as respond with compassion rather than frustration because we know there is something else to this behavior.

Human beings are complex, as are the systems in which we operate every day. Knowing when and how to respond to someone whose stress response is activated can be challenging. Thus, developing positive relationships with each other and with students is essential. Trusting relationships serve as protective factors and buffers to stressful events and interactions. Additionally, when we know someone well, we can better understand what activates their stress responses and what they need to become regulated again. Thus, every moment we have with another person is an opportunity to build a safe and supportive connection.

Pause and Reflect

Describe some ways you have used or might use the 3 Rs (regulate, relate, and reason) to respond to staff or students (or yourself) whose stress response system is activated. Consider how you have helped or might help them or yourself:

- **Regulate**—Pause; get grounded and centered. How do you learn to recognize the signs in your mind and body that indicate that you (or your student or colleague) are stressed or about to react?
- **Relate**—Get connected in safe and supportive relationships and environments. How do you and others support each other feeling included and connected by attuning to each other's needs?
- **Reason**—How do you create cultures of care that allow people agency over their own minds, bodies, and behaviors that support effective learning, teaching, and decision-making? How do you support your growth and that of your students and staff?

TRAUMA-INFORMED, HEALING-CENTERED PRACTICE IN CONTEXT

When we understand the ways stress and trauma influence ourselves and others, we can support others at an **individual** level (Figure 12.1).

For example, an educator may model and practice self-regulation skills (breathing, focused attention) with a student in their classroom to support student and educator well-being. When we work together to provide safe and supportive relationships, environments, routines, practices, and community

Figure 12.1. Ecological Systems Lens (created based on work of Bronfenbrenner, 1979)

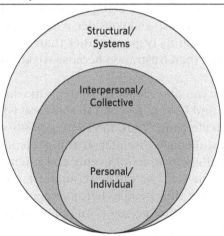

Structural/Systems

Interpersonal/Collective

Personal/Individual

care strategies, we can support people at the **collective** level. For example, when teachers gather their students in a circle to discuss "what's good" that morning, they are engaging in collective care strategies to support the school community's well-being. Finally, when we create policies, processes, and practices that offer equitable opportunities for all people, we can support people at the **systems** level. For example, when administrators and school board members institute nonexclusionary discipline policies, implement restorative practices, and create equitable access to culturally responsive supports and services, they are cultivating trauma-informed, healing-centered systems.

There are six guiding principles of trauma-informed practice that are useful for school and district leaders to consider (CDC, n.d.). These are described briefly as follows.

1. **Safety:** Create an environment where people feel physically and emotionally safe.
2. **Trustworthiness and Transparency:** Develop trust. Share information with everyone who is involved.
3. **Peer Support:** Offer opportunities for people who have experienced trauma to share their stories. Sharing promotes recovery and healing.
4. **Collaboration and Mutuality:** Understand that healing happens in relationships. Everyone has an important role. Share power and decision-making in meaningful ways.
5. **Empowerment, Voice, and Choice:** Acknowledge and build on people's strengths and experiences.
6. **Cultural, Historical, and Gender Issues:** Create policies, protocols, and processes that actively interrupt identity-based biases. Acknowledge and address historical trauma.

One way educational leaders can begin building resilience and healing to support people is through a process called a healing-centered approach (Ginwright, 2018), which combines **healing** (i.e., becoming well again) and **resilience** (i.e., the ability to overcome serious hardship or adverse experiences) (APA, n.d.). A healing-centered approach does the following:

- Builds on the six guiding principles of trauma-informed practice
- Focuses on the whole person, not only their experience of trauma
- Highlights ways that trauma and healing are experienced collectively
- Supports people to take control of their own well-being
- Helps people move beyond "what happened to you" to "what's right with you"

Overall, stress and trauma are not destiny. Prevention of and healing from toxic stress can happen at any stage in life. Thus, education leaders play a critical role in preventing harm, providing protective factors and positive childhood experiences (PCEs), and promoting healing from its effects. Overall, trauma-informed practice can be used to support all people. It can help individuals, groups, and communities, including staff and students.

Pause and Reflect

What are some ways you have or might apply the principles of trauma-informed practice and promote healing and resilience in your school community? Consider:

- Individual-level (identification, supports, self-awareness, self-care, etc.)
- Collective-level (safe and supportive relationships and environments, culturally responsive approaches)
- Systems-level (system-wide practices, programs, processes, policies, resources)

STRATEGIES

The following are simple strategies and practices that school and district leaders can practice themselves as well as encourage others to integrate into their work and daily lives. This overarching list of strategies is not exhaustive nor prescriptive. Rather, it is an invitation and a foundation upon which to build and strengthen your trauma-informed practice in the personal, collective, and systems contexts. One suggestion is for leaders to share and discuss these strategies during leadership team meetings. As you adopt and adapt any of these (or other) practices, you are encouraged to model these with your colleagues and students to normalize trauma-informed practices and institutionalize a culture of safety. This list is adapted from several resources (see Pate, 2020; Pate et al., 2022; 2023).

Strategies to Support Safety and Security (Regulate)

- Facilitate grounding and centering activities.
- Create structure and consistency.
- Create more opportunities for breaks, physical activities, and nonacademic activities.
- Promote self-awareness and communication of feelings.
- Practice and facilitate self-regulation.
- Provide choices for student and staff input and output.
- Offer suggestions for meeting sensory needs.

Strategies to Support Connection and Belonging (Relate)

- Understand behavior is communication.
- Model positive interactions.
- Emphasize caring connections.
- Create opportunities and systems for responsiveness and attunement.
- Foster collaboration and teamwork.
- Create structures for co-regulation.

Strategies to Support Agency, Self-Management, Decision-Making, and Growth (Reason)

- Establish systemwide commitments and policies centering equity, well-being, and care.
- Apply an asset frame.
- Implement healing-centered, culturally responsive practices.
- Support executive functioning and self-management skills.
- Ensure materials are nonviolent and free of activating content.
- View students and staff as experts and prioritize their choice.

CONCLUSION

Altogether, trauma-informed and healing-centered approaches can support the lived experiences and understandings of all people, especially those who have experienced chronic or toxic stress or trauma. For education leaders, trauma-informed and healing-centered approaches can support our ability to maintain control, self-awareness, and authenticity in difficult interactions as well as build our capacity to explore emotional and physical concerns and healthy connections to others. For staff and students, having the systems and structures in place to support regulation, connection, agency, and decision-making allows for the school community to thrive, academically and nonacademically.

Again, the foregoing list of strategies and practices is not exhaustive nor prescriptive. Rather, it is an invitation and a foundation upon which to build and strengthen your trauma-informed, healing-centered practice in the context of community and systems. As you adopt and adapt any of these (or other) practices, you are encouraged to model these with your colleagues and students to normalize trauma-informed, healing-centered practices and institutionalize a culture of care. Thus, not only is it important for us to shift our way of *doing*, but we must shift from a way of *doing* to a way of *being*—and *you* model the way.

Reflect Further and Take Action

- What mindsets and strategies have supported you in the past when managing your own or others' stress or the effects of trauma? In what ways might those approaches apply during particularly stressful times?
- In what ways do you experience a sense of safety and connection when you are with others? What educational environment factors have supported your well-being? How might you adapt these strategies to develop and maintain healthy relationships and create safe and supportive environments?
- In what ways do you create systems and structures to support agency, self-management, decision-making and growth for yourself? How might you apply these to your staff and students?

REFERENCES

American Psychological Association (APA). (n.d.). *Resilience*. https://www.apa.org/topics/resilience

Bartlett, J. D., & Sacks, V. (2019). Adverse childhood experiences are different than child trauma, and it's critical to understand why. *Child Trends*. https://www.childtrends.org/adverse-childhood-experiences-different-than-child-trauma-critical-to-understand-why

Blodgett, C., & Dorado, J. (2016). *A selected review of trauma-informed school practice and alignment with educational practice*. The California Endowment. https://www.pacesconnection.com/g/aces-in-education/fileSendAction/fcType/5/fcOid/478274755608928450/fodoid/478274755608928447/CLEAR-Trauma-Informed-Schools-White-Paper.pdf

Bronfenbrenner, U. (1979). *The ecology of human development*. Harvard University Press.

Centers for Disease Control and Prevention (CDC). (n.d.). Six guiding principles to a trauma-informed approach. https://www.cdc.gov/orr/infographics/6_principles_trauma_info.htm

Centers for Disease Control and Prevention (CDC). (2020). *Adverse childhood experiences (ACEs)*. https://www.cdc.gov/violenceprevention/childabuseandneglect/acestudy/index.html

Center on the Developing Child. (2007). *InBrief: The impact of early adversity on child development*. Harvard University. https://developingchild.harvard.edu/resources/inbrief-the-impact-of-early-adversity-on-childrens-development/

Felitti, V. J., Anda, R. F., Nordenberg, D., Williamson, D. F., Spitz, A. M., Edwards, V., Koss, M. P., & Marks, J. S. (1998). Relationship of childhood abuse and household dysfunction to many of the leading causes of death in adults. The Adverse Childhood Experiences (ACE) study. *American Journal of Preventive Medicine*, 14(4), 245–258. https://doi.org/10.1016/s0749-3797(98)00017-8

Ginwright, S. (2018). *The future of healing: Shifting from trauma informed care to healing centered engagement.* Medium. https://ginwright.medium.com/the-future-of-healing-shifting-from-trauma-informed-care-to-healing-centered-engagement-634f557ce69c

Maggi, S., Irwin, L. J, Siddiqi, A., & Hertzman, C. (2010). The social determinants of early child development: An overview. *Journal of Pediatrics and Child Health, 46*(11), 627–635. https://doi.org/10.1111/j.1440-1754.2010.01817.x

Office of the California Surgeon General (OSG). (2023). *Safe spaces: Foundations of trauma informed practice for educational and care settings (professional learning modules).* CA OSG and WestEd. https://osg.ca.gov/safespaces/

Pate, C. M. (2020). *Strategies for trauma-informed distance learning.* Center to Improve SEL and School Safety, WestEd. https://www.wested.org/resources/trauma-informed-distance-learning/

Pate, C. M., Pfister, T., & Ripma, T. (2023). *Creating a culture of care: A guide for education leaders to develop systems and structures that support educator well-being.* Center to Improve Social & Emotional Learning at WestEd.

Pate, C. M., Tilley-Gyado, T., & Betz, J. (2022). *Connecting the brain and body to support equity work: A toolkit for education leaders.* WestEd. https://www.wested.org/wp-content/uploads/2022/03/Brain-Body-Educ-Equity-Leaders_Brief.pdf

Perry, B. D. (2006). The neurosequential model of therapeutics: Applying principles of neuroscience to clinical work with traumatized and maltreated children. In N. B. Webb (Ed.), *Working with traumatized youth in child welfare* (pp. 27–52). The Guilford Press.

Perry, B. D. (n.d.). *The 3 Rs: Reaching the learning brain.* https://beaconhouse.org.uk/wp-content/uploads/2019/09/The-Three-Rs.pdf

Shonkoff, J. P., Boyce, W. T., & McEwen, B. S. (2009). Neuroscience, molecular biology, and the childhood roots of health disparities building a new framework for health promotion and disease prevention. *JAMA: Journal of the American Medical Association, 301*(21), 2252–2259. http://dx.doi.org/10.1001/jama.2009.754

Shonkoff, J. P., Garner, A. S., Siegel, B. S., Dobbins, M. I., Earls, Garner, A. S., M. F., McGuinn, L., Pascoe, J., & Wood, D. L. (2012). The lifelong effects of early childhood adversity and toxic stress. *Pediatrics, 129*(1), e232–e246. http://dx.doi.org/10.1542/peds.2011-2663

Substance Abuse and Mental Health Services Administration (SAMHSA). (2014). *SAMHSA's concept of trauma and guidance for a trauma-informed approach.* HHS Publication No. (SMA) 14-4884. Substance Abuse and Mental Health Services Administration.

Van der Kolk, B. (2014). *The body keeps the score.* Penguin Random House.

CHAPTER 13

Building on Family and Community Strengths

Maria Paredes

Pause and Reflect Before Reading

- How would you describe the interactions and relationships between educators and families in your school or district? What are strengths, and what opportunities exist for growth in this area?
- What family engagement policies and practices have you identified as priorities in your school or district?
- What steps have you taken to strengthen family engagement in your school or district?

INTRODUCTION

When education leaders work together with families to improve outcomes for students, it strengthens the unity and common purpose in schools. Therefore, it is important to elevate the family engagement practices in schools and districts by adopting innovative perspectives and implementing systematic approaches that are integrated with student learning priorities and continuous school improvement efforts. In addition to strengthening the bonds between educators and families, effective family engagement practices have enormous payoff potential. As noted in the research base section later in the chapter, effective family engagement can lead to higher student attendance, improved student academic outcomes, healthier school climate, and greater teacher retention. It can also improve relationships and trust between educators and families, better equip families to monitor and support student learning and transitions through educational environments, as well as extend home and community learning opportunities.

At its best, effective family engagement is entwined in the culture of the school and is powered by leaders who believe that all families can contribute as advocates, role models, and leaders themselves in their children's schools. This chapter aims to provide practical information and tools that support school and district leaders' efforts to engage all families, especially families who feel unheard, unseen, and underserved.

RESEARCH BASE

The profound benefits of family engagement in student learning, self-efficacy, and well-being have been well documented over the last 50 years. A critical resource came in 2002 when *New Wave of Evidence: The impact of School, Family, and Community Connections on Student Achievement* was published (Henderson & Mapp, 2002). It presents a synthesis of the research and a window into the many ways family engagement contributes to student success. According to this report, students with engaged families, no matter their background or income level, are more likely to do the following:

- Earn higher grades and test scores, and enroll in higher-level programs
- Be promoted, pass their classes, and earn credits
- Attend school regularly
- Have better social skills, show improved behavior, and adapt well to school
- Graduate and go on to postsecondary education

Other research reveals that open lines of communication, monitoring progress, and learning support by parents and families tend to increase student academic outcomes. For example, one series of meta-analyses found that parental high expectations and parents' beliefs in their child's potential had the strongest relationship to student academic outcomes (Jaynes, 2005, 2007). This research also found that parents and families' capacity to contribute to their child's educational success is strengthened when they are in partnership with their child's school.

A groundbreaking 2010 study by the Chicago Consortium on School Research showed that strong connections between families, schools, and the community can have systemic and lasting effects on learning outcomes for students and school improvement. The effects were higher when combined with other essential supports, such as strong school leadership, student-centered learning, effective instruction, and professional learning (Bryk et al., 2010).

In sum, experts advocate for family engagement as a necessary strategy of a systems approach to continuous school improvement, student learning, and an inclusive school culture (Mapp & Kuttner, 2013; Weiss et al., 2010).

DEFINING EFFECTIVE FAMILY ENGAGEMENT

For education leaders to have an image of the capacity of their schools to effectively engage families, it is important to understand what effective engagement consists of. Some leading scholars have described effective family engagement as "an intentional and systemic partnership of educators, families, and community members who share responsibility for a student's preparation for school, work, and life, from the time the child is born to young adulthood" (Weiss et al., 2010). To accomplish this, educators, families, and community members must develop the skills, knowledge, and disposition needed to work collaboratively. In addition, schools and districts must integrate family and community engagement into their structures and processes, including training and professional development, teaching and learning, community collaboration, and the use of data for continuous improvement and accountability. Families also need regular access to student progress data and must be afforded opportunities to acquire the skills to interpret and recognize the full picture of their child's needs and strengths.

According to two leading researchers (Bodenhausen & Birge, 2017), effective family engagement in schools and districts also requires the continuous strengthening of two critical dimensions of family engagement: trusting relationships between educators and families, and the direct connection between family engagement activities and student learning.

Trusting relationships are strong when the following conditions are met:

- Educators are culturally responsive and reach out to families to build partnerships.
- All families feel welcome, valued, and respected at their child's school.
- Educators and family leaders jointly plan and lead family engagement activities.

Connections to student learning are strong when the following are true:

- Family engagement activities are aligned with district goals for student outcomes.
- Families and educators engage in two-way communication about what students are learning at school, including the review of student progress data.

- Family engagement activities help families to monitor their child's progress and to provide learning support at home.

Finally, to achieve the foregoing, effective home and school partnerships must rely on consistent communication that is linked to learning. Families cannot wait for report cards or parent–teacher conferences to hear a very short, camouflaged version of their child's skills and abilities on assessments. According to a national survey, over 90 percent of parents believe their child is at or above grade level, while only 44 percent of teachers say their students are prepared to do grade-level work (Learning Heroes, 2023). Families take meaningful action to support learning and to advocate for their children when they have a clear and complete picture of their child's progress on a regular and consistent basis. The stakes are highest for families.

Pause and Reflect

- How does the foregoing description of family engagement align with your previous understanding?
- Consider the extent to which your school or districts approach to family engagement aligns with the foregoing definition. What are the similarities and differences?

BEGIN BY DEVELOPING A PLAN

Designing and implementing effective family engagement based on research and evidence is a responsibility shared among educators, parent leaders, and community partners. It begins with developing a plan. A meaningful and equitable family engagement plan should be designed in collaboration with parent leaders and community partners, and it should align with school and district improvement priorities.

To lay the foundation for effective family engagement planning, begin by establishing a family and community engagement (FACE) team. The FACE team should include educators and school leaders from multiple departments, union leaders, other district- and school-level staff members, parent leaders, students, and community partners. This team should meet regularly and functions much like a professional learning community. When assembling the team, consider how the needs of different educators, families, and students will be represented. Incorporate key individuals who have roles in different school programs to help align family engagement activities across school and district initiatives.

Throughout the identification and planning process, it is essential to consider the capacity of families and staff to engage in planning effective family engagement work. Consider professional learning for the FACE team to ground all members and guide them toward evidence-informed practices.

The following are some questions to consider when forming a FACE team.

- Who has been successful at engaging diverse families in the district's schools?
- Who will represent the voices of classroom teachers and school staff to the team?
- Who are parent leaders who can speak for underrepresented families in the district and schools? Families of students with disabilities? Recent immigrant families?
- What barriers could be mitigated so that traditionally underrepresented families have the opportunity to engage in the FACE planning team? Could the district:
  » Provide childcare?
  » Provide interpretation services?
  » Adjust meeting times?
- Who is influential in your district and can help promote the goals of the plan?
- How will you bring voices from underrepresented communities to the forefront?

A Framework for Family Engagement Plans

Once a FACE team is in place and foundational knowledge and understanding have been acquired, planning work can start. When developing a plan, consider including the following four components.

1. Capacity. School staff and families develop skills, confidence, and the disposition for authentic home and school partnerships.

Building capacity in the area of family engagement is a prerequisite for doing meaningful work in partnership with families. Professional learning helps educators understand why it is important to work with families and helps them value families' perspectives and experiences. Developing capacity encompasses learning new skills and abilities. It also includes developing or strengthening healthy core beliefs about families, which is necessary for enabling educators to recognize and remove barriers that stand in the way of families fully participating in their children's education.

2. Process. Districts and schools adopt and implement practices that are research- and evidence-informed; families are engaged at all levels of the system.

The process is how the work gets done—the practices and procedures that are adopted and implemented by schools to engage families in their children's learning and in collaborative decision-making. Research and practice demonstrate that effective engagement requires intentional processes to be implemented: Barriers must be identified and removed, parents must be informed and empowered as advocates, and schools must collaborate with families and community partners to support robust student and family experiences at all levels of the system.

3. Infrastructure. Districts and schools allocate time, resources, and staff; they also establish policies to protect, expand, and sustain effective practices.

Infrastructure is the foundation of resources and coordinated efforts that support and sustain equitable home and school partnerships. Family engagement infrastructure within schools and communities can be established, protected, expanded, and sustained through the purposeful allocation of staff time and resources. As knowledge is gained about which engagement practices work or do not work, schools must review and alter practices to ensure they achieve stated goals and objectives.

4. Outcomes. Districts and schools monitor, evaluate, and report progress.

Evaluation is critical to understanding the effects that engagement opportunities have on children, families, and schools. Schools must review their efforts to determine if they are achieving their desired outcomes. Outcome data empower educators and families to set and achieve high expectations, make informed decisions, and strengthen effective practices while changing those that are ineffective. Data are most useful when they are meaningful, user-friendly, actionable, and regularly shared with community partners.

Pause and Reflect

- To what extent does your school or district have a structured framework or plan for strengthening family engagement?
- Based on the foregoing information, how could your school or district strengthen its approach to engaging families?

EVIDENCE-BASED PRACTICES TO STRENGTHEN CAPACITY
TO ENGAGE FAMILIES

In addition to having a plan, schools and districts benefit from having a sound organizational structure that articulates their family engagement vision, priorities, and goals. The regular and explicit communication of these priorities to educators, families, and community partners by school and district leaders helps elevate expectations and increase the visibility for the work and should also be a part of any family engagement plan. Ultimately, the goal is to build strong alliances between home and school, develop capacity, share meaningful information, and create a clear plan of action for home and school partnerships that advance outcomes for students.

Once they begin implementing their plan, many schools struggle to get a high turnout at school family engagement events. Understandably, it can be frustrating for staff when a lot of effort in planning and organizing the events yield disappointing attendance results. To change this tendency, schools must elevate the experience and the added value for families. The following evidence-informed practices can help enhance family participation in activities and events.

Cultivate Trusting Relationships

The ability and disposition of educators to form genuine bonds and connections with families is a critical factor for effective family engagement that impacts student outcomes. The bonds improve when educators invest time and effort in getting to know each family. Educators learn about the family's education goals and aspirations for their child and become aware of their values and priorities, and this information helps educators differentiate learning for that child. This close connection with families helps develop trust, and trust is at the center of effective family engagement.

In the author's observations from professional experience over the last 25 years working closely with teachers and administrators, less than a half of educators recognize the power and benefits of working in partnership with families, lean into this practice as an instinctive part of teaching, and know how to go about forming relationships with their students' families. On the other hand, a majority of educators are on the fence or feel uncomfortable, awkward, and often disagreeable about extending themselves to families outside the traditional parent–teacher conferences. This reality is unsettling and comes down to individual values, beliefs, social, racial, and economic perceived differences with the families and communities they serve. Fortunately, the perceived differences and fear of the unknown can be mediated by continuous professional learning, coaching, mentoring, and experiencing success by doing. Mindsets are flexible.

Embrace a Strengths-Based Mindset

An educator's mindset related to family engagement is an essential foundation for doing engagement work well. Effective family engagement activities and strategies should be strengths-based and focus on the potential of each student's family and the community as a whole. A strengths-based approach focuses less on trying to address perceived problems or deficits and more on recognizing capacities and building upon assets.

Learning more about each family and what they bring to the table helps reveal the abundance of individual and combined experiences and resources already present within your school's families and community. This awareness helps shape a strengths-based family engagement approach that is meaningful and relevant in your school community.

Address Common Barriers and Challenges

There are a variety of common barriers and challenges that education leaders encounter when implementing family engagement plans. Table 13.1 lists some of the most common barriers and suggested strategies for overcoming them.

Table 13.1. Overcoming Barriers to Engaging Vulnerable Families

Overcoming Barriers to Engaging Vulnerable Families	
Common Barriers	Strategies to Mitigate These Challenges
Negative experiences with schooling in the past	• Conduct home visits with new families and get to know them personally. • Find out how and when families prefer to be contacted.
History of receiving only negative school calls about their child	• Start the school year with positive calls home.
Lack of understanding about the education system and expectations of family involvement	• Use an interpreter during calls or meetings with families whose primary language is not English.
Difficulty communicating because the primary language is not English	• Use an interpreter or a communication platform that uses multiple languages to help families understand grade-level learning priorities. • Connect families to tools and resources in their first language.
Work during school hours	• Give tips for how families can support learning at home.
Lack of technology or internet access	• Survey families to understand their needs and assets.

Communicate Clearly and Consistently With Families

The communication that flows from the school to the students' home is often unreliable. Sometimes it is a requirement that teachers communicate regularly with families, and sometimes the communication is left up to teachers' discretion. That being the case, families are most likely to experience inconsistent messaging and gaps in communication from different teachers in the same school. Additionally, the quality and content of the communication that families receive tend to reflect what educators and leaders in the school perceive as important.

A good practice to communicate effectively is to collaboratively design with families a communication strategy that all teachers agree to honor and that families can depend on for engaging with learning. Consistent communication about classroom key learning objectives, strategies for home practice, and how and when students are assessed, can enable families to be actively engaged. Effective communication helps families to proactively monitor, support, and advocate for their children.

Teachers who extend themselves to build relationships and trust with families through ongoing communication are better equipped to join forces with them in culturally responsive engagement and partnership. Being culturally responsive goes beyond multilingual communication, it includes awareness and understanding of traditions, foods, holidays, religion, history, books, geography, and other unique qualities that support inclusion in the classroom and the school.

Ultimately, good communication with families is about building strong partnerships and trust. Just as with any healthy relationship between two people, trust is a must for a successful partnership between groups. A responsive relationship that respects cultural differences lays the foundation to build just that.

Develop Educator Capacity to Form Partnerships

Engaging families in student learning while also developing relationships and trust with them represents a big change in mindset and practices for teachers. It is essential not to assume that educators already have the skills, confidence, and disposition to work in partnership with families. Teachers and education leaders identify family engagement as one of the most challenging aspects of their work (Metlife, 2013). This underscores the importance of professional learning. Schools often focus capacity-building efforts at families through programs and workshops, but strengthening the capacity of educators is equally important. It is ultimately educators who will lead the way to genuine partnerships with families, and the educators need to be equipped with knowledge and competence to be successful.

Developing capacity is an ongoing process. Every year, administrators must collect evidence and identify the required knowledge and competencies; secure the professional learning, coaching, and resources necessary; then support the implementation of the new skills through coaching and feedback for continuous improvement; and, during staff meetings, review the data gathered and engage school staff in family engagement data conversations to deepen their understanding. Yearly professional learning and data conversations signal to the school and district that family engagement is a key priority and is valued by the administrative team.

As an essential part of professional learning, make sure to promote greater attention to equity, both by addressing equity concerns in professional learning and by ensuring that teachers and school leaders who work in high-poverty schools and those with concentrations of students of color have access to high-quality preparation, professional learning, and coaching. This can be done by directing professional development resources to those school sites.

Keep in mind that the goal of ongoing professional learning is to develop local experts and to grow and sustain the evidence-informed practices that yield positive results for school culture, student learning, and school improvement. Identify instructional coaches, teachers, and school leaders who are committed to this work, continue to develop their skills, and provide them with leadership roles and responsibilities to create the needed district infrastructure.

Pause and Reflect

- Reflect on the foregoing practices. Which are the strongest in your school or district?
- Which could be stronger and what steps could you take to strengthen them?

STRATEGIES TO UPGRADE SCHOOL EVENTS AND ACTIVITIES

Effective family engagement is much more than single events and activities in which families are regarded as visitors. School family engagement events are prime opportunities for applying the practices described previously. The objective is to strengthen the knowledge and skills families need to be full partners in education.

Shift the Focus of Open House

During an open house, have a designated time for all the families to meet in their child's classroom. Use this time for introductions and for families to meet and learn about each other. Have the chairs placed in a circle to make it easier to see and talk to each other. You can even sit outside if the weather allows. The goal is for families to network and feel connected to their teacher and to their peers. This is the team—these are the families who the teacher will be partnering with to help the students learn and thrive.

Share with families key academic and nonacademic skills that students are expected to master over the course of the school year. Share real stories and end-of-year work samples so families understand what they are helping their children work toward. The main messages of the family open house meeting should be mutual collaboration, high expectations, and partnership.

Activities for Making the Open House Meeting Personal and Engaging

- Ask every family member to wear a name tag so everyone can be on a first-name basis.
- Start the meeting with a fun team-building activity. (This activity is about the adults getting to know each other.)
- Ask families about the information they want to receive from the teacher and their preferred mode of communication.
- Have teachers and staff introduce themselves, share what they do, and how they can be contacted.

Make Parent–Teacher Conferences a Mutual Learning Experience

Parent–teacher conferences are often stressful for both families and teachers, but they do not have to be, especially if you have taken the time to get to know each of the families.

Build upon Relationships. Parent–teacher conferences should build upon the relationships that teachers have been working to establish. The more the teachers know and understand about the families, the more mutually meaningful and genuine conferences become.

Provide Practical Information and Guidance. When planning, teachers should remember that parent–teacher conferences are most effective when teachers provide families with a complete and accurate picture of how their children are progressing academically and personally; model practical ways that families can support academic, social, and emotional development at home; and listen to families and learn more about them and the students.

Place Families' Needs at the Center. To make the conferences more collaborative and inclusive, ask families in advance what they are most interested in sharing and learning. Make family voice the centerpiece of the meeting experience.

Tips for Enhancing the Parent–Teacher Conference Experience

- Offer a flexible conference schedule and spread the meetings with families over many days and even weeks. Teachers should meet with the most vulnerable students first so their families can be better equipped to offer home learning support. For a student who is receiving academic interventions, the teacher should explain clearly how those interventions work and what teachers do during this time.
- Based on the students' needs, teachers should prepare activities for families to practice at home with their children and should demonstrate how to do the activities at home and how to assess children's progress.
- Teachers should share and discuss progress data and co-create learning goals based on that data to inform family learning support.
- Teachers should also draw from personal experience, if possible, and facilitate the kind of conferences they would want from their own child's teacher—that perspective should provide the motivation and inspiration.

Share and Discuss Student Progress Data With Families. Schools collect vast amounts of data about students, from attendance records, classroom activities, and standardized assessment scores to homework completion and behavior data. School leaders and educators are becoming increasingly skilled in sharing and using data to make needed decisions about programs, interventions, resources, and policies. Unlike educators, families are mostly unaware of where to access data and how to interpret available data sources.

Having data conversations with families is a growing strategy being implemented in many schools and districts. The purpose of data conversations with families is to increase knowledge and understanding of grade-level measures of success, cultivating high expectations and shared responsibility for student learning. Sharing progress data with families is likely the biggest shift teachers face in working closely with families. Professional learning and coaching help to clarify the type of data that is practical and actionable for families, timing, and the steps families can take to improve outcomes. Professional learning and coaching can also help to boost self-confidence.

Tips for Inviting Families to Data Conversations

- Host regular data-sharing meetings to strengthen families' comfort with data and their capacity to review and discuss data. Consider hosting these sessions virtually or at different times to accommodate family schedules and encourage more families to participate.

- Communicate a clear purpose and significance for using data.
- State goals and limitations upfront. Discussions about data will be most successful if all participants are clear about the goals they are trying to achieve and the parameters they are working within. For example, if there are specific criteria that will measure the success of a new program or if there are funding limitations for what can be done to address a problem, all participants should know about these upfront.
- Allow ample time for families to ask questions, offer suggestions, and provide solutions. Honor family perspectives and assets.
- Show a real commitment to using the feedback from families during data conversations. Asking for input from families and then not taking any action will slowly erode trust and willingness to engage.

Tips for Engaging Families in Data-Centered Conversations

- Make the data meaningful: Help families understand the context for the data and focus on how the data highlight areas of strength and opportunities for growth.
- Make the data user-friendly: Display the data in a visually appealing and accessible manner. Use visual aids to model how to read and interpret the data.
- Make the data actionable: Tell a story and show families tips, ideas, and resources so they can consider a range of options.
- Define the goals: Explain the goals that the school is trying to reach. Ask for their input on the goals. Help families understand any compliance requirements, resource allocations, or other potential barriers related to the decisions they are being asked to make.

CONCLUSION

This chapter includes concrete ideas to make family engagement in a school or district a well-coordinated initiative. To be clear, what is proposed here is a substantial undertaking, but it is intended to be a team effort between the district and the schools and can be accomplished over time. Equally, if not more, important are the lessons from research and practice about effective family engagement.

First, all students benefit personally and academically from their families being engaged, especially students in low-income and Black and Brown communities. As educators, we have the ability to change the narrative and bring families from the education periphery to a permanent seat at the table.

Second, educators cannot be expected to make substantial changes to the way they connect and engage with families without appropriate professional learning and support. Genuine family engagement requires that educators hold core positive beliefs about the promise and potential of families and students, and that educators have the knowledge and influence to help families reach their goals and aspirations for their children.

Third, family engagement efforts and activities need to be focused on developing trusting relationships and need to be connected to student learning. This requires planning strategically and allocating time for teachers to do outreach and connect with families early and often. Close connections with families are what allow all family engagement efforts to produce outcomes for students.

Finally, family engagement is not a program. It is a set of beliefs, behaviors, and practices designed to bring educators and families together, as a team, connected by the mutual goal of helping students thrive. As an education leader, you can help to create the organizational conditions for these relationships to grow and flourish.

Reflect Further and Take Action

- In what ways did the information in this chapter affirm prior knowledge?
- What new insights did you gain from this chapter, and how might you leverage these insights to support continuous improvement related to family engagement?
- What are some immediate next steps you can take to strengthen family and community engagement in your school or district?

REFERENCES

Bryk, A. S., Sebring, P. B., Allensworth, E., Luppescu, S., & Easton, J.O. (2010). *Organizing schools for improvement: Lessons from Chicago.* University of Chicago Press.

Bodenhausen, N., & Birge, M. (2017). Family engagement toolkit: Continuous improvement through an equity lens.

Henderson, A. T., & Mapp, K. L. (2002). *A new wave of evidence: The impact of school, family, and community connections on student achievement.* National Center for Family and Community Connections with Schools and SEDL. https://files.eric .ed.gov/fulltext/ED536946.pdf

Jeynes, W. H. (2005). Effects of parental involvement and family structure on the academic achievement of adolescents. *Marriage & Family Review, 37,* 99–116. http://dx.doi.org/10.1300/J002v37n03_06

Jeynes, W. H. (2007). The relationship between parental involvement and urban secondary school student academic achievement: A meta-analysis. *Urban Education, 42*(1), 82–110. https://doi.org/10.1177/0042085906293818

Learning Heroes. (2022). Hidden in Plain Sight: A Way Forward for Equity-Centered Family Engagement – Parents 2022, L-12 Parent, Teacher & Principal Survey Findings, June 2022. Edge Research. https://bealearninghero.org/wp-content/uploads/2022/06/Parents22-Research-Deck-1.pdf.

Mapp, K., & Kuttner, P. (2013). Dual capacity-building framework for family–school partnerships. Austin, TX: Southwest Educational Development Laboratory (SEDL) and the US Department of Education. https://files.eric.ed.gov/fulltext/ED593896.pdf.

MetLife, Inc. (2013). *The MetLife survey of the American teacher: Challenges for school leadership*. https://files.eric.ed.gov/fulltext/ED542202.pdf

Weiss, H. B., Lopez, M. E., & Rosenberg, H. (2010). *Beyond random acts: Family, school, and community engagement as an integral part of education reform*. National Policy Forum for Family, School and Community Engagement. Harvard Family Research Project.

CHAPTER 14

Deepening Understanding to Support Transgender Youth

Deborah A. Bradley and Stephen C. Hamilton

Pause and Reflect Before Reading

- Take a few minutes to think about what you currently know regarding transgender individuals.
    - » What is your understanding of transgender students and issues related to schools?
    - » Do you know anyone who is transgender? Do you have friends or know families with transgender relatives?
    - » What have you heard from news or other sources about this topic?
    - » Jot down some of your current thoughts and feelings.
- Imagine you are the parent of child who has recently told you they are transgender.
    - » Write down some of the emotions you might have.
    - » Note what actions you might want to take as a parent, given these emotions.
- Describe in your own words what you think is the meaning of the following terms.
    - » Gender identity
    - » Cisgender
    - » Transgender
    - » Nonbinary
    - » Gender nonconforming

INTRODUCTION

How concerned would you be if 84 percent of the students within a subgroup in your district felt unsafe at school? How would you respond if these students felt unsafe due to verbal harassment, online harassment, physical harassment, or physical assault? What if you learned that nearly half of them skipped school during the previous month due to safety concerns? Unfortunately, this is the reality for far too many transgender and gender nonconforming (GNC) youth within our public schools (Kosciw et al., 2020).

These were similar to the statistics that we, as parents, found ourselves confronted with in 2014. At the time, our 25-year-old had recently expressed her true gender identity. Being unfamiliar with what it means to be transgender, we were stunned. With this realization, we began to understand why our daughter, who was assigned male at birth, had such a challenging experience through her primary and secondary public school years. As a physician and an educational professional, neither of us had encountered transgender individuals during our lengthy careers. This led us to a tremendous amount of research and exploratory learning. A monthly support group with parents who had similar family experiences proved invaluable in helping us process our new reality. We discovered that many of the group members' children had identified as transgender during primary or secondary school years. Our daughter eventually shared with us that she had the initial sense of being transgender at the age of ten but had no words to describe her feelings.

As is often said, with new challenges come new possibilities and opportunities for growth. For us, learning and becoming a part of a community of parents, families, and educators dedicated to supporting the needs of transgender individuals and families took on new understanding and commitment. It has become our privilege to meet and learn about children similar to our own, whose lives have grown in happiness and success upon realizing their gender identity. For these individuals, expressing their gender identity allowed them to overcome the depression, fear, and anxiety that often prevented them from realizing their full potential.

We are now fortunate to recognize the trials our child faced, as well as the challenges currently confronting families and schools as they work to support the unique needs of transgender and GNC students. While we celebrate new guidance developed to protect these students within many of our states and school systems, we're deeply concerned by the antagonistic initiatives facing transgender and GNC students today.

In recent years, a growing number of state and local policies have purposefully failed to protect transgender students from discrimination. As a result, many are struggling to have their basic needs met in their school environments. The intent of this chapter is to offer committed educational leaders the insight and resources to address the needs of this growing subset of students. This chapter begins by exploring general information relative to the topic. The unique concerns of students and parents are then discussed, along with the challenges confronting districts and schools supporting them. The chapter closes with several suggestions and resources for further consideration.

TERMINOLOGY

LGBTQ+ is an umbrella term referring to individuals who are lesbian, gay, bisexual, transgender, or queer. LGBT (lesbian, gay, bisexual, and transgender) has been used more commonly in the past. The Q has also been known to stand for those who are questioning their gender or sexuality. The "+" includes individuals for whom LGBTQ does not reflect their identity (PFLAG, 2023). Many variations exist. For the purpose of this chapter, the acronym(s) used are consistent with those found within the various resources referenced.

- *Gender identity* refers to a person's internal, deeply held sense of being male, female, or something else (American Psychological Association, 2016).
- *Gender expression* is how a person communicates their gender identity to others through behavior, clothing, hairstyles, voice, and/or body characteristics (American Psychological Association, 2016).
- *Cisgender* describes a person whose gender identity corresponds to the person's assigned sex at birth (GLAAD, 2022).
- *Transgender* describes a person whose gender identity does not conform to the sex they were assigned at birth. This should not be confused with sexual orientation, which is a person's sense of attraction or sexual desire for other individuals. A transgender boy or man is a person who was assigned female at birth, and a transgender girl or woman is an individual who was assigned male at birth. Transgender individuals may describe themselves generally or more specifically using one or more of a wide variety of terms including transgender, trans, transgender man or woman, nonbinary, gender fluid, gender nonconforming (GNC), or genderqueer (GLAAD, 2022).
- *Nonbinary* is an umbrella term describing a person who does not identify exclusively as a man or a woman. Many nonbinary individuals consider themselves transgender; others do not (GLAAD, 2022).
- *Gender nonconforming* is a term used to describe people whose gender expression differs from conventional expectations of masculinity and femininity. Simply having a nonconforming gender expression does not make someone trans or nonbinary (GLAAD, 2022).

Minnesota's Department of Education guidance document observes, "Language around gender is evolving. In some Native American communities, the term *'Two Spirit'* is used for a person possessing a blend of male and female spirits" and they traditionally do not "use the language of transgender nor gender nonconforming" (Minnesota Department of Education, 2017).

RELEVANT DATA

Recent studies have found that transgender and GNC students experience discrimination, harassment, and physical violence at higher rates than their peers.

- 83 percent of transgender students and 75 percent of nonbinary students experienced victimization based on their gender identity (Kosciw et al., 2020).
- Transgender and GNC students experienced higher rates of verbal harassment and were twice as likely to report feeling unsafe at school as their cisgender peers (Kosciw et al., 2014).
- 57 percent of LGBTQ students who were harassed or assaulted did not report their experience to school staff (Kosciw et al., 2020).
- 60 percent of students who reported harassment or assault to school staff received no response or were told to ignore it (Kosciw et al., 2020).

Pause and Reflect

- What challenges might transgender students have within their school environment?
- What reactions might their friends, parents, and other family members have upon their coming out as transgender?
- How might the challenges you noted affect transgender students' experience and performance in school?

TRANSGENDER STUDENT CHALLENGES AND CONCERNS

For some students, the realization of their true gender identity comes at a young age. Fortunately, new information and support are enabling more parents to understand, accept, and advocate for their children even during their early primary years. For other students, however, self-realization and a need to express their gender identity come much later. This delay in self-acceptance is often due to fear, confusion, and social concerns. The 2015 U.S. Transgender Survey of 27,715 individuals found 60 percent of respondents began to feel their gender was different than the sex they were assigned at birth before they were 10 years old, with 94 percent reporting they sensed their gender was different before they reached 20. It was years before many of them had the vocabulary and perspective to realize they might be transgender (James, 2016).

For transgender students, concerns with acceptance and rejection by family and friends is complicated by lack of knowledge and societal stigmas. They find themselves on the receiving end of comments and actions, whether intended or unintended, that cause further isolation and distress. Recent anti-LGBTQ+ legislation, policies, and political rhetoric have intensified these concerns.

As students come to terms with expressing their gender identity, they are confronted with a range of personal challenges in their school environments. In 2013, GLSEN responded to the need for data pertaining to the school experiences of LGBTQ+ youth by creating the first National School Climate Survey. They have conducted a survey on a biennial basis ever since. The majority of the transgender students surveyed in 2016 felt unsafe at school because of their gender expression and were more likely to experience verbal harassment, physical harassment, and physical assault than their peers (Kosciw et al., 2016). Their 2021 survey of 22,298 youth documented the following information related to school environment and student well-being (Kosciw et al., 2022).

- Derogatory comments about gender expression, both from students and school staff, had increased since their survey of 2019.
- Only 8.5 percent of students reported they were aware their school had a policy or guidelines supporting transgender and nonbinary students.
- 77.9 percent of transgender and 57.0 percent of nonbinary students reported exclusionary or discriminatory gender-based rules, programs, or policies.
- 29.2 percent of respondents had been prevented from using their chosen name or pronouns in their schools.
- Due to fear for personal safety, students avoided school spaces traditionally segregated by sex, including bathrooms, locker rooms, and athletic facilities.
- Transgender and nonbinary students felt unsafe at school due to in-person experiences and online harassment. Many did not report harassment or assault to school staff due to confidentiality concerns. They were worried about being "outed" to the staff or family members if they reported their experiences.
- Transgender and nonbinary students were more likely than their cisgender peers to have been sent to the principal's office, received detention, and been placed in a room, hallway, or another space in the school building alone.

A number of national surveys over the last 12 years have brought to light the significant educational consequences of feeling unsafe at school.

- 45 percent of transgender students who felt unsafe had missed school during the previous month (Kosciw et al., 2022).

- 20 percent of students who felt unsafe changed schools (Kosciw et al., 2022).
- 15 percent of students who suffered harassment left school (Grant et al., 2011).
- 7.6 percent of transgender students reported they did not expect to complete high school. Of those who provided a reason for not planning to graduate, more than half indicated an unsupportive or hostile school environment was a contributing factor (GLSEN, 2016).

It is not hard to imagine that for many students, their relationship with their peers and the atmosphere in middle and high school have a significant impact on their self-perception and mental health. In recent years, numerous national surveys have confirmed that social support and school environment have a critical influence on the mental health of transgender youth.

- Discriminatory school policies, high levels of in-person victimization, and online in-school harassment were each found to be associated with high levels of depression and low self-esteem in LGBTQ students (Kosciw et al., 2022).
- 51 percent of transgender students who were harassed or physically assaulted in school, or expelled due to their gender expression, reported a history of attempted suicide (Grant et al., 2011).
- The most common reason LGBTQ students gave for not planning to complete high school was mental health concerns (Kosciw et al., 2020).
- Transgender youth who were able to use their chosen name had significantly fewer depressive symptoms, a 29 percent decrease in suicidal ideation, and a 56 percent decrease in suicidal behavior (Russell, 2018).

The positive impact of acceptance and support of children and youth was evident in the 2009 Family Acceptance Project's study of family reactions to their LGBT children. This research explored how family behaviors affect their children's risk for depression, suicide, substance abuse, HIV, and sexually transmitted diseases (STDs). It also looked at issues of self-esteem, outlook, life satisfaction, and social support. Researchers found significant differences when they compared LBGT young adults who had experienced extensive rejection to LBGT youth who were well accepted. The research found that young adults who were highly rejected as adolescents were eight times more likely to have attempted suicide, six times more likely to report significant depression, and three times more likely to use illegal drugs or be at high risk for HIV and STDs (Ryan, 2009).

PARENT CONCERNS AND REACTIONS

When a child comes out and parents learn they have a transgender or gender nonconforming child, their responses can range from utter rejection to total acceptance. How they react can significantly impact a student's health and well-being. There are a number of stages some parents may experience in the process of accepting and supporting their child.

- **Shock, denial, or disbelief** are not unusual, initially. Parents may react with anger, fear, sadness, or disgust. Many parents hope their child is just going through a phase (Strong Family Alliance, 2017).
- **Guilt or blame** occurs when parents question whether they did something wrong or whether their child was influenced by their peers or media (Strong Family Alliance, 2017).
- **Grief** over the loss of their cisgender child and the future they envisioned for them is common (Pullen-Sansfaçon et al., 2022).
- **Fear** of being judged by others and losing friends and family support can make parents feel isolated. They often fear for the safety of their child as they anticipate the transphobia and discrimination they may encounter (Strong Family Alliance, 2017).
- **Acceptance** develops as parents process their emotions, develop a greater understanding of what it means to be transgender, and realize their child is happier. With acceptance often comes advocacy for their child within the family, their greater social network, and through the school system (Strong Family Alliance, 2017).
- **Advocacy** occurs when parents work to achieve supportive relationships for their child, who is entitled to happiness and security. If they feel their child is being marginalized, their advocacy may be manifested in a collaborative role with school personnel or may be confrontational. This can be influenced by a variety of factors, including how vulnerable parents feel as they protect their child while facing challenges they have never confronted (Abreu et al., 2022).

Unfortunately, not all parents achieve total acceptance. Even partial acceptance can lessen the negative outcomes for students who are highly rejected. Throughout their process of coming to understand and accept their child, many parents feel the need for their own support. The importance of dialogue, discussion, and support become critical to parents as they seek to understand the emotional, social, and potential physical challenges affecting their child and them (Ryan, 2009).

Pause and Reflect

- Jot down what you know about laws and guidance that protect or limit protections for transgender students in your school(s).
- Using two columns, record your best estimate of states that have created laws and guidance to **support** transgender student rights and those that have developed **exclusionary** policies.

GUIDANCE AND OPPOSITION

Understanding state and federal laws protecting individual rights, while being empathetic to student and parental concerns, is an essential first step in providing a supportive school environment. For more than a decade, many states implemented guidance and policies affirming protections for LGBTQ+ students. The New York State Education Department's 2015 "Transgender and Gender Nonconforming Guidance Document" for school districts is an example of a state guidance "intended to help districts foster an educational environment safe and free from discrimination for transgender and gender nonconforming (GNC) students" (New York State Education Department, 2015). This trend reached a highpoint in 2019 with 12 states enacting policies supporting LGBTQ+ students; refer to Figure 14.1 (Temkin et al., 2022).

Beginning in 2020, a shift began to emerge as opposition to transgender and GNC students' protections increased in a number of states.

Figure 14.1. Number of State Policies That Affirm or Exclude LGBTQ+ Students

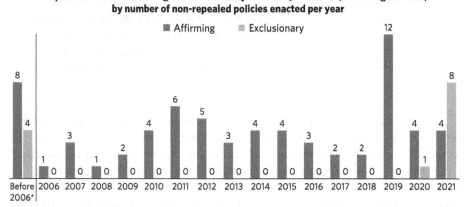

State policies that are affirming and exclusionary of LGBTQ+ students, as of August 2021, by number of non-repealed policies enacted per year

* Cumulative since 1979
Note: *The graph reflects the current statutory and regulatory landscape when these data were collected (August 2021) and does not include statutes and regulations repealed before this date.*

Anti-transgender rhetoric brought protections to the forefront of educational issues. The trend of enacting exclusionary policies increased despite evidence of the detrimental effect on the education, health, well-being, and safety of LGBTQ+ students. It is noteworthy that in 2021, eight states enacted exclusionary policies (Temkin et al., 2022).

Federal policies and actions have fluctuated through multiple administrations. A 2016 Dear Colleague letter, concerning civil rights protections for transgender students, was rescinded in 2017 and remained on the Department of Education (DOE) website for historical purposes only (Lhamon & Gupta, 2016). In early 2021, an executive order was signed "Guaranteeing an Educational Environment Free from Discrimination on the Basis of Sex, Including Sexual Orientation or Gender Identity," directing the DOE to review the Title IX regulations (Biden, 2021). This order did not reinstate the previous Title IX guidance but placed it under a period of comment through 2022, prior to revision. In June of 2022, the Biden Administration proposed new regulations and invited public comment (U.S. Department of Education, 2022). The DOE received over 250,000 comments and, as a result, the office of Civil Rights (OCR) announced October 2023 as its revised deadline to release the revised Title IX regulations, as well as the final rule related to Title IX athletics gender equity (Sokolow, 2023). At the time this was written in October 2023, no new regulations had been announced.

It is notable that the Supreme Court also reaffirmed transgender and GNC student protections in 2021. They refused to hear *Grimm v. The Gloucester County School Board*, upholding the 4th Circuit Court of Appeals decision that the school board had violated Grimm's civil rights. He had been excluded from the boys' restroom because he was transgender. The Circuit Court twice found this policy unconstitutional, based on the equal protection clause of the 14th Amendment and Title IX, prohibiting sex-based discrimination (ACLU, 2021).

The upcoming Title IX guidance revision will not address the issue of transgender and nonbinary student participation in sports. The administration has stated this will be covered in an additional ruling, allowing for a separate period of commentary. At a briefing on the proposal, Education Secretary Miguel Cardona specifically commented, "Some states are passing laws targeting LGBTQ+ students. Standing up for equal access and inclusion is as important as ever before," and "The department recognizes that standards for students participating in male and female athletics teams are evolving in real time, so we decided to do a separate rule making, on how schools may determine eligibility while upholding Title IX's nondiscrimination guarantee" (Brink, 2022).

Changing state and federal laws, policies, and guidance underpin the need for continual monitoring of new and shifting regulations. It will be critical for educational leaders to watch them closely in the coming years. To help with this task, links to state and federal laws and policies can be found in the resource section following this chapter.

CHALLENGES FOR DISTRICT AND SCHOOL LEADERS

Educators share a common goal of creating safe and supportive school environments that allow their students to thrive. In this time of rapidly changing state policies, it's not unusual for school staff to be unfamiliar and possibly uncomfortable with recommended approaches for supporting and protecting transgender and GNC students. Professional development informing staff about federal and state guidance and implementation of best practices will help address staff, student, and parent concerns.

As of March 2023, 23 states and two territories provide guidance of varying degrees on how to support LGBTQ+ students and their parents. The Movement Advancement Project (MAP) also provides access to a list of state laws and related policies that are updated on a regular basis. (MAP, 2023)

Districts and school staff who are knowledgeable of their state policies and utilize them to inform actions are much more likely to be seen as providing a supportive culture. Conversely, lack of knowledge could leave staff, schools, and districts at greater risk for allegations of sex-based discrimination exemplified by the Arvada Unified Schools District Civil Rights Complaint (DOJ/OCR, 2011).

Pause and Reflect

- Expand the list of those actions to include additional steps to support transgender students and their families.
- What actions could build greater community support and awareness?

HOW TO BE PROACTIVE IN ADDRESSING CHALLENGES

Community and staff awareness and their reactions to LBGTQ+ issues vary and are sometimes unpredictable. The topic can easily become a contentious issue for schools and districts. For this reason, being proactive is a strategy to consider for addressing school–community interactions. While not necessarily an easy subject to raise, initiating dialogue and discussion *before* issues become personal can result in more productive and less reactionary responses than when dealing with urgent student matters after they have arisen.

The following list, while not exhaustive, incorporates a few of the numerous state recommendations for various stakeholders to build awareness and promote more inclusive school environments.

For School Boards and Community Members

- Proactively schedule information sessions for board and community members to provide opportunities for stakeholder dialogue and discussion.
- Be aware of the atmosphere of the community when engaging in open discussion and dialogue around these topics. Consider what, if any, security precautions might need to be addressed.
- Offer school-based support groups for LGBTQ+ students.
- Review, modify, and/or create school policy aligned with state and federal law that support LBGTQ+ individuals.
- Work with other local entities and organizations to promote greater community awareness and understanding.
- Anticipate privacy and individual student needs when designing renovations or new building projects (e.g., consider adding or naming gender-neutral facilities).
- Implement curricula that reflect gender and sexual diversity.

For Colleagues, Faculty, and Staff

- Provide professional learning opportunities on applicable laws, regulations, and the specific needs and concerns affecting transgender and GNC students.
- Build awareness that student gender transitions are unique, individual processes that may happen at any time and have implications relative to the privacy and support needed by students and their families.
- Define and identify roles and responsibilities for staff most likely to act as resources and guides when students, parents, or staff have questions or need support.
- Develop and share talking points to help guide staff communications and maintain student confidentiality.
- Analyze a variety of data related to bullying, suspension, expulsion, and attendance to note any inequalities related to sexual orientation or gender identity.
- Develop procedures to review and update school record systems on a regular basis to ensure students' information is consistent with how they want to be identified.

For Parent and Student Support

- Act proactively rather than reactively when addressing concerns.
- Identify and communicate resources that students and families can access for support both within and outside of school (literature, support groups, counseling, etc.).
- Maintain confidentiality by supporting a student's or family's choice in how, or if, they want to disclose transgender status.
- When possible, develop systems and procedures to support individual students who might be fearful of choosing not to disclose to parents or family.

For Everyone

- Identify districts, schools, and individuals who have already made progress dealing with the issues; schedule opportunities to learn from their experiences.
- Schedule engagements and opportunities to hear from transgender and GNC individuals and/or their parents to develop greater staff and community understanding.

CONCLUSION

As Horace Mann noted with his principles for public education 180 years ago, education is best served in schools that support the dignity of children from diverse backgrounds, teaching them with the nonsectarian spirit and methods of a free democratic society (Cremin, 2023). The challenges of meeting Mann's principles for *all* students continue through today. This is exemplified by the school desegregation struggles that led to the landmark *Brown v. Board of Education* decision (1954) and the establishment of "least restrictive environment" guidelines for students with disabilities via the Individuals with Disabilities Education Act (IDEA, 1975/2004). Accepting and supporting individual student gender identity appears to be yet another important challenge in an effort to fully embrace *all* children within our public schools. This will take an ongoing effort from our communities at large, along with effort from caring and concerned educators and educational leaders.

Knowing that we had a transgender daughter, a friend sent us a link to a radio broadcast that captured the hopes and desires we have held for our daughter, as well as so many other individuals and families we now know who have experienced similar realizations. In an essay written and read by Will, an 8th grade student, Will comments, "It took me a long time to realize and sort out who I really was. It was a realization, not a decision. The decision part came with what I decided to do with my realization." He goes on to say, "The support I received was absolutely incredible. . . . This experience has taught me to be thankful for the people who surround me, because so many people in my position are not as lucky. Being fully accepted is truly a miracle, a miracle I am living every day. A miracle I hope to continue to live, and I hope others get to live it too" (Malloy, 2016).

Reflect Further and Take Action

- What information in this chapter resonated most with you? Why?
- Take time at the conclusion of this chapter to watch the testimony from Debi Jackson, a mother of a young transgender child, titled "That's good enough." Then, listen to the audio recording "This I believe" from an 8th grade student, Will. Both are available on YouTube.
- Reflect on how Horace Mann's principles are relevant to building a supportive school environment for students like Will and Debi Jackson's daughter.
- What are some concrete next steps you can take to strengthen support for LGBTQ+ students in your school or district?

REFERENCES

Abreu, P. D., Andrade, R. L. P., Maza, I. L. S., Faria, M. G. B. F., Valença, A. B. M., Araújo, E. C., Palha, P. F., Arcêncio, R. A., Pinto, I. C., Ballestero, J. G. A., Almeida, S. A., Nogueira, J. A., & Monroe, A. A. (2022). Support for mothers, fathers, or guardians of transgender children and adolescents: A systematic review on the dynamics of secondary social networks. *International Journal of Environmental Research and Public Health, 19*(14), 8652. https://www.ncbi.nlm.nih.gov/pmc/articles/PMC9319694/

ACLU. (2021). *Grimm v. Gloucester County School Board.* https://www.aclu.org/cases/grimm-v-gloucester-county-school-board

American Psychological Association. (2016). *Understanding transgender people, gender identity and gender expression.* APA. https://www.apa.org/topics/lgbtq/transgender-people-gender-identity-gender-expression

Biden, J. (2021, March 8). *Executive Order 14021. Guaranteeing an educational environment free from discrimination on the basis of sex, including sexual orientation or gender identity.* DCPD202100214. https://www.govinfo.gov/content/pkg/DCPD-202100214/pdf/DCPD-202100214.pdf

Brink, M. (2022). Protections for trans athletes in Title IX proposal still unknown. *Inside Higher Ed.* https://www.insidehighered.com/news/2022/07/05/title-ix-transgender-athletes-be-considered-separately

Brown v. Board of Education of Topeka, Opinion. (1954, May 17), Records of the Supreme Court of the United States, Record Group 267, National Archives. https://www.archives.gov/milestone-documents/brown-v-board-of-education

Cremin, L. (2023). Horace Mann. *Encyclopedia Britannica*. https://www.britannica.com/biography/Horace-Mann

Department of Justice, Office of Civil Rights. (2011). *Arcadia unified school district letter*. https://www.justice.gov/sites/default/files/crt/legacy/2013/07/26/arcadialetter.pdf

GLAAD. (2022). *GLAAD media reference* (11th ed.); *Glossary of Terms: Transgender*. https://www.glaad.org/reference/trans-terms

GLSEN. (2016). *Educational exclusion: Drop out, push out, and school-to-prison pipeline among LGBTQ youth*. GLSEN. https://www.glsen.org/sites/default/files/2019-11/Educational_Exclusion_2013.pdf

Grant, J. M., Mottet, L. M., Tanis, J., Harrison, J., Herman, J. L., & Keisling, M. (2011). *Injustice at every turn: A report of the National Transgender Discrimination Survey*. National Center for Transgender Equality and National Gay and Lesbian Task Force. https://transequality.org/sites/default/files/docs/resources/NTDS_Report.pdf

Individuals with Disabilities Act (IDEA). (1975/2004). Title 20, Chapter 33 § 1412 5 *Least restrictive environment*. https://www.govinfo.gov/content/pkg/USCODE-2011-title20/pdf/USCODE-2011-title20-chap33.pdf

James, S. E., Herman, J. L., Rankin, S., Keisling, M., Mottet, L., & Anafi, M. (2016). *The report of the 2015 U.S. Transgender Survey*. National Center for Transgender Equality. https://transequality.org/sites/default/files/docs/usts/USTS-Full-Report-Dec17.pdf

Jimenez, K. (2023). Biden administration will release new Title IX rules in May. What to expect. *USA Today*. https://www.usatoday.com/story/news/education/2023/02/08/biden-administration-release-new-title-ix-rules-may/11163003002/

Kosciw, J. G., Clark, C. M., & Menard, L. (2022). *The 2021 National School Climate Survey: The experiences of LGBTQ+ youth in our nation's schools*. GLSEN. https://www.glsen.org/sites/default/files/2022-10/NSCS-2021-Full-Report.pdf

Kosciw, J. G., Clark, C. M., Truong, N. L., & Zongrone, A. D. (2020). *The 2019 National School Climate Survey: The experiences of lesbian, gay, bisexual, transgender, and queer youth in our nation's schools*. GLSEN. https://www.glsen.org/sites/default/files/2020-10/NSCS-2019-Full-Report_0.pdf

Kosciw, J. G., Greytak, E. A., Giga, N. M., Villenas, C. & Danischewski, D. J. (2016). *The 2015 National School Climate Survey: The experiences of lesbian, gay, bisexual, transgender, and queer youth in our nation's schools*. GLSEN. https://files.eric.ed.gov/fulltext/ED574780.pdf.

Kosciw, J. G., Greytak, E. A., Palmer, N. A., & Boesen, M. J. (2014). *The 2013 National School Climate Survey: The experiences of lesbian, gay, bisexual and transgender youth in our nation's schools*. GLSEN. https://www.glsen.org/sites/default/files/2020-03/GLSEN-2013-National-School-Climate-Survey-Full-Report.pdf

Lhamon, C. E., & Gupta, V. (2016, May 13). *Dear Colleague Letter on Transgender Students*. U.S. Department of Justice, Office for Civil Rights. https://www2.ed.gov/about/offices/list/ocr/letters/colleague-201605-title-ix-transgender.pdf

Malloy, W. (2016, February 23). *This I believe Rhode Island: Acceptance* [radio series episode]. Rhode Island Public Radio. http://ripr.org/post/i-believe-rhode-island-acceptance

Minnesota Department of Education. (2017, September 25). *A toolkit for ensuring safe and supportive schools for transgender and gender nonconforming students.* https://education.mn.gov/mdeprod/idcplg?IdcService=GET_FILE&dDocName=MDE072543&RevisionSelectionMethod=latestReleased&Rendition=primary.

Movement Advancement Project (MAP). (2023b). LGBTQ *youth: School nondiscrimination laws & related policies.* https://www.lgbtmap.org/img/maps/citations-schools-nondisc.pdf

New York State Education Department. (2015). *Transgender and gender nonconforming students guidance document now available for schools and districts.* Author. http://www.nysed.gov/Press/Transgender-and-Gender-Nonconforming-Students-Guidance-Document

PFLAG. (2023). LGBTQ+Glossary. https://pflag.org/glossary/

Pullen Sansfaçon, A., Medico, D., Gelly, M., Kirichenko, V., & Suerich-Gulick, F. (2022). Blossoming child, mourning parent: A qualitative study of trans children and their parents navigating transition. *Journal of Child and Family Studies, 31*, 1771–1784. https://link.springer.com/article/10.1007/s10826-021-02178-w

Russell, S. T., Pollitt, A. M., Li, G., & Grossman, A. H. Chosen name use is linked to reduced depressive symptoms, suicidal ideation, and suicidal behavior among transgender youth. *Journal of Adolescent Health, 63*(4), 503–505. https://pubmed.ncbi.nlm.nih.gov/29609917/

Ryan, C. (2009). *Supportive families, healthy children: Helping families with lesbian, gay, bisexual and transgender children.* Family Acceptance Project, Marian Wright Edelman Institute, San Francisco State University. https://familyproject.sfsu.edu/sites/default/files/documents/FAP_English Booklet_pst.pdf

Sokolow, B.A. (2023, August 8). It Looks Like We Won't Have Final Title IX Regulations by October 2023... Now What? Association of Title IX Administrators (ATIXA). https://www.atixa.org/blog/it-looks-like-we-wont-have-final-title-ix-regulations-by-october-2023-now-what/.

Strong Family Alliance. (2017). *The journey for parents of transgender.* https://www.strongfamilyalliance.org/parent-guides/parent-guide-trans/the-journey-for-parents-2/

Temkin Cahill, D., Lao, K., Nuñez, B., Kelley, C., Kelley, S., & Stuart-Cassel, V. (2022, March). LGBTQ+ students in schools are affirming, despite recent trends toward exclusion. *Child Trends.* https://www.childtrends.org/publications/most-state-policies-that-address-lgbtq-students-in-schools-are-affirming-despite-recent-trends-toward-exclusion.

U.S. Department of Education. (2022, June 23). The U.S. Department of Education Releases Proposed Changes to Title IX Regulations, Invites Public Comment [Press release]. https://www.ed.gov/news/press-releases/us-department-education-releases-proposed-changes-title-ix-regulations-invites-public-comment.

Afterword

Over a decade ago, the New York State Council of School Superintendents (NYSCOSS), through the Leadership for Educational Achievement Foundation (LEAF), partnered with WestEd to produce a series of articles meant not only to inspire school leaders but also to provide them with practical ideas on how to face everyday challenges.

As you have learned through your reading, within these pages lies a collection of chapters that delve into the heart of educational leadership. As the education landscape constantly shifts, the need for leaders who can inspire rapid and impactful change becomes increasingly crucial. This compilation offers a treasure trove of insights, strategies, and experiences that illuminate the path toward not just improvement but transformation.

From leading with empathy to implementing a program for special needs students, the chapters in this book are a testament to the power and duty of leadership. Hopefully this book will continue to serve as a guiding light for school leaders who are driven to turn challenges into opportunities and lead their schools toward a brighter future.

May the knowledge shared here assist you to become an architect of change, to mold the future, and to embody the essence of transformational leadership.

Charles S. Dedrick
Executive Director
The New York State Council of School Superintendents

Index

Note: Page numbers followed by *t* indicate tables and *f* indicate figures.

About the Editor and Contributors

Kevin Perks (he/his/him) is the director for the Quality Schools and Districts team at WestEd. In this role he is responsible for directing the development and implementation of school and district improvement services and projects across the country. In his work with schools, districts, and state education agencies, Kevin applies his expertise to lead a team of over 35 staff who provide a wide range of services in the areas of school improvement, leadership coaching, standards-aligned and evidence-based curriculum, instruction, assessment, literacy, student engagement, and adult learning to drive equitable school improvement, particularly for students who have been historically underserved. Kevin is also the principal designer for WestEd's VITAL Collaboration in PLCs and Reading to Learn services. He is the coauthor of *Motivation to Learn: Transforming Classroom Culture to Support Student Achievement*. Kevin's experiences before joining WestEd include being a district leader, school leader, instructional coach, and teacher at the elementary, middle, and high school levels.

ABOUT WESTED

As a national leader in research, development, and service, WestEd is reimagining solutions to a more equitable society by taking on the most demanding and enduring challenges in education and human development. As a nonpartisan research, development, and service agency, WestEd's mission is to work with education and other communities to promote excellence, achieve equity, and improve learning for children, youth, and adults. To achieve this mission, WestEd staff work collaboratively systemwide to provide a broad range of services—including research and evaluation, professional learning, technical assistance, and policy guidance—that are tailored to the needs of clients. As a nonpartisan partner, WestEd generates knowledge and applies evidence and expertise to improve policies, systems, and practices. A steadfast commitment to equity, diversity, and inclusion is central to WestEd's work to advance equitable opportunities, increase well-being, and promote positive outcomes for all children, youth, and adults. Visit Wested.org to learn more.

ABOUT LEAF, INC.

Established in 2006, the Leadership for Educational Achievement Foundation, Inc. (LEAF, Inc.) is a 501(c)3 organization that serves as the professional development arm of the New York State Council of School Superintendents (NYSCOSS). LEAF, Inc. provides high-quality professional learning to support the development of superintendents and their leadership teams. LEAF's programs are research-based, aligned to the needs of the field, responsive to changing expectations for school leaders, and cost-effective. The mission of LEAF, Inc. is to be a premier organization offering comprehensive professional development to ensure the success of educational leaders and the students they serve through opportunities that are excellent in quality, pertinent in focus, and readily accessible to all.

ABOUT THE CONTRIBUTORS

Jenny Betz (she/they) is a senior program associate with WestEd's Resilient and Healthy Schools and Communities, leading coaching, training, and technical assistance to support efforts to assess and improve school climate and wellness, with an emphasis on equity, trauma-informed practices, SEL, community engagement, youth leadership, bias-based bullying, LGBTQ+ students, data use, and sustainability. Betz currently provides leadership and technical assistance with the national Center to Improve Social and Emotional Learning and School Safety at WestEd, the California Center for School Climate, California's Learning Communities for School Success Program, and the development of trauma-informed practice modules for the California Office of the Surgeon General. With more than 20 years of experience in the nonprofit sector, Betz has worked with state education agencies (SEAs), as well as hundreds of local education agencies (LEAs) and community organizations to create and sustain safe, supportive, and equitable learning environments.

Deborah A. Bradley is a retired physician and a board certified fellow of the American College of Obstetrics and Gynecology. She is the mother of a transgender daughter and has served as a volunteer coordinator and facilitator of a support group for parents of transgender and nonbinary children for many years. Her pronouns are she/her.

Andrea Browning is a senior policy advisor on WestEd's Culturally Responsive Systems team, through which she provides equity-focused professional learning and coaching for school, district, and state education practitioners and policymakers. Her expertise spans social and emotional learning, personalized learning, systems change, and culturally responsive pathways to a well-rounded education. Ms. Browning directs the Engaging Equity project for the Oregon Department of Education to design and implement professional learning about equity mindsets, practices, and systems for educators. She also co-directs the Lyon County, Nevada, Portrait of a Learner project to design and implement a student-centered learning vision. Prior to joining WestEd, Ms. Browning led the U.S. Department of Education's $500 million Race to the Top-District program supporting school districts in their transformation to next generation, personalized learning environments. Her career in education began more than two decades ago as a community liaison in the Boulder Valley School District in Colorado.

Rebeca Cerna is an area director; she supports districts, schools, and community partners in strengthening educational, prevention, and health outcomes while centering equity and inclusion. Cerna's areas of expertise include school culture and climate, data use practices, health and wellness, and partner/cross-sector collaboration. Her expertise has been developed by working with communities that have been challenged by infrastructure deficiencies and in lifting the voices of all community and educational partners. Currently, Cerna directs the California Center for School Climate, funded by the California Department of Education, focused on building the capacity of schools and districts across California in understanding and using school climate data and in strengthening school climate practice. She has also served as an evaluator for multiple federal, state, and local evaluation projects. Prior to coming to and joining WestEd, Cerna taught in adult education, and she worked for the University of California, Riverside, on research about resilience and reducing risk factors.

Nancy Gerzon provides national leadership in formative assessment implementation. She and her team have developed models of technical assistance and professional learning at all levels of the education system—for teachers, school and district leaders, and state department teams—to guide widespread implementation. Nancy specializes in advancing teacher and leader learning models that lead to significant changes in the student role, including how to develop students' metacognitive skills and develop instructional routines that enable students to monitor and guide their own learning. Since 2005, when Nancy led the development of the first statewide implementation of formative assessment, she has been at the forefront of developing teacher-led learning in formative assessment. She has designed models for formative assessment peer coaching, site-based communities of practice, teacher-led video study groups, and intensive blended digital professional learning. Nancy is co-author, with Sonia Caus Gleason, of *Growing into Equity: Professional Learning and Personalization in High-Achieving Schools* (Corwin, 2013), which outlines principles of teacher support, leadership, and systems that contributed to significant improvements in learning.

Stephen C. Hamilton is a retired educator with experience as a former elementary teacher, principal, and locally elected school board member in Vermont and Massachusetts. For 20 years he worked with a national educational organization as a consultant to schools, districts, and state departments of education, focused on school improvement, data informed practices and policy development. He is the father of a transgender daughter and volunteers as a support group facilitator for parents of transgender and nonbinary children.

Shazia Hashmi is a program associate at WestEd. In this role, she leads research and technical assistance projects that focus on improving practices in social-emotional learning, school climate, and community engagement. She uses expertise in data collection and analysis, evidence-based policy and practice, and research and evaluation to create equitable, inclusive, and supportive learning environments. She currently provides research and technical assistance support for the California School Climate Center and the National Center to Improve Social Emotional Learning and School Safety. She began her career providing technical assistance and coaching to adult education and digital literacy practitioners for the City of Philadelphia.

Shandy Hauk is a professor of mathematics at San Francisco State University and senior research associate at WestEd. With a bachelor's degree in theater and film, a doctorate in mathematics, and a post-doc in mathematics education, Shandy specializes in video-rich mixed-methods research and development. She studies in-person and digitally mediated student, teacher, teacher-leader, and administrator learning in the context of mathematics, science, and engineering in grades K–20. She directs the *Video Cases for College Mathematics Instructor Development* project and regularly serves as an advisor on research and development projects, including *Making Sense of Science* and *Mathematics and Culture in Micronesia: Integrating Societal Experiences*. Shandy has widely disseminated work on interculturally attentive leadership, teaching, and learning. Prior to her graduate work, Shandy taught mathematics and English/language arts at socioeconomically and ethnically diverse middle and high schools in southern California.

Nancy Hurley, a retired senior research associate at WestEd, conducted numerous program evaluations in a variety of topic areas, including special education; teacher induction, retention, and mentoring; effective school leadership; smaller learning communities; use of technology in the classroom; science education; mathematics and social studies curricula; and school and district systems of support and change initiatives. Throughout her career, Hurley collaborated with colleagues and clients to design quantitative and qualitative evaluations that met the needs of all constituents and contributed to the writing and development of *Collaborative Evaluation Led by Local Evaluators: A Practical, Print- and Web-Based Guide to Program Evaluation* (Brackett, A. 2004). Subsequently, Brackett and Hurley developed the Collaborative Evaluation Institute to build the capacity of educators to conduct program evaluation. They and other colleagues facilitated institutes across the northeast and in Puerto Rico and Alaska, including several summer institutes for the Massachusetts Department of Education: Effective Evaluation of Special Education Programs (2006–2011).

Joyce S. Kaser was a senior program associate in the Science, Technology, Engineering, and Mathematics (STEM) Program at WestEd. Coauthor (with Shandy Hauk) of a chapter that appears in this volume, Joyce died in late 2021. She had extensive experience in program evaluation, primarily the evaluation of STEM programs, and she served as a team member for the development of three frameworks for the National Assessment of Educational Progress: Science (2009), Technology and Engineering Literacy (2014), and Mathematics (2021). Joyce was first author of *Enhancing Program Quality in Science and Mathematics* (1999) and *Leading Every Day* (2013)—a guide for STEM educators. Before joining WestEd, Joyce's professional contributions included directing the Washington D.C. office of The NETWORK, heading an equity assistance center, serving as a district administrator and high school teacher, and four years as facilitator of the New Mexico Secretary of Education's Advisory Council for Math and Science.

Nakanya Magby is a senior program associate in WestEd's Resilient and Healthy Schools and Communities (RHSC) area. In this capacity, she provides coaching, training, and curriculum development in all areas related to school climate and culture. Currently, she serves as a technical assistance provider for the California Center for School Climate, an initiative of the California Department of Education. She also served as one of the lead content developers for the Office of California Surgeon General's Foundations of Trauma-Informed Practice professional learning modules. Prior to WestEd, Nakanya worked as a special education teacher, school counselor, dean of students, and at the LEA and state levels in Washington, DC, supporting elementary, middle, and high schools.

Dona Meinders is a senior project director for the Special Education Policy and Practices team at WestEd, where her focus has been the improvement of academic and behavioral outcomes for students with disabilities at the systems levels. One such area of focus has been the work on Special Education Program Reviews. Over the last 10 years, she has completed more than 30 program reviews in LEAs across the country. This experience has provided her team with a deep understanding of the challenges and solutions that LEAs face when working to improve outcomes for their students receiving special education services. This knowledge, along with the experience and expertise of the team, is then brought to use in the program review process. Additionally, the team has also focused on refinement of the process to improve the efficiency and effectiveness through the use of technology.

Michael Middleton serves as the provost and vice president for teaching, learning, and growth at Ramapo College of New Jersey. He conducts research on the relation of classroom and cultural contexts on adolescent achievement motivation in diverse community settings and has received funding for this work through the National Science Foundation. His scholarship includes the book *Motivation to Learn: Transforming Classroom Culture to Support Student Achievement*. At the University of New Hampshire, he held the John and H. Irene Peters Professorship in Education and was a recipient of a UNH Faculty Excellence in Teaching Award. He also served as dean of the College of Education and Human Development at University of Massachusetts Boston and as the Klara and Larry Silverstein Dean of the School of Education at Hunter College, City University of New York. He has focused on leading academic communities in increased community engagement, strategic planning, and addressing issues of equity and justice.

Mike Nagler is the Superintendent of the Mineola School District, a suburb of New York City (NYC). He began his career as a social studies teacher in NYC. While teaching, he earned his doctorate from Columbia University and accepted an administrative position with Mineola in 1999. During his 23 years with the district, he has been a big proponent of using technology to engage students in rigorous content. All five schools in Mineola have been recognized as Apple distinguished schools. Mineola is also a member of the League of Innovative Schools, Dr. Nagler is the chairperson of the Advisory Board. Dr. Nagler was also the 2020 New York State Superintendent of the Year and was a finalist for the 2020 National Superintendent of the Year. He recently published a book entitled *The Design Thinking, Entrepreneurial, Visionary Planning Leader—a Practical Guide for Thriving in Ambiguity*.

Maria Paredes is a senior engagement manager at WestEd. In her role she is responsible for the development and expansion of integrated family and community engagement services across the country. Dr. Paredes applies research and evidence in her work with schools, districts, and state education agencies to develop the capacity of educators, families, and the community to work collaboratively to improve learning outcomes for students. Paredes developed Academic Parent-Teacher Teams (APTT) in 2010, a family engagement framework used in schools and districts across 27 states. The model incorporates the development of relationships and trust between educators and families, data discussions, modeling of home practice activities, and goal setting to engage families as partners in education. Paredes is a prolific writer; she has authored a multitude of articles, briefs, blogs, toolkits, and guides to support educators and families. She is a highly regarded speaker at national conferences and webinars. Before joining WestEd, she was a district family engagement director, middle school teacher, adult education teacher, and university teaching assistant.

Christina Pate leads WestEd's Safe & Supportive Learning Environments body of work and serves as deputy director of the National Center to Improve Social and Emotional Learning and School Safety. She is a psychologist by training and a facilitator of learning, development, and transformation. An accomplished strategist, designer, coach, facilitator, author, and public speaker, Pate helps people and organizations transform from the inside out. With over 20 years of experience in the public and private sectors, she has led the development and implementation of organization- and state-wide strategies, programs, and initiatives to facilitate change. Pate also coaches clients in development, implementation, and sustainability efforts to promote healthy personal and organizational development. Pate brings a range of expertise in strategic planning, professional learning and development, program design, systems thinking and change, social-emotional development and mental health, leadership and collaboration, and organizational climate and culture.

Kristin Reedy is a career-long special educator. At her retirement in 2017, Kristin was the co-irector of the National Center for Systemic Improvement (NCSI) at WestEd, funded by the U.S. Office of Special Education Programs (OSEP) to provide technical assistance (TA) to state agencies, nation-wide, in the implementation of the Individuals with Disabilities Education Act (IDEA) and the improvement of outcomes for children and youth with disabilities. She has provided consultation, professional development, program evaluation, and technical assistance to school districts and states across the United States. Kristin has over 30 years' experience in special education as a teacher, therapist, state education agency consultant and manager, local special education director, and regional/national TA provider. She holds an Ed.D. in educational leadership and policy studies from the University of Vermont.

Robert Rosenfeld, a senior engagement manager with WestEd's Quality Schools and Districts team, has over two decades of experience providing coaching to state- and district-level leaders, principals, and teachers. He supports states, districts, and schools to create systems that enhance leadership, strengthen teaching, and increase student learning. He leads projects that support the review and implementation of local curricula, assessments, and innovative teaching practices. He is a former math and science teacher and is bilingual (Spanish and English). Rosenfeld received his master's in education from Stanford University and his B.A. in ecology, behavior, and evolution from the University of California, San Diego.

Alexis Stern (she/her) is a research associate with WestEd's Justice & Prevention Research Center. She supports research and evaluation projects in areas including early childhood education and care, school climate, school safety, juvenile justice, and community health. Before joining WestEd, Alexis worked for a community grant maker in Rhode Island, where she collaborated with local partners to develop a policy agenda for adult basic education in the state.

Saroja Warner is the director for culturally responsive systems and provides strategic leadership for WestEd's technical assistance, research and evaluation services, and policy development, with state education agencies, school districts, regional education agencies, and institutions of higher education focused on creating, implementing, and sustaining culturally responsive and equitable systems, including sustaining a racially and linguistically diverse educator workforce. She is a nationally recognized expert in educator workforce issues and culturally responsive teaching, leading, and school cultures. Prior to coming to WestEd, Saroja launched a national initiative at the Council of Chief State School Officers to increase educator diversity and culturally responsive practice (CRP) and authored an anchor paper for that work, *A Vision and Guidance for a Diverse and Learner-Ready Teacher Workforce,* which provides guidance to states to meet these goals and identifies model best practices. Saroja taught high school social studies for 15 years and is a nationally board-certified teacher.